The Fictional Labyrinths of Thomas Pynchon

by

David Seed

Lecturer in English
University of Liverpool

University of Iowa Press   Iowa City

International Standard Book Number 0–87745–165–6
Library of Congress Catalog Card Number 86–51086
University of Iowa Press, Iowa City 52242
Copyright © 1988 by David Seed
All rights reserved
First edition, 1988

THE FICTIONAL LABYRINTHS OF
THOMAS PYNCHON

For Nana

Contents

List of Illustrations

Foreword

Criticism is by its very nature an incremental process and while I have recorded particular debts in the following pages I would also like to acknowledge the general influence of the following critics: Tony Tanner, Thomas H. Schaub, William M. Plater, Richard Poirier and Joseph W. Slade. Professor Slade has also kindly given his permission for the calculus diagram (Figure 2) to be reproduced from his 1974 study *Thomas Pynchon*. I am grateful for financial assistance from the University of Liverpool and the US Information Service which enabled me to pursue research in New York. I am grateful too for the help and assistance of my friend and colleague Brian Nellist who read parts of this study in its early stages. Sections of Chapter 1 have previously appeared in the *Journal of Narrative Technique* and the *Rocky Mountain Review of Language and Literature*; a part of Chapter 3 first appeared in *Pynchon Notes*; and several parts of this book first appeared in a very different form in the *Critical Quarterly*. I am grateful to the editors of these journals for their permission to reprint the material. I would also like to record my thanks to the secretaries of the Liverpool University English Department for their patience and accuracy in typing this book. My thanks must go to Thomas Pynchon himself for granting permission to quote from his works and particularly for his generosity in allowing me to print the letter which forms my appendix in spite of his misgivings about its style. Lastly I must record a great debt to my wife Nana for her patience and support during the writing of this book, which is dedicated to her.

Acknowledgements

The author and publishers wish to thank the following publishers for permission to quote from the works of Thomas Pynchon: A. M. Heath & Co., Harper & Row Inc. and Lippincott & Crowell, for the extracts from *V.* (US copyright Thomas Pynchon 1961, 1963) and *The Crying of Lot 49* (US copyright Thomas Pynchon 1965, 1966); A. M. Heath & Co., Jonathan Cape Ltd and Viking Penguin Inc., for the extracts from *Gravity's Rainbow* (US copyright Thomas Pynchon 1973); A. M. Heath & Co., Jonathan Cape Ltd and Little, Brown & Co. for the extracts from *Slow Learner* (US copyright Thomas Pynchon 1984). The extracts from Thomas Pynchon's article 'A Gift of Books' are reprinted from *Holiday* magazine, now published by *Travel-Holiday*, Floral Park, New York 11001. The extracts from 'Is It O.K. to Be a Luddite?' are reprinted with permission from *The New York Times Book Review* (US copyright New York Times Co. 1984). The extracts from Kirkpatrick Sale's 'The World Behind Watergate' are reprinted with permission from *The New York Review of Books* (copyright 1973 Nyrev Inc.).

The following publishers are also thanked: Random House Inc., for the extracts from Peter Matthiessen's *Far Tortuga* (US copyright Peter Matthiessen 1975); Faber & Faber Ltd and Grove Press Inc., for the quotation from Samuel Beckett's *Endgame* (US copyright Grove Press 1958); Faber & Faber Ltd and Alfred A. Knopf Inc., for the extract from Laurel Goldman's *Sounding the Territory* (US copyright Laurel Goldman 1982); George Weidenfeld & Nicolson Ltd and Grove Press Inc., for the quotation from Vladimir Nabokov's *The Real Life of Sebastian Knight* (US copyright Grove Press 1941, 1959); Little, Brown & Co. for the extract from M. F. Beal's *Amazon One* (US copyright M. F. Beal 1975); and Houghton Mifflin & Co., for the extracts from Tom Robbins' *Even Cowgirls Get the Blues* (US copyright Tom Robbins 1974).

Every effort has been made to trace the copyright-holders, but if any have been inadvertently overlooked the publishers will be pleased to make the necessary arrangements at the first opportunity.

Introduction

In December 1965 the American magazine *Holiday* carried an article entitled 'A Gift of Books' where distinguished writers and critics suggested books which in their opinion had failed to receive the public recognition that they merited. The contributors included Joseph Heller, Alfred Kazin and Thomas Pynchon. Pynchon's nomination went to *Warlock* (1958), a Western by Oakley Hall which is set in the 1880s. The eponymous town has no law and order so the citizens' committee offers the office of marshall to one Clay Blaisedell who already has a reputation as a feared gun-figure. Although he immediately reduces the number of hold-ups and lynchings a new anxiety immediately springs up that Blaisedell is arrogating the law to himself, an anxiety that even touches Blaisedell too so that he submits himself for trial in a neighbouring town. One of the central issues of the novel is the precarious and problematic nature of legality in a place where no creditable legal institutions exist. The town embodies this precariousness in physical terms:

> Warlock lay on a flat, white alkali step, half encircled by the Bucksaw Mountains to the east, beneath a metallic sky, with the afternoon sun slanting down on it from over the distant peaks of the Dinosaurs, the adobe and weathered plank-and-batten, false-fronted buildings were smoothly glazed with yellow light, and sharp-cut black shadows lay like pits in the angles of the sun. The heat of the sun was like a blanket; it had dimension and weight. The town was dust- and heat-hazed, blurred out of focus.[1]

The surrounding mountains dwarf Warlock, and the heat and dust almost obliterate it. Hall shrewdly composes a visual image with just the right suggestions of film-set (false-fronts) and stereotype to resonate metaphorically through the narrative. The visual clarity of the town becomes a metaphor of its legal orderliness which is constantly threatening to break down and revert to anarchy. Hall increases this tension by alternating passages of mental objective narrative with excerpts from the journals or 'testimonies' of the helpless townsfolk.

1

Pynchon identifies this central tension in his comments on the novel: 'the collective awareness that is Warlock must face its own inescapable Horror: that what is called society, with its law and order, is as frail, as precarious, as flesh and can be snuffed out and assimilated back into the dust as easily as a corpse can'.[2] The opposition which Pynchon sets up here between fragile social construct and threatening non-human landscape also informs his first novel *V.* where wastelands constantly encroach on human settlement. Even in his first published story Pynchon deals with the disasterous effects of hurricane on southern Louisiana and repeatedly refers to the weather in his early fiction in an inverted pathetic fallacy, as if to imply that his characters reflected the tone of their surroundings instead of vice versa. The ironic and metaphysical implications of this emphasis in Pynchon are complex and are related to another comment he makes on *Warlock*. At a late stage in the novel one of Blaisedell's antagonists reads about himself in a pulp magazine, noting with amusement that he has become converted into an image of evil (as the 'Black Rattlesnake of Warlock'). The novel as a whole both recognizes and resists the mythologizing process by proliferating points of view on Blaisedell in particular so that he never becomes an unambiguous hero. As Pynchon notes, Blaisedell's self-esteem has been fed by magazine images, but ultimately he cannot live up to them. Pynchon is not so much interested in this novel as a dramatization of individual failure, but rather as a comment on the projection of melodramatic images where good confronts evil. The citizens of Warlock invite Blaisedell to become a hero they could never be, thereby rendering the projection of such images as inseparable from the civilizing process itself. This link helps to explain Pynchon's ironic attitude towards American society in his early fiction and takes us to a social commentator whose insights he incorporated into his works – Marshall McLuhan.

One of McLuhan's basic arguments in *The Mechanical Bride* (1951) is that the 'mechanical agencies of the press, radio, movies, and advertising' are exerting a pressure on modern man which he does not realize. Again and again McLuhan stresses the need to counter the passivity induced by these agencies. He describes this state variously as narcosis (*Understanding Media*) or somnambulism (*The Gutenberg Galaxy*) but his basic assertion stays the same: that modern man is unconscious of the effects these agencies are having on him. Therefore *The Mechanical Bride* tries to reverse this process 'by providing typical visual imagery of our environment and dislocating it into meaning by inspection'.[3] McLuhan takes specimens of advertising and then, drawing on methods he had acquired in literary criticism, proceeds to analyse them, to clarify their latent content and underlying cultural assumptions. Although McLuhan modestly underplays his purpose in the preface to *The Mechanical Bride*, he consistently attacks the twin processes of standardization and mechanization which he sees as uniting such diverse phenomena as success manuals, cosmetics advertisements and body-development courses. His sub-title (*Folklore of Industrial Man*) cleverly confronts the contemporary with the primitive and implies that McLuhan is engaging in a quasi-anthropological investigation of modern culture. A similar tactic was used by Thorstein Veblen in *The Theory of the Leisure Class* for a similar purpose: to reveal the contemporary in a strange and therefore informative light. McLuhan's method might vary in details but basically he too is defamiliarizing the familiar, presenting the ordinary in an unusual light.

Pynchon confirmed in a letter of 1968 (see Appendix) that he had read McLuhan and we shall see unmistakable signs of *Understanding Media* influencing his second novel. By the same token two sections in particular of McLuhan's study ('Love-Goddess Assembly Line' and 'the Mechanical Bride') explain the bearings which Pynchon takes from Henry Adams in his short story 'Entropy' and *V.* to diagnose a drift towards the mechanical. Pynchon renders his contemporary environments bizarre by emphasizing their cherished consumer-objects (radio, hi-fi sets, etc.) in varying contexts and then naming or depicting characters in such a way that they cannot be separated from their environments. Behaviour-styles in *V.*, for instance, are shown deterministically as the unconscious imitations of patterns from film and television. McLuhan argues that modern advertising methods are annihilating the ego and Pynchon similarly demonstrates how technology pre-empts human activity, offering his characters a voice, sexual partner or behavioural model. In the central sections of *The Mechanical Bride* McLuhan notes the 'interfusion of sex and technology' in advertising and the popular press, and comments: 'It is not a feature created by the ad men, but it seems rather to be born of a hungry curiosity to explore and enlarge the domain of sex by mechanical technique, on one hand, and, on the other, to *possess* machines in a sexually gratifying way.'[4] Almost as if he were glossing this passage Pynchon creates an important motif around the erotic satisfactions of the mechanical. Prosthetics becomes part of a general process of atrophy where the human body is becoming redundant. One of Pynchon's characters then has a mock-orphic vision of the ultimate erotic woman:' . . . skin radiant with the bloom of some new plastic; both eyes glass but now containing photoelectric cells, connected by silver electrodes to optic nerves of purest copper wire and leading to a brain exquisitely wrought as a diode matrix could ever be'.[5] This grotesque mixture of eroticism and technology exactly demonstrates the cultural process identified by McLuhan. In *V.* robots, artist's lay-figures and automata symbolize the possible inanimate end-point to such a process.

The central image of *The Mechanical Bride* shows a pair of nylon-clad legs on a pedestal advertising stockings McLuhan explains:

> To the mind of modern girls, legs, like busts, are power points which she has been taught to tailor, but as parts of the success kit rather than erotically or sensuously. She swings her legs from the hip with masculine drive and confidence. She knows that "a long-legged gap can go places". As such, her legs are not intimately associated with her taste or with her unique self but are merely display objects like the grill work on a car. They are date-baited power levers for the management for the male audience.
>
> Thus, for example, the legs "on a Pedestal" presented by the Gotham Hosiery company are one facet of our "replaceable parts" cultural dynamics. In a specialist world it is natural that we should select some single part of the body for attention.[6]

McLuhan is claiming here that advertisements promote a notion of 'technique' which in effect breaks down the human body and human behaviour into components which can either be replaced or rendered more efficient. He quotes an example from Margaret Mead of a film star achieving success after having cosmetic work on her nose and teeth – exactly the two areas Pynchon uses in *V.* to draw attention to the domination of certain stereotyped images. Here he creates a fanciful and modish mock-science of 'psychodontia', a cross between psychiatry and orthodontia which implicitly brings the former into ridicule as a kind of mental 'servicing'.

Pynchon's attention to hidden persuaders implies a notion of 'mass society' which would closely fit Irving Howe's diagnosis of 1959, i.e. from the period when Pynchon was beginning to write seriously. Howe states:

> By mass society we mean a relatively comfortable, half welfare and half garrison society in which the population grows passive, indifferent, and atomized; in which traditional loyalties, ties, and associations become lax and dissolve entirely; in which coherent publics based on definitive interests and opinions gradually fall apart; and in which man becomes a consumer, himself mass-produced like the products, diversions, and values that he absorbs.[7]

Howe predicts the contemporary scenario of *V*. where consumerism helps to induce a 'feeling that life is a drift', a passivity which the novel's protagonist rationalizes as a means of evading action and which becomes increasingly difficult to relieve through rounds of party-going. Vance Packard's 1960 report *The Waste Makers* examines the systematic promotion of extravagance and built-in obsolescence by American business, and the rubbish-heaps which litter Pynchon's cityscapes stand as sombre warnings of a cultural destiny. The scrapyards of *V*. are implicitly linked to the piled corpses of the Nazi concentration camps, suggesting that the latter represent an extreme case of the reduction of human beings to objects or statistics.

Pynchon's extreme sensitivity to promoted images and stereotyped cultural patterns places him in a line of American fiction which would include Dos Passos and Nathanael West. In *U.S.A.* Dos Passos assembles examples of how the media create voices which drown out human speech and become means of political control. In West's *The Day of the Locust* his characters have converted themselves into mechanisms, routines which monopolize the self. The most bizarre case is Harry Greener who exploits an anachronistic vaudeville routine to sell polish. In the middle of his routine he suffers a seizure:

> Suddenly, like a mechanical toy that had been overwound, something snapped inside of him and he began to spin through his entire repertoire. The effect was purely muscular, like the dance of a paralytic. He jigged, juggled his hat, made believe he

had been kicked, tripped, and shook hands with himself. He
went through it all in one dizzy spasm, then reeled to the couch
and collapsed.[8]

To vary West's own analogy, the effect is as if he has turned the
camera on Harry and then speeded up the film. The reader is too
aware of mechanistic movement to be emotionally involved in
Harry's fate even though he is literally acting himself into the
grave. He becomes a case, one of many examples which pack the
novel, of characters who only exist as routines or images. Both
Pynchon and McLuhan cite Hollywood as reinforcing cultural
mimicry and image-promotion. Like West Pynchon flattens out
the characters in his early fiction into two-dimensional figures
who ludicrously define themselves through single repeated
actions, verbal mannerisms or obsessions. The protagonist of his
first published story tries out a wisecrack which immediately
reminds him of a caption from *Life* magazine and his disgusted
reaction is typical. Wherever Pynchon's characters turn they find
their environment – mental and physical – packed with clichéd
images. Pynchon reserves his sharpest ironies for those who
deceive themselves that they are dropping out of the system
when in fact they are continuing the very passive imitations
which that system promotes. Disenchantment leads to repeated
gestures of disengagement in his early fiction. It is not until the
mid-1960s that absurdist techniques become complicated by
political interests.

   Of course part of a would-be novelist's environment consists of
the novelistic styles already available to him. The Cornell English
Department introduced Pynchon to the Modernists (Hemingway
and T. S. Eliot figure prominently in his stories and first novel)
and yet it was his discovery of the Beats around 1956 which
marked a turning-point in his ambition to become a writer. In his
introduction to *Slow Learner* (1984), his recent collection of early
stories, Pynchon writes that he became aware of opposing notions
of language and fictional practice even though it was an oblique
influence:

We were at a transition point, a strange post-Beat passage of
cultural time, with our loyalties divided. As bop and rock'n'roll
were to swing music and postwar pop, so was this new writing
to the more established modernist tradition we were being

exposed to then in college. Unfortunately there were no more primary choices for us to make. We were onlookers: the parade had gone by and we were already getting everything secondhand, consumers of what the media of the time were supplying us. This didn't prevent us from adopting Beat postures and props . . .[9]

Pynchon singles out Kerouac for particular praise perhaps because his colloquial, free-flowing style contrasted so strongly with the Modernists he had been studying at Cornell, and he has subsequently confirmed that 'of all the influences I remember then being in the air, his was most glamorous'.[10] The problem here is that we need to distinguish clearly between Kerouac's stylistic influence and the life-style he depicted in novels like *On the Road*. Kerouac (and for that matter Saul Bellow, Herbert Gold and Philip Roth) all receive mention by Pynchon as indicating a new direction towards the colloquial and away from literary decorum. This is a direction which Pynchon himself has followed in his novels. *V.* maintains a generally impassive narrative voice, articulating events without overt comment; *The Crying of Lot 49* inches towards the verbal style of its protagonist without completely identifying with her; and by *Gravity's Rainbow* Pynchon has adopted the ribald voice of a stand-up comedian. This does not mean that he simply became a Beat novelist after the fact because for one thing Pynchon scrupulously avoids the confessional mode, adopting instead what he calls a 'strategy of transfer' whereby autobiographical materials are obliquely assimilated into his narrative structures. It is rather that Pynchon recognized certain possibilities in Kerouac's fiction and turned them to his own uses. Certain materials central to the Beats occur in his early fiction but always in inverted or modified forms. Some time in January 1950 John Clellon Holmes and Kerouac planned a 'decade of parties' and the party became in Beat fiction a set piece, a supposedly spontaneous event which extravagantly contradicted such bourgeois values as thrift or sobriety.[11] As many critics have noted the party is equally a set-piece in Pynchon's fiction but this time dramatizing either an entropic drift towards disorder or a purely mechanical process. The 'feeling of separateness' which Lawrence Lipton saw as unifying the Beats ('it is *we* against *they*') was reinforced by jargon, a 'cool' stance and a common enthusiasm for jazz.[12] Here again Pynchon rings the changes. The slang of the fifties ('flip', 'roach', 'benny', etc.) is divorced from its immediate social context and woven into the humorous texture of his fiction. 'Roach' becomes an army camp, 'benny' becomes the protagonist of *V.*, and so on. Jazz figures either in terms of individual skill or as an ironic stimulus to argument in 'Entropy' of which Pynchon has stated 'it is as close to Beat story as anything I was writing then'.[13] Here jazz creates no solidarity but figures in fantastic speculations about music phrased in what amounts to a parody of Beat idioms. Whereas in the fiction of Chandler Brossard and Kerouac the quest pattern gives the narrative impetus, Pynchon's ambivalence about meaningful goals renders his characters' quests ludicrous. They become pretexts for action or self-perpetuating process. Kerouac's open road, full of the possibilities of discovery, narrows down to the street in Pynchon's first novel, a place of alienation, anonymity and threat.

Did Kerouac's fiction offer Pynchon a possible life-style? Biographical details are notoriously thin on the ground but the signs are that Pynchon followed a conventional enough course from his birth in 1937 to a well-to-do Republican Long Island family to his graduation from Cornell in 1959. Although he was offered a Woodrow Wilson Fellowship to begin graduate studies he spent the next year with friends in New York. Thereafter he worked as a technical writer for the Boeing Company in Seattle from 1960 to 1962.[14] There the details stop. From 1962 onwards Pynchon has apparently subsisted entirely off his writings and has studiously avoided any personal publicity, so much so that one journalist has even claimed that Pynchon is in fact J. D. Salinger![15] His reported comments suggest that Pynchon has avoided the public gaze partly because he has an absurdly low opinion of his own writings in spite of the fact the *V.* won the Faulkner Award in 1964, *Lot 49* the Rosenthal Memorial Award in 1967, and *Gravity's Rainbow* only narrowly missed a Pulitzer Prize in 1974. In 1975 he was awarded the Howells Medal of the American Academy for his third novel but declined it without giving any reason.[16] Apart from this rather exaggerated modesty, Pynchon's avoidance of publicity is perfectly consistent with his sensitivity to public images. He could have gone to the opposite extreme like Mailer who, in the 1960s particularly, blended personal and fictional performances together so that the two are virtually inseparable. Pynchon's course ensures that his fiction is valued on its own merits and avoids the complication of promotional publicity. In effect he has chosen to withdraw from American public life, perhaps influenced partly by the example of Sal Paradise and certainly influenced by a completely different book, Helen Waddell's *The Wandering Scholars* which was reissued in a paperback edition in 1955. By his own account Pynchon discovered the Beats while doing national service in the mid-1950s, and probably came across the Waddell study at about the same time. He was fascinated by the *vagi*, the Medieval poets 'who left the monasteries in large numbers and took to the roads of Europe, celebrating in song the wider range of life to be found outside their academic walls'.[17] The analogy he draws is with the contemporary universities, and exactly the same book is cited by Lawrence Lipton as an important influence on the Beats as a whole, containing 'poems by those on-the-road twelfth-century beatniks, the goliards'.[18] Lipton sees the goliards as proto-Beats. Pynchon seems to have adopted their life-style and become a writer at large. Reports from his friends testify to his nomadic existence, and his unpredictable appearances now in Mexico, now in California; and the monastic bareness of his apartments, all of which parallel Waddell's wandering scholars who are only seen in glimpses and 'who owe no allegiance to any man, but follow their own will'.[19]

This uncommitted life-style with its related theme of freedom bear directly on a friend of Pynchon's from his Cornell days, Richard Fariña. Fariña wrote only one novel, *Been Down So Long It Looks Like Up to Me* (1966) which was reissued in 1983 with a new introduction by Pynchon. This introduction implicitly idealizes Fariña into the nonconformist which Pynchon would have liked to be in the late fifties. Fariña is descirbed as a wary, detached presence, a loner who leaves Cornell without getting his degree, and certainly his subsequent life until his death in a motorcycle accident in 1966 confirms this impression. His first wife described Fariña as an 'incredible adventurer' which is if anything an understatement.[20] He was active in Cuba during Castro's rebellion, worked with the IRA in Northern Ireland; was a singer, composer, playwright as well as author of short stories and his one novel; he issued two record albums with his second wife Mimi Baez, and led a nomadic life between Paris, London, New York and California. *Been Down So Long* is a comic parable on the state of America. Its protagonist Gnossos Pappadopoulis attempts to exercise freedom by (what he variously calls 'exemption' or 'immunity') by shifting manicly through a whole series of roles drawn mainly from popular culture. These roles offer an ideal ease of manoeuvre through situations potentially full of threat. Gnossos reflects at one point: 'who to be? Green Arrow, Billy Batson? Plastic Man still best, do the metamorphosis, be a Mingus side, feel the crystal vibration in my grooves . . .'[21]. By momentarily pretending to be a consumer-object Gnossos avoids fixity or social definition. His playfulness is anarchic and disruptive, trading off pre-existing situations as spring-boards to new roles. This freedom is expressed in images of light or mobility through cherished figures such as Plastic Man, Pooh Bear or Captain Midnight which anticipate many of the references to popular culture in *Gravity's Rainbow* (dedicated to Richard Fariña). Gnossos defines his freedom through negative reactions, firstly against the diseased landscape of America over which broods the threatening image of the atom bomb's mushroom cloud, and secondly over the forces of standardization at work in American life. Most of the novel is set in a thinly disguised version of Cornell University which is used as an emblem of the republic as a whole. The process is stereotyping:

> All about them the golden girls, shopping for dainties in Lairville. . . . A generation in the mould, the Great White Pattern Maker lying in his prosperous bed, grinning while the liquid cools. . . . Ah, the regimented good will and force-fed confidence of those who are not meek but will inherit the earth all the same.[22]

Gnossos ducks and weaves through the novel trying to avoid this sort of conformity but his freedom turns out to be largely verbal. His joking has a shrill edge to it as he constantly struggles to fight down paranoia or superstitious images of dread. His bravado in the face of death ('Oh, Thanatos baby, come give your easy kiss') is only possible while death remains remote, but the tone of the novel darkens dramatically when Gnossos' closest friend is shot in Cuba. For all of its verbal antics this is ultimately a novel about betrayal. As Pynchon points out, 'Gnossos looks at a number of possibilities'.[23] He has been on the road; he toys with Catholicism and drugs; he visits friends who embody a modish orientalism or ecological self-sufficiency; and he tries to find fulfilment through love but is infected by the very girl he thought was a virgin. The riots loosely based on the 1958 student protests over the regulation of women's dormitories which almost conclude the novel seem to imply a defiance of the forces of authority but nemesis finally catches up with Gnosses when he is called for military service. Fariña's novel resembles Pynchon's fiction in presenting comically masked cultural criticism. His range of allusion is far more limited than Pynchon's but nevertheless he evokes a similarly complex set of conspiratorial or threatening agencies which underline the vulnerability of the individual. Fariña also uses many narrative tactics which resemble Pynchon's: the alienating effect of bizarre names, alternation between fantasy and realism, and the construction of parable-like sequences.

If Kerouac acted as a catalyst on Pynchon, opening up his sense of narrative possibilities, by the latter's own account he also sharpened his distrust of literary decorum; but this distrust has not led Pynchon to produce totally self-reflexive fiction. While each of his novels to date has incorporated ironic and sometimes facetious allusions to their own processes, these allusions only represent a post-modernist anxiety about the scope of literature and are counter-balanced by another equally prominent characteristic of Pynchon's fiction – its factual density. One of his agents has described the astonishing lengths to which Pynchon will go to collect information for his novels and when he was working on *V.* it is reported that he wrote to friends from Mexico asking them to check details from an almanack.[24] The immediate comparison that springs to mind here is with Joyce's obsessive efforts to verify topographical details of Dublin while working on *Ulysses*. Pynchon is consistently sceptical of of the procrustean patterns into which information is forced but he never allows this scepticism to exclude data as such. Rather the difficulties of organizing and verifying that data are incorporated into his narrative structures with the result that the reader is often as entrapped within a labyrinth of reference as his characters. Pynchon's combination of Engineering Physics and English at Cornell peculiarly fitted him for unpredictable non-literary reference and is scholastic imagination has made even his short stories astonishingly dense and complex ('why should things be easy to understand?' he allegedly retorted to a friend who complained about the difficulty of *V.*).[25] In 1978 *Newsweek* carried a report that Pynchon was currently working on a 'science-fiction thriller' and a novel that required detailed research on the Mason–Dixon Line.[26] These two

works could be taken as symbolic of contrasting strands in
Pynchon's fiction which manages to combine popular art-forms
with abstruse information. The pages that follow examine in
detail what sort of fiction these interests produce.

1

The Short Stories

Although it has been reported that Pynchon wrote 'several loosely connected stories which form a kind of picaresque novel' centring on one Meatball Mulligan only one story in this series was ever published – 'Entropy'.[1] He originally planned to make Pig Bodine, a similar figure, central to the story 'Low-Lands' but in the event he was given a secondary role not only in that story but also in *V.* and *Gravity's Rainbow*. Pynchon's published stories then are individual works using radically different techniques which all move away from realism. Even his first story establishes a realistic narrative on to which Pynchon then superimposes – with varying degrees of success – layers of symbolism. In spite of their varied subjects the stories usually bear, however obliquely, on contemporary American themes – on diplomacy, consumerism, espionage and so on.

1 'THE SMALL RAIN'

Pynchon's first story dates from his undergraduate days at Cornell. He struck up friendship with Kirkpatrick Sale (then editor of the *Cornell Daily Sun*) and Richard Fariña both of whom were involved in *The Cornell Writer*.[2] Pynchon served for a time on the editorial staff and it was in this journal that his story 'The Small Rain' appeared in March 1959.[3] Jules Siegel, another fellow-student at Cornell, has recorded that Pynchon was writing short stories (and even French quatrains) earlier in the 1950s and, since 'The Small Rain' draws on events which took place in mid-1957, it is possible that the story dates from that year.[4] At any rate part of its interest lies in the glimpses it gives us of Pynchon's later preoccupations.

The story centres on one Nathan 'Lardass' Levine, a soldier at Fort Roach, Louisiana. Levine's impending leave has to be postponed when he is sent south to help in hurricane relief work in the Bayou district near Lake Charles. While there he has a casual sexual encounter with a student called Buttercup. Levine is the first in a whole series of disengaged protagonists which includes Benny Profane and Tyrone Slothrop. He is introduced to the reader as 'an inert figure in fatigues lying on a bunk, reading a paperback'.[5] The story's humour grows out of the irritating effects which this inertia has on others. He doesn't react at all when Dugan, the company clerk, tells him the Lieutenant wants him. He engages briefly in repartee with the first sergeant and with a friend; when the latter asks him what is happening, Levine mockingly inflates his own self-importance by saying 'Oh, the Pentagon again . . . just won't let me alone' (30). On one level Levine's manner is an exercise in brinkmanship. He pushes his disrespectful style as far as he can without over-stepping the limits but, more basically, Levine displays a constant anxiety to avoid being classified. His lack of respect reflects his resistance to the role of private. Equally he dislikes the labels of 'college boy' or 'intellectual' which his friends try to pin on him. His mannerisms are drawn from Marlon Brando films, vaudeville, etc, and he has 'gone native' in the sense of adopting a Southern drawl and switching his taste from jazz to hillbilly music. He does the latter with a conscious sense of mimickry, as if once again he was trying to avoid stereotyping as the Jewish boy-made-good from the Bronx.

Levine has deliberately cultivated the manner of a lazy slob to articulate his sense of pointlessness. When other characters criticize him he ducks their criticism by facetious evasions. He is urged to become an officer, for instance; is charged with being a romantic or simply afraid of experience. Given the pointlessness of everything then, immobility takes on a positive value for Levine as do his throw-away jokes since they prevent commitment. In the latter respect Levine resembles the hero of Richard Fariña's novel, *Been Down So Long It Looks Like Up to Me* (1966). As we have seen, Gnossos Pappadopoulis adopts a variety of guises and postures to avoid being identified with any of the situations in which he participates. This so-called 'exemption' can only be maintained by a style which Pynchon, in his introduction to the novel, has described as 'an extended version of 1950s Cool'.[6] Levine similarly draws on wise-cracks, 'in' slang and roles from the cinema to as it were free-wheel through the story.

If Levine were the only substantial subject the story would very quickly become tedious. But circumstances force movement upon him. The company is sent south to help in the rescue work after a hurricane has struck in the Lake Charles area. Here, as Mathew Winston has pointed out, Pynchon is drawing on fact.[7] On the night of Thursday, 27 June 1957 (not mid-July, as Pynchon's story states) Hurricane Audrey swept up from the Gulf of Mexico and inflicted wide-spread destruction on the Bayou communities of Creole and Cameron. Pynchon follows the details closely. McNeese State College, where Levine goes, was in fact an emergency relief centre, and the *Lake Charles American Press* for Saturday, 29 June, did carry a headline reading 'Toll May Hit 250'.[8] Although Pynchon has altered some of the names involved (Fort Polk becomes Fort Roach; Creole not Cameron became the worst hit township), he preserves the factual nature of the news-story and thereby anticipates on a very small scale the extensive use he will make of historical information in *V.* and *Gravity's Rainbow*.

Details of fact aside, Pynchon draws on the disaster to give a rudimentary shape to his story which dramatizes a series of shocks to Levine's studied indifference. His main problem is how to react to a spectacle of death. His participation in the 'death detail', in the work of gathering corpses, causes existential anxieties about himself to grow and his detachment and flippant manner diminish correspondingly. The pivotal passage of description probably draws on Hemingway for its hard edge and for its grotesque rendering of the corpses:

It was mostly this that Levine remembered afterward, the peculiar atmospheric effect of gray sun on gray swamp, the way the air felt and smelled. For ten hours they cruised around looking for dead. One they unhooked from a barbed wire fence. It hung there like a foolish balloon, a travesty; until they touched it and it popped, hissed and collapsed. They took them off roofs, out of trees, they found them floating or tangled in the debris of houses. Levine worked in silence like the others, the sun hot on his neck and face, the reek of the swamp and the corpses in his lungs, letting it all happen; not exactly unwilling to think about it nor quite unable; but realizing somehow that the situation did not require thought or rationalization. He was picking up stiffs. That was what he was doing. When the tug pulled in around six to offload bodies, Levine walked off as carelessly as he had climbed aboard.   (47–8)

'The Small Rain' establishes a fairly conventional narrative perspective close to Levine's. His is the only consciousness to which we gain access. Even in the passage quoted above the factual apparently dead-pan prose suggests that the job gives Levine a grim satisfaction in relieving him from thought. The first corpse he encounters becomes an emblem of futility and this marks a difference between Pynchon's treatment of the dead and Hemingway's 'A Natural History of the Dead' sketch from *Death in the Afternoon*. In the latter Hemingway uses calculatedly non-heroic descriptions in a polemic against literary glamourizing and on behalf of a naturalistic accuracy. In Pynchon's story, on the other hand, the corpses are engrossed into Levine's general sense of pointlessness. The local power of the description leads nowhere, however, because Levine blocks off any reaction to the deaths around him. Pynchon has subsequently found this the besetting fault of the whole story: 'In "The Small Rain" characters are found dealing with death in pre-adult ways. They evade; they sleep late, they seek emphemisms' (5). Levine's activities trigger off a parodic image of himself as 'Lardass Levine the wandering Jew' as if to suggest that even his dissatisfaction is moving through stereotyped grooves.

The concluding event of the story is Levine's sexual encounter with the student Buttercup, but to understand the ironies involved we need to return to the beginning. There Levine is reading a pornographic paperback called *Swamp Wench*. During the journey from Fort Roach to Lake Charles Levine is taunted with the romantic dream of withdrawing into the wilderness to live with a girl in a swamp shack. Levine's meeting with Buttercup suggests that this fantasy is going to be realized when she takes him to an isolated cabin. But the mattress and Buttercup's sexual repartee also suggest a familiar routine which blocks Levine's pleasure and makes him fall back on his cherished detachment. After they had made love he tries to joke ironically, but even that turns into cliché:

'In the midst of great death', Levine said, 'the little death'. And later, 'Ha. It sounds like a caption in *Life*. In the midst of *Life*. We are in death. Oh god.'   (50)

His sour punning turns in on itself as he shows disgust with his own literary comments. At this point the significance of the title emerges.

'The Small Rain' comes from the anonymous Renaissance quatrain:

> Western wind, when will thou blow,
>   The small rain down can rain?
> Christ, if my love were in my arms
>   And I in my bed again!

One version of this poem is quoted by Hemingway's Frederic Henry during his retreat from the Austro-Italian front in *A Farewell To Arms*.[9] The quotation forms part of his yearning for his lover Catherine as he travels through the rain-swept landscape, and is made with a consciously ironic contrast with the actual scale of the rain. Pynchon's title contains an identical irony, particularly as it refers to hurricane damage, and Levine's contrast between the death-toll and the Renaissance notion of orgasm as a little death perhaps signposts the title's significance and at the same time expresses a certain embarrassment at its literary nature. Pynchon leaves us in no doubt about the association between rain and death since near the end of the story a character names Hemingway and Eliot as precedents. On the strength of these allusions Joseph Slade has argued that Levine is the first of Pynchon's redeemer-figures who fail to rejuvenate the waste land.[10] In fact rain promises fertility and hope in *The Waste Land*, whereas in Pynchon's story it has brought death and destruction, a *literal* waste land. It would be wrong to inflate Levine's status even though Pynchon allows a certain amount of pathos to accrue around him.

The story's limitations lie in other areas. Pynchon is, for instance, rather self-conscious about using army slang and terminology. He draws out the narrative to excessive length. He also sets up a context which is hostile to any literary rhetoric that goes beyond the terse and the immediately physical. One point where Levine's language jerks awkwardly away from his usual laconic wise-cracks comes when he expresses his feelings through a technical analogy.

'What I mean is something like a closed circuit. Everybody on the same frequency. And after a while you forget about the rest of the spectrum and start believing that this is the only frequency that counts or is real. While outside, all up and down the land, there are these wonderful colors and x-rays and ultraviolets going on.'   (42)

This is Pynchon's first literary application of science and it fails because Levine cannot bear this kind of rhetoric. Slade has commented that the analogy expresses a longing for a community but it actually articulates Levine's dissatisfaction.[11] Immediately after Levine's statement another soldier dismisses the analogy as false but the damage has been done. It is not until his second story, 'Mortality and Mercy in Vienna', that Pynchon can create a stylistic context hospitable to quite diverse literary allusions.

In spite of his ostensible ease at the beginning of the story Levine exists in an awkward state of imbalance. He is far more intellectual than he would care to admit and his intellect can find no corresponding support from his feelings, certainly not from Buttercup because he was disillusioned with her even before he set out for her cabin. 'The Small Rain' dramatizes Levine's recognition of his dissatisfaction but in a deliberately inconclusive way. At the end of the story he is merely setting off on leave.

2   'MORTALITY AND MERCY IN VIENNA'

Pynchon's second story also appeared in a Cornell journal, *Epoch*, in Spring 1959. The story describes one Cleanth Siegel who is a member of a political commission and who has returned to Washington from overseas expecting to meet his girl Rachel at a party. He is instead met at the door by the host, David Lupescu, who packs an overnight bag and leaves him to host the party. Once the guests arrive Siegel allows the party to run under its own momentum and listens instead to the 'confessions' of two girls present. One of them introduces him to Irving Loon, an Ojibwa suffering apparently from melancholic depression. When Siegel sees Loon taking a rifle down from the wall, he leaves as unobtrusively as possible. As he is walking away he hears sounds presumably from Loon running amok.

The party is to become a set piece in Pynchon's fiction, reappearing to 'Entropy', in the activities of the Whole Sick Crew in *V.* (whose lives seem to revolve around a series of unplanned parties), and in the orgy on the *Anubis* in *Gravity's Rainbow*. In 'Mortality and Mercy' Siegel is drawn to the party but is by no means a participant in it. The preliminary pages of the story make it clear that, unlike Levine, he is more intellectual and more self-conscious. Extended sentences track out the wanderings of his thoughts:

> he would shake his head like a drunk who is trying to stop seeing double, having become suddenly conscious of the weight of the briefcase and the insignificance of its contents and the stupidity of what he was doing out here, away from Rachel, following an obscure but clearly marked path through a jungle of distrainments and affidavits and depositions;[12]

Siegel's disengagement from his own actions is, unlike Levine's, a fairly constant state and so no particular stimulus to recognition is needed. Detached from the value of his actions, Siegel feels free to enjoy their style (the political manoeuvrings of Washington become a Machiavellian game for him) and indeed throughout the story Siegel demonstrates an ironic awareness of the various styles and roles he is adopting. Since he can examine himself so shrewdly the rhetorical distinction between narrator and character ceases to be particularly important.

Allon White has given one of the most cogent readings of this story which he sees as dramatizing the contradictions within American liberalism (mortality and mercy: violence and sympathy). He locates these contradictions in David (i.e. 'saviour') Lupescu (i.e. 'wolfish') and Siegel (who is half-Jewish, half-Catholic), and in the whole rhetoric of the story:

> Terms which under ordinary circumstances are mutually exclusive are forced into a kind of identity where the one becomes a version of the other. The form is rather like a metaphor in which we cannot see which is the vehicle and which the tenor – there is no one referential set which controls the narrative . . .[13]

White has identified one characteristic of this story which distinguishes it strikingly from 'The Small Rain'. In the latter Pynchon works basically within a realistic mode and then expresses restiveness with that mode because it restricts his rhetorical scope. 'Mortality and Mercy' begins in a deceptively realistic way and then uses bizarre events and literary allusion to subvert its own realistic base. It constantly disorientates the reader by rendering uncertain the level on which it is working. Two examples from the passage quoted above all will show this process at work. In Siegel's thoughts 'seeing double' and the 'jungle' of legal documents appear as incidental rhetorical details, the one an analogy the other a metaphor. But once Siegel enters the party both tropes become literally true. He sees a wild mirror-image of himself in Lupescu and is told that Washington is a jungle. In each case the reader's realistic expectations are thwarted; our surprise is as great as Siegel's.

The main weakness in White's discussion of the story is that he oversimplifies its rhetorical complexity into pairs of oppositions. There is some justification for this in that Pynchon several times juxtaposes the wild and the civilized, as when a girl tells Siegel that Lupescu was 'going native'. Siegel's puzzled reaction ('going native in Washington, D.C.?': (201) and his memory of a *New Yorker* cartoon nudges the reader into admitting that the story's humour and surrealism grows out of a disparity between its various elements. We jerk unsettlingly from anthropological reference to party small-talk to literary allusions, all of which pull against each other rather than settle down into stable oppositions.

At the heart of this story lies a belief in the inauthenticity of contemporary life and a split in the self between feeling and intellect. Siegel inherits the western cultural tradition from his parents – his father is Jewish and his mother a lapsed Catholic. But because connections have disappeared culture becomes either as arsenal for private role-playing or a mechanical memory-bank; when the Ojibwa is identified he 'began flipping over a stack of mental IBM cards frantically' (206). The story thus consists to quite a large extent of perceiving resemblances. Repeated comparisons with artefacts suggest that character has become mimicry. Siegel compares Rachel to a Modigliani; the pig foetus which Lupescue nails to the wall is a mock-Dada exhibit; the chanting of a dirty limerick reminds Siegel of a climactic point in *Faust* and a list of affairs of the catalogue aria from *Don Giovanni*. These resemblances can include parody (the first girl Siegel meets is an exact reproduction of a 1940s bohemian; in fact the apartment, conversation and characters at the party all resolve into stereotypes), but Siegel is not exempt from these ironies. When he complains to Rachel about the party-guests she tells him to 'stop acting like a war flick' (200).

'Mortality and Mercy' then demands recognitions which complicate the textual surface of the story. When Siegel meets Lupescu he recognizes himself in the other; Lupescu in turn recognizes a quality in Siegel and says to him '*mon semblable, mon frere*'. At this point the reader recognizes a quotation from another recognition-scene in *The Waste Land* which bizarrely juxtaposes the ancient and modern, and which draws the 'hypocrite lecteur' into complicity with the writer.[14] Immediately after this point in the story Lupescu quotes from a quotation – 'Mistah Kurtz – he dead', which Eliot uses as epigraph to 'The Hollow Men'. These complex allusions transform the text of 'Mortality and Mercy' into a kind of palimpsest, teasing the reader's sense of familiarity and creating increasingly ambiguous effects. Is Pynchon, for instance, setting up meaningful connections with past texts, or are these cases of intellectual party chitchat? Because of such uncertainty the allusions resemble gestures towards referents which are never fixed.

The same ambiguity surrounds the story's Shakespearian title. As several critics have noted, it comes from the Duke's commission to Angelo in *Measure for Measure*:

> In our remove be thou at full ourself;
> Mortality and mercy in Vienna
> Live in thy tongue and heart.

(i.i.43–5)

Allon White has argued that mortality and mercy represent opposed qualities but the Duke's casual linkage of the two terms in fact begs the issues which the play will deal with. He delegates his authority to Angelo with the injunction to exercise mercy because of the inescapable fact of mortality, and to express that which is truly felt. The play demonstrates a complex shifting relation between justice and legality which shows the very opposite to a harmony between mortality and mercy, tongue and heart. The delegation of authority obviously finds an analogue in Lupescu leaving Siegel to take charge of the party. In other words Siegel parallels Angelo. But the Duke does not leave Vienna and instead lurks in disguise, watching Angelo's administration. Siegel too is an on-looker, detached from events by his age and a period abroad. The Duke adopts the disguise of a friar and prescribes penance to Juliet for sexual wrongdoings just as Siegel acts as father-confessor the two girls at the party. Here he parallels the Duke. The very fact that the Shakespearian analogy is shifting and also to a problem play fits the ambiguities of Pynchon's story, and details like the theme of disguise bear directly on Siegel's sense of role-playing.

'Mortality and Mercy' makes repeated reference to areas of myth and religion, again in a context of roles. Lupescu forces a role on Siegel in giving up the party to him. He has to play father-confessor to a girl called Lucy, then to a second girl called Debby, and finally to Brennan, the cause of the triangular tension. Lupescu (facetiously?) converts Siegel into a deity (a 'fisher of souls') which in effect extends his own private sense of himself as a healer, and puns on the title of 'host'. Allon White has commented shrewdly on the anthropological relevance of Lupescu's pig totem, showing that the pig regularly represents penitence. Frazer's *The Golden Bough*, which Pynchon used extensively in *V.*, also gives examples of the wolf being a predatory corn-spirit.[15] These, however, are connotations raised retrospectively by the blocks of information on Ojibwa culture. We need first to recognize the ironies in Siegel's confessional role. As Joseph Slade has pointed out, he performs as a mock-priest partly because he is forced to act out his resemblances to Lupescu.[16] His quotations from ritual verge on parody because they are mimicking an empty form, a relic of Siegel's cultural inheritance which was dead even before it reached him. The religious references thus gesture towards absent spaces and strengthen our sense of the hollowness of contemporary culture.[17]

As Pynchon juxtaposes references to the primitiveness and sophistication of urban America he both undermines Washington's assumption of superiority and questions the values of high culture. The two figures who polarize these two extremes are Grossmann, Siegel's former room-mate at college, and the Ojibwa Irving Loon. Grossmann 'gets culture', partly from reading Santayana and T. S. Eliot, and adopts the correct dress and speech; in other words, adopts a certain role. Siegel at least recognizes the element of theatre in such behaviour:

. . . having committed himself . . . by the very act of lying next to a girl he did not know and playing the role of crying towel for half an hour, resolved in true British-staff-officer style to bite the jolly old bullet and make the best of a bad job. (205)

Like Porpentine in Pynchon's later story 'Under the Rose', Siegel wryly shifts role, mocking himself as he does so. His performance as priest is no more privileged than any other role he plays.

Directly contrasted to Grossmann and to the whole party ethos is Irving Loon, the Ojibwa, who personifies the wildness and inner demons which other characters are trying to suppress. The mortality of the story's title bears on Siegel's memory of his cousin's death, on Lucy's revelation of semi-hysteria, and above all on Loon who stands as a ludicrous *and* powerful *memento mori*. Pynchon challenges our sense of plausibility by making the information about the Ojibwa seem preposterous; first it is released in a carefully documented way, then mocked, then converted into nightmare, and mocked once again as party talk.[18] Siegel's memory of the Windigo psychosis puts him in a privileged position at the end of the story and forces on him a moment of choice: should he tell the others that Loon might run amok or not? Allon White states disapprovingly that the story 'dissolves its revulsion and guilt about modern America into literary analogues and stylish paradox' but I have been arguing that allusion functions as an integral part of the story's irony.[19] Siegel toys with offering the party-goers 'a kind of miracle' but withdraws instead leaving a grotesque revelation to come from Loon's mania. This withdrawal was implicit from the very start and it is a logical continuation of the story's attention to resemblances that Siegel should compose a pastiche Hemingway image to articulate his sense of impending death. His general detachment and the opposition between the two halves of his sensibility would both work against a positive decision.

3 'LOW-LANDS'

Pynchon's third story, 'Low-lands' (1960), repeats the gesture of disengagement which closes 'Mortality and Mercy' but this time the withdrawal is into pure fantasy. The story opens with a scene where its protagonist Dennis Flange is drinking with his garbageman. Upstairs his wife paces angrily to and fro, waiting for them to stop. The last straw comes with the arrival of Pig Bodine (a sailor who is AWOL) which sends Cindy (the wife) into paroxysms of fury. She drives the three men out of the house, Flange 'for good', and they go to the local rubbish dump which is presided over by a negro named Bolingbroke. In his shack they swap sea stories over wine until lights out. During the night a girl's voice summons Flange from the shack and lures him into a secret part of the dump where she lives with other gypsies. The story ends with Flange promising to stay with her.

There is a simple but well-defined plot-sequence to the story which opens with a scene of flawed domesticity and then moves off in pursuit of more satisfying pleasure and fulfilment. Flange and his wife Cindy live in a mock-English cottage on the north shore of Long Island. Cindy has become a personification of the restraints and futility of domesticity; she has persuaded Flange to spend $1000 on a stereo set and then used it as a stand for cocktail trays. She even objects to Flange's friends, including Squarcione the garbage collector. The story does not concern itself with *why* Flange's marriage has broken down. Suffice it that the monotony of his life with Cindy, his job (he works for a firm of attorneys in New York) and of his suburban surroundings gives impetus to Flange's withdrawal. The domestic references here are as ironic as at the beginning of *The Crying of Lot 49* when Oedipa Maas fusses over her cooking, with the difference that Flange is more aware of his dissatisfaction. This does not mean that he consciously rejects monotony, however, because, as we shall see, passivity has a positive value for him. The theme of the story thus emerges as Flange's desire for pleasure or happiness, pleasure figured in terms of escape from restriction into irresponsibility. The story examines two avenues open to Flange whereby he might find relief from his dissatisfaction at home.

The first of these is psychoanalysis. Flange plays regular visits to Geronimo Diaz (a 'crazed and boozy wetback'), the prototype of Dr Hilarius in *The Crying of Lot 49*, who complicates the normal doctor–patient relationship in being himself manic, obsessed with certain analytical theories, and driven by a delusion that he is Paganini. It is this insanity which delights Flange:

> . . . it was a wonderful, random sort of madness which conformed to no known model or pattern, an irresponsible plasma of delusion he [Diaz] floated in, utterly convinced, for

example, that he was Paganini and had sold his soul to the devil. (58)[20]

Within the story's reversal of conventional values Diaz represents an unusually manic kind of freedom, offering to Flange a therapy derived not from the procedures used by the analyst but from his very lunacy. It offers relief from the rationality of his home life. Early in the story, Flange's house is described in a way which demonstrates its imaginative importance for him and which alerts the reader to his yearning for withdrawal. The house's cellar has 'innumerable tunnels . . . writhed away . . . into dead ends, storm drains, abandoned sewers and occasionally a secret wine cellar' (56). This warren of rooms and tunnels stimulates Flange's imagination just as the boys in Pynchon's later story, 'The Secret Integration' (1964), can give their fancies free reign in a derelict mansion. The attraction of the house is expressed through a Freudian image:

Flange at least had come to feel attached to the place by an umbilical cord woven of lichen and sedge, furze and gorse; he called it his womb with a view . . . (57)

As the first image which refers to Flange's psyche, it explains why Diaz should be brought into the story at about this point. It tempts the reader to engage in a quasi-psychological analysis of the text, perhaps to search for sexual complexes which Flange is not admitting. But Pynchon, through Flange's response, anticipates this approach and dismisses his predilection for labyrinthine enclosures with an outrageous pun. Furthermore Flange does not get much out of Diaz's psycho-analytical procedures because he is so familiar with the works of Freud. His explicitness prevents the womb-image from giving us access to his unconscious and dismisses at once the value of his psycho-analysis and of a psycho-analytical reading of the text. Despite its references to Freud the story clearly does not work on a Freudian level. Rather it sets up certain metaphorical linkages which give us access to Flange's fantasies. Apart from giving Flange relief from domesticity, Diaz is also important in reinforcing some of these linkages – specifically those which relate to the sea. He repeats Freud's own outline of dream symbolism in pointing out the evolutionary importance of the sea as the cradle of life and therefore 'the true mother image for us all' (59). Freud also indicates the literal relevance of water of individual birth in the amniotic fluid, which the story recognizes explicitly.[21] But this still does not mean that Freud's theories deepen the psychological scope of the story; rather Freudian linkages strengthen and are incorporated into Flange's fantasy-life and into the metaphorical themes of the story. Of the two possible avenues of response open to him, the fantasy receives far more attention.

The frequently ironic and joking activities of the fantasizing self rather than Freudian psychology supply the main language for 'Low-lands', and the sea supplies many of the images. On the most literal factual level it has played and is still playing a part in Flange's life since he – like Pynchon – has served a spell in the navy, and is now living on the shore of Long Island Sound.[22] Other allusions to traditional tropes, like the sea representing the unconscious, or the Moon breaking away from the Pacific and then being personified as a goddess of change set up a context for Flange's obsession. The sea offers him a Conradian self-image:

A peculiar double of his was sole inhabitant to this tilt of memory: Fortune's elf child and disinherited darling, young and randy and more a Jolly Jack Tar than anyone human could conceivably be; thews and chin taut against a sixty-knot gale with a well-broken-in briar clenched in the bright defiant teeth; standing OOD on the bridge through the midwatch with only a dozing quarter-master and a faithful helmsman and a sewer-mouthed radar crew and a red-dog game in the sonar shack, along with the ripped-off exile moon and its track on the ocean for company.   (59–60)[23]

This humorous portrait makes one thing clear at least – that neither Flange nor anyone else was ever like this. This double is a 'sole inhabitant' of a dream-like or imaginary scene where the other crew-members form part of the setting. The physical improbabilities and a phrase like 'Fortune's elf child' prevent Flange from sliding into self-pity. He clings on to this fantastic image of himself as a buttress against the increasing signs of middle age, and is thus ideally distanced from any signs of suburban domesticity. Although the story is narrated in the third person we rarely sense a sharply defined ironic gap between narrator and protagonist, as we do in *The Crying of Lot 49* for example, because Flange demonstrates a humorous self-consciousness about his own fantasies. This may be useful to Pynchon in helping to rule out solemnity but, as we shall see, it raises a critical problem in making it difficult to decide how far events ironize Flange.

Similarly it is difficult to be sure how the story treats Flange's expulsion from home. Does it raise any alternative to suburban boredom? The main answer would be Flange's fantasy life, but the story distractingly raises another possibility. The garbage-collector Squarcione is one discordant element in the Flange household. A far more direct threat materializes when 'an ape in a naval uniform' (60) arrives on the doorstep. The new arrival is Pig Bodine, an ex-shipmate of Flange's who has been a pet hate of Cindy's since he diverted Flange from his honeymoon on to a fortnight-long binge. Many of the details surrounding him are simply repeated in *V.* He has gone AWOL, has led riotous parties involving fights with the naval police, and he is a close buddy of both Flange and Benny Profane. Since Pynchon was working on *V.* at the time of the publication of 'Low-lands' these parallels are not surprising. Is Pynchon then using Bodine as a spokesman for some alternative to unsatisfactory domesticity? In the short story he certainly figures as a catalyst in Flange's expulsion from home, personifying a reckless energy which is subversive to Cindy's domesticity. At this point it seems as if Pynchon is joining Hemingway and Kerouac in celebrating the pleasures of male cameraderie as against the irritating entanglements of domesticity. The impression persists until Flange, Bodine and Bolingbroke swap sea-stories in the dump. Certainly in this scene Flange appears to be more relaxed and at ease. It does not follow, however, that Pynchon is setting up an alternative way of life for Flange. To do so would be too solemn for his purposes in the story, too close to what Flange calls the 'relentless rationality' of his wife and would shift the story's focus away from Flange's fantasies which are the constant source of vitality in the story. In his eagerness to try out themes and characters for *V.* Pynchon runs the risk of damaging the story's unity because he does not have the space to develop the free-wheeling picaresque humour of Pig Bodine's escapades.

Flange's expulsion from home leads the reader to the central image of the whole story and the prime example of how structure and subject coincide. When Dennis is driven out his garbageman,

Squarcione suggests that they drive to his dump. The dump immediately catches Flange's imagination and introduces the imagistic core of the story where the two settings (sea and dump) converge. The dump is in the middle of a housing development, some fifty feet below street level. At first Flange is fascinated by the 'fated' way in which the dump's surface is inching upwards year by year. Then he realizes a more important correspondence. From a sea-ballad he has taken the term 'Low-lands', detached it from its normal meaning of southern Scotland and attached it to an optical impression of the sea:

> Anyone who has looked at the open sea under a special kind of illumination or in a mood conducive to metaphor will tell you of the curious illusion that the ocean, despite its movement, has a certain solidity; it becomes a gray or glaucous desert, a waste land which stretches away to the horizon, and all you would have to do would be to step over the lifelines to walk away over its surface; . . .   (65)

There is no question here of anything as portentous as a hidden truth. Pynchon insists on the illusion of Flange's feeling, but then this is not really the point. The sea offers Flange a borderless expanse which his imagination can fill and this is figured in the liberating movement of stepping 'over the lifelines'. Once he senses the spatial dimensions of the sea – and it is important that this only happens after he has left home – he projects a human figure on to the area, an imaginary surrogate of himself. The action of stepping over the bounds of life itself predicts the end of the story when Flange will withdraw into a realm of pure fantasy.

The dump may be an ironical presence in the story because Flange's responses to it may be in themselves examples of waste, but Pynchon resists a predictable satirical onslaught on bourgeois contentment. The dump itself offers Flange more tangible satisfactions to the imagination than the sea because it is a 'discrete kingdom' with its own geography and texture. The objects in the dump have a purely visual or aesthetic appeal. They form an enormous collage of all the things Flange has left behind, a collage represented in miniature on the walls of Bolingbroke's shack which are lined with cuttings from periodicals dating back to the Depression. Bolingbroke, the overseer, no doubt takes his name from *Henry IV* and, as Joseph Slade suggests, is the ruler of this miniature kingdom.[24] Indeed he even has a mock-crown in the form of a pork-pie hat.

The dump is an 'enclave in the dreary country around it' (67) within the set of inversions which Pynchon has established. It lies in the centre of the Long Island suburbia from which Flange is withdrawing. Its surroundings are 'dreary', i.e. a metaphorical waste land, whereas the dump itself has all kinds of startling eminences and depressions – 'acres' of abandoned refrigerators, and a 'valley' of tyres. In other words the dump possesses its own variable and fascinating landscape. There are other ironies present too. Despite the presence of consumer articles the values of consumerism do not operate here since anything is free for the taking. Bolingbroke invites them to choose any bed they like. Unlike Cindy's stereo set, nothing here has a price. The dump thus gives Pynchon a chance to ironize briefly the same values of consumerism which he will later mock in Oedipa Maas' tupperware parties at the beginning of *The Crying of Lot 49*. In that novel Oedipa must leave this behind just as Flange must leave home. Bolingbroke's dump obviously stimulates his imagination in a positive way, and thereby plays on double meanings to the notion of waste.

In a survey of Pynchon's short stories Richard Patteson has argued that a central preoccupation is with 'the conflict between the human need to create meaningful form and the unavoidable tendency towards formlessness in the universe.'[25] Junk, he suggests, is one example of such formlessness and relates to the other breakdowns in the story: Flange's marriage, Diaz' insanity, etc. The 'dead centre' of the dump thus contrasts with T. S. Eliot's 'still point' in representing the culmination of this process of collapse without any saving spiritual insight. Patteson's argument skilfully identifies a kind of counterpoint in 'Low-lands'. On the one hand the dump is gradually rising towards street-level and therefore heading inevitably towards an entropic loss of differences ('this peculiar quality of fatedness', as Flange puts it). On the other Flange's imagination fastens on to the texture of the dump's surface and projects life on to it. Thus it is quite appropriate for us to discover that people actually live in the dump after it has been vitalized imaginative by Flange.

The first stage of the story has been accomplished. The reader has been invited to consider events in terms of Freudian psychology or of 'dropping out', but both possibilities have been discounted. Flange's preservation of passivity has a central importance and leads to one of the major theoretical statements of the story. He has left home and exchanged his wife's company temporarily for that of Bodine and Bolingbroke, which they formally celebrate by telling sea-stories over their win in Bolingbroke's shack.[26] Flange's story is the odd one out in having no connection with the sea at all; it recounts how he and other fellow-students stole a corpse and deposited it in the bedroom of his fraternity president. Flange's reason for not telling a sea-story makes an important gloss on 'Low-lands' as a whole:

> . . . the real reason he knew and could not say was that if you are Dennis Flange and if the sea's tides are the same that not only wash along your veins but also billow through your fantasies then it is all right to listen to but not to tell stories about that sea, because you and the truth of a true lie were thrown sometime way back into a curious contiguity and as long as you are passive you can remain aware of the truth's extent but the minute you become active you are somehow, if not violating a convention outright, at least screwing up the perspective of things, much as anyone observing subatomic particles changes the works, data and odds, by the act of observing. So he had told the other instead, at random.   (69)

Despite the complexity of this sentence it basically expresses a rationalization of passivity. We have already encountered the proposition that the sea embodies life (in evolutionary sequence as the amniotic fluid) and also provides rich fuel for fantasy (metaphor, etc.). Flange here balances life precariously against fantasy and deliberately refuses to tell a sea-story because it would upset that balance. Life and fantasy can only be counterpoised against each other by maintaining passivity. Because we have already seen the existential value of fantasy for Flange, maintaining passivity paradoxically becomes a positive action. He draws an analogy with Heisenberg's uncertainty principle which states that the position of a subatomic particle cannot be measured accurately without interfering with the system. Since qualities are paired the position of a particle *and* its momentum cannot both be measured simultaneously. This whole passage bears directly on the ambiguity of the story's ending.

The only critic to examine this story-telling episode in any detail, J. O. Stark, argues that it introduces an element of self-reflexivity into the story and should alert us to the existence of other fictions. Stark uses the term 'fiction' to cover any kind of imaginative construct or explanation; thus the metaphor of the sea as a woman and the comparison of Flange's house to a prehistoric mound are as much fictions as the more obvious examples of the Noel Coward song and the ballad which gives the story its title. Stark's discussion does justice to the complexity of the story's texture but it leads him to a rather tendentious conclusion, that 'two of the most important themes in 'Low-lands' are the creation and validity of fictions . . . his [Pynchon's] main purpose is to analyse fictions'.[27] The generally relaxed tenor of the story, its light humour and play on the unexpected would not imply anything as tensed or deliberate as analysis. Indeed the central passage just discussed explains why Flange never examines his own fantasies; within his logic to do so would be to damage their vitality and equilibrium. There may not be anything as solemn as analysis in the story but there are nevertheless ironies in Flange's situation and resemblances which counteract his sense of pleasing change.

When the men were picking their way around the debris outside the shack, Bolingbroke had thrown out cryptic references to other inhabitants in the dump. Before Flange goes to sleep (and only *he* notices this) Bolingbroke bolts the door and gives him a piece of pipe in case the gypsies get in, for they prove to be the other presences. Night-time characterizes the last section of the story which follows the same clear logic of withdrawal. Flange has left his home, gone to the dump and encountered one fascinatingly self-enclosed world. Once he has finished celebrating his new-found freedom with his friends, he is ready to withdraw again, this time into a dream. Flange suddenly jerks awake in the darkness and hears a girl's voice calling 'Anglo . . . Anglo with the golden hair. Come out. Come out by the secret path and find me' (72). It is as if a dream is taking place. Flange recognizes his own imaginary *Doppelgänger* in her description. Both the girl's foreign idiom and phrase 'the secret path' hint at mystery, as if Flange will know her. Flange at last decides to risk going outside, picks his way through the winding path from the shack, but then knocks over a stack of snow tyres which temporarily stun him. When he comes to, he gets his first look at the girl. This is a key moment in the story.

> He finally managed to get to his feet, and it was only then that
> he had a good look at her. In the starlight she was exquisite:
> she wore a dark dress, her legs and arms were bare, slim, the
> neck arching and delicate, her figure so slender it was almost a
> shadow. Dark hair floated around her face and down her back
> like a black nebula; eyes enormous, nose retroussé, short upper
> lip, good teeth, nice chin. She was a dream, this girl, an angel.
> She was also roughly three and a half feet tall.   (73–4)

The girl's very perfection suggests unreality and Pynchon
brilliantly avoids giving the description a hard edge. The girl is so
delicate her figure is 'almost a shadow', her hair 'floats' like a
'nebula', thus continuing the impression of her in a watery
medium and in the sky. It is to Pynchon's credit that he can force
meaning on to a slangy cliché like 'she was a dream' which
becomes literally true. The girl's name proves to be Nerissa, but
Pynchon's girl bears no resemblance at all to Portia's vigorous
waiting-woman and he probably chose the name for its
resemblances to 'Nereis', i.e. a mythical sea-maiden. The fact that
this girl has a rat called Hyacinth gives us sufficient clue that
Pynchon is basing Flange's 'epiphany' on a similar moment in
Eliot's hyacinth garden at the beginning of *The Waste Land*.[28]

Nerissa guides Flange along another path and then enters a
General Electric refrigerator whose back is missing. The fridge is
simply an updated form of the usual entry point into a fantasy-
world. It could be compared with Alice's rabbit-hole and indeed
Flange does have to worm his way through a tunnel of junk
before they reach a large concrete pipe. This they follow until they
arrive at a 'dead end' where a door opens on to 'a room hung
with arrases and paintings'. These Gothic furnishings perhaps
recall Esmeralda's room in Hugo's *Notre Dame de Paris* where
Gringoire is brought to the Court of Miracles, the enclave of the
beggars in the heart of medieval Paris. This, like Bolingbroke's
dump, is a self-enclosed world, one which literally exists but
which seems too fantastic to be real. The appeal which Nerissa's
world bears for Flange is individual and lyrical; he feels pleasure
at the sheer distance he has come from his home.

In view of the extensive references to the sea throughout the
story, it is hardly surprising that Pynchon draws on *The Tempest* to
underpin Flange's reaction to Nerissa. Shakespeare's play begins
with a similar progression away from ordinary life to a place

where special magical values operate. Ferdinand awakens to the sound of ethereal music and sees Miranda just as Flange encounters Nerissa. Both men are transfixed by their respective maiden's beauty and both wonder whether they are dreaming. The parallels are confirmed by a brief allusion to Ariel's song when Flange reflects that he has suffered a 'sea change' as he drifts off to sleep.[29] The sea has already been associated with the imagination and Ariel's evocation of submarine transformations only reinforces the connection.

In Nerissa's room Flange meets her pet rat Hyacinth (a forerunner of the rat Veronica in *V*.) and the name of the rat completes, for Joseph Slade, a long series of references to Eliot's *The Waste Land* which runs throughout the story. Slade concludes that Pynchon blurs his story by too closely adopting Eliot's motifs which are anyway ambiguous. Certainly the number of parallels with Eliot's poem suggests a caution on Pynchon's part, a tentative attitude towards his own story, although the sea provides a thematic umbrella which is broad enough to assimilate a considerable amount of allusion. One drawback in Slade's approach is that he tends to moralize the story and to look for signs of affirmation which simply do not exist: 'no real healing or redemption seems forthcoming, even if we assume that Flange has symbolically died and risen; he is a miserable messiah'.[30] 'Of course he is; in fact he is not a messiah at all. Pynchon dismisses that very possibility when discussing Flange's attitude to the sea (Diaz mocks his fantasy of walking on its surface as a 'messiah complex'). Slade in fact comes much nearer to the tone of the story when he describes Flange as another of Pynchon's schlemiels.

Enough has been said about the story by now to show that Pynchon is more concerned to establish a series of polarized associations in 'Low-lands' than to make an explicit comment on the nature of society or the possibility of renewal. The monotony of Flange's naval manoeuvres is contrasted with the jack-tar image he fashions of himself; urban development areas with the dump; domestic routine with passive fantasy, and so on. Although Pynchon now sees the story as a static character-sketch, the main impetus of the story is towards total withdrawal into dream and that is why it begins appropriately with references to dream images. While Pynchon borrows details from *The Waste Land* and from 'The Love Song of J. Alfred Prufrock' (which ends with a fatal awakening from undersea fantasy) this does not prove that he is trying to follow up all the motifs of that poem, especially as Pynchon draws on other works. Hugo's novel offers one possible parallel, the Alice books another (they might explain the rat for example) and also *The Tempest*. There is no equivalent moment to Prufrock's awakening in 'Low-lands'. In a scene strongly reminiscent of *Alice in Wonderland* (in Flange's wide-eyed reaction to the most fantastic things, for example) Nerissa offers herself as a wife, but Flange hesitates until he realizes that both she and her rat resemble children. Pynchon gives a misleading impression of insight ('So of course he knew': 77), misleading because Flange's decision to stay with Nerissa has been latent throughout the story and in such a passive character his 'decision' is nothing more than a final yielding to his own fantasy. Flange's awakening in the shack and his regaining consciousness after the tyres fall on him are devices which insist on the increasingly dream-like level of action; they suggest penetration into deeper levels of the mind. By the end of the story, Flange has turned, as it were, into pure consciousness and the last lines show his swoon of pleasure into the sea-image he has created for himself: 'White caps danced across her eyes; sea creatures, he knew, would be cruising about in the submarine green of her heart' (77). By this point the withdrawal into fantasy is complete.

I have been suggesting that Flange's fantasy has a richness and vitality lacking in his everyday life. As Slade puts it, Flange 'prefers withdrawal underground to the void, the emptiness above'.[31] Floating, for instance, takes on connotations of freedom from fixity and monotony, and in the workings of Flange's imagination we can clearly observe an effort to resist the void or the formless. The change in the dump's level is analogous to the spiral downwards towards the 'dead centre'. Both mark entropic declines towards 'perfect, passionless uniformity' (66). Flange uses the latter phrase to describe what might be an optical illusion or the result of a passing mood – the impression that the sea offers a solid surface. It is this uniformity which Flange's imagination or fantasy tries to counteract. That is why he projects a figure on to the sea's surface and why he imagines himself travelling from city to city. One ironic possibility which the story raises is that entropic decline may even be infecting Flange's fantasies and that he may be enacting the very process he is trying to resist. This suggestion emerges in the similarity between the enclosures he enters and his house which is both womb-like and a labyrinth; in the former respect it resembles his police booth; it also resembles Bolingbroke's shack (explicitly a second 'home') and Nerissa's dwelling in the middle of a labyrinthine network of paths and pipes. Thomas Schaub has noted some of these similarities and has argued that the story has an hour-glass shape.[32] The ending thus becomes almost a mirror-image of the opening. These resemblances certainly pull ironically against the more linear narrative sequence of withdrawal and suggest that Pynchon is distancing himself from his protagonist. Flange links his life metaphorically to natural processes like the change in the dump's level and tries to resist the pull of such processes towards anonymity and uniformity by indulging his fantasy life. The story's main irony is that his withdrawal into Nerissa's world is both a partial repetition of the opening scene and a 'dead end'; it is, in short, the very opposite of liberation.

'Low-lands' is an enigmatic treatment of dream and fantasy, all the more puzzling because it is difficult to find the right vocabulary to describe it. Again and again Pynchon blurs the distinction between dream or fantasy and reality. The story makes extensive use of metaphor to pull apparently disparate levels of experience into a continuum. The sea, for example, constantly shifts in representative significance until it is completely internalized in the concluding image. 'Low-lands' rather defensively wards off any such seriousness by its witty and joking surface, but nevertheless represents an important early treatment of dream in Pynchon's fiction.

4 'ENTROPY'

Of all Thomas Pynchon's short fiction 'Entropy' (1960) has attracted the most critical attention. Tony Tanner describes it roundly as 'his first important short story' and other critics have paid tribute to its sophisticated structure.[33] It also represents the first explicit application of a scientific concept to his fiction. The story is set in an apartment block in Washington, D.C. The date is February 1957. In one flat (the lower of the two which provide the setting) a party being given by one Meatball Mulligan is about to get its second wind. People are sprawled about in various stages of drunkenness and a quartet of jazz musicians are sitting in the living-room, listening to records. Quite early in the story a man named Saul climbs into Mulligan's flat from the fire-escape and explains that he has just had a fight with his wife Miriam. Subsequently the other people enter, the drunkenness and noise increase, a fight breaks out and the party seems to be on the verge of chaos. After due consideration Mulligan decides to calm everyone down and restore order. This he does. The action of 'Entropy' in fact alternates between Mulligan's party and the apartment above his where one Callisto and his companion Aubade are trying to heal a sick bird. The apartment is a kind of hot-house, a perfectly self-contained ecological system. Like Henry Adams, Callisto is obsessed with energy running down and – perhaps for posterity, but more likely as a solipsistic exercise – he is dictating his memoirs. The bird dies and, abandoning the ecological balance they have built up for the past seven years, Aubade goes to the window and smashes it. The story ends with the two waiting for the internal and external temperatures to equalize and for night to fall.

This bald summary of the action does not of course explain its relevance to the title and to understand this we must apply the various definitions of 'entropy' offered by a standard modern dictionary. *Webster's Third New International Dictionary* defines the concept as follows:

1. [In thermodynamics]   A quantity that is the measure of the amount of energy in a system not available for doing work . . .

2. [In statistical mechanics]   A factor or quantity that is a function of the physical state of a mechanical system . . .

3. [In communication theory]   A measure of the efficiency of a system (as a code or a language) in transmitting information . . .

4. The ultimate state reached in the degradation of the matter and energy of the universe: state of inert uniformity of component elements; absence of form, pattern, hierarchy, or differentiation . . .[34]

Of these meanings the second is the least important for Pynchon's story, being only glanced at briefly. In Callisto's hot-house, Mulligan's party and finally in Saul's apartment below we can see that the apartments form a schematic analogue to the fourth, first and third definitions respectively. Callisto is preoccupied above all with the final run-down of energy, the 'heat-death' of the universe. Mulligan's party-goers are all characterized by apathy and inertia and so ironically exemplify energy which is unavailable for work. And lastly Saul has had an argument with his wife over communication theory and discusses with Mulligan (very inconclusively) what a high proportion of sheer 'noise' human speech contains. Outside the apartment block is the street and the weather which, by implication, are also outside this multi-level metaphor.

Tony Tanner had suggested another interpretation of the building as follows:

> The house . . . is some sort of paradigm for modern consciousness; the lower part immersed in the noise of modern distractions and sensing the failing of significant communication, while the upper part strives to remain at the level of music, yet feels the gathering strain as dream is encroached on by life. Life, in this context, is not only the party downstairs, but the weather.[35]

Certainly this would explain the broad contrast between Callisto's 'hot-house' and Mulligan's party. The former is dream-like and enclosed; the latter is earthy and open to newcomers. But Tanner makes evaluations which the story does not really invite. Callisto's world is like a dream but Pynchon does not ironize it by contrast with outside 'life'. It too is part of life, the life of the mind, and if it is inadequate to external pressures, Mulligan's party seems equally so. Pynchon does not set up a distinction between 'life' and 'non-life'; he dramatizes different meanings of the central concept and explores their inter-connection.

Already then it should be obvious that Pynchon is not using the term 'entropy' loosely. While an undergraduate at Cornell Pynchon took several courses on physics which certainly help to explain the precision of the scientific references in this story. And yet, although the basic concept is difficult to grasp, Pynchon's story requires little more technical knowledge than that offered in the dictionary definitions. Indeed the story's epigraph, taken from Henry Miller's *Tropic of Cancer*, introduces us straight away to one area of metaphor. The passage prophesises no change in the weather and asserts, with gloomy fatalism, a chain-gang image for man's future: 'We must get into step, a lockstep towards the prison of death' (81)[36]. Already we have metaphor proposed to us – constant weather as an emblem of the lack of hope. By juxtaposing the epigraph and title Pynchon now invites us to broaden the metaphor, particularly in the direction of the fourth dictionary definition of 'entropy'. The passage in fact omits two sentences immediately preceding the one quoted above, namely: 'Our heroes have killed themselves, or are killing themselves. The hero, then, is not Time, but Timelessness.'[37] These lines occur at the beginning of the novel and give an opening statement of theme – the absence of change and the deliberate stress on negative or inverted values. But it is important to recognize that Miller is summarizing Boris's views. Miller's surrogate narrator does not give in to his friend's apocalyptic gloom and even regards him as comically melodramatic. Indeed, only three lines after the summary of Boris's 'prophecies', the narrator comments 'I am the happiest man alive', a remarkably cheerful statement for a man preoccupied with universal decline. In Miller's novel the interchange between the narrator and Boris creates a considerable amount of humour, and, by choosing such a passage for an epigraph, Pynchon leads the unwary reader into a kind of trap. On the other hand the weather metaphor makes the abstract concept of entropy easy to grasp, on the other the prophecies lack authority even in Miller's novel. And so we should not jump to the conclusion that Pynchon is endorsing the metaphor. He is rather introducing one theme, one strand of meaning, which will be taken up in the early stages of the story.

Outside the apartment block the weather has been very unusual.[38] Pynchon stresses this detail in order to mock a Romantic identification of soul and air. This identification can induce a modish passivity in those who merely 'recapitulate' the weather:

And as every good Romantic knows, the soul (*spiritus*, *ruach*, *pneuma*) is nothing, substantially, but air; it is only natural that warpings in the atmosphere should be recapitulated in those who breathe it. So that over and above the public components – holidays, tourist attractions – there are private meanderings, linked to the climate as if this spell were a *stretto* passage in the year's fugue: haphazard weather, aimless loves, unpredicted commitments: months one can easily spend *in* fugue, because oddly enough, later on, winds, rains, passions of February and

March are never remembered in that city, it is as if they had
never been.   (83)

Pynchon sets randomness ('meanderings') against order ('fugue')
to ironize the party-goers whose passivity differs from Flange's in
leading nowhere. It does not release imagination but stays inert,
hence Pynchon's play on the second psychological meaning of
'fugue'.[39]

Against this notion of apparently random change Pynchon
contrasts Callisto's view of the weather. He too has noted its
changeability, but is far more preoccupied with the eventual
general run-down of energy, the final heat-death of the universe
predicted by some cosmologists following Clausius's original
proposition that entropy tends towards a maximum. Accordingly
Callisto pays no attention to the prosaic details of the rain and
snow; he is more disturbed by the fact that the temperature
outside has stayed at a constant 37°F. for three days. Like Miller's
Boris he is 'leery at omens of apocalypse' (85). When dictating his
memoirs the combination of terms like 'vision' and 'oracle' with
scientific information suggests that Callisto is fitting his materials
into a non-scientific, quasi-religious pattern. Indeed, for all the
differences between his obsession with endings and the party-
goers' version of the pathetic fallacy, both outlooks could loosely
be described as 'Romantic'. Three times in the course of the story
Callisto asks Aubade to check the external temperature, thereby
paralleling a similar action in an earlier modernistic work –
Beckett's *Endgame* (1958). Early in the play Hamm sends Clov to
the window:

Hamm: (gesture towards window right). Have you looked?
Clov: Yes.
Hamm: Well?
Clov: Zero.
Hamm: It'd need to rain.
Clov: It won't rain.[40]

The relation and clipped idiom between Hamm and Clov parallels
that between Callisto and Aubade. Like Callisto Hamm delivers
lengthy monologues, the longest one trailing away into silence at
the end of the play. In Beckett's play the gloom is relieved on-
stage by the dialogue whose humour literally fills the time before

the final end. Both works have pre-apocalyptic elements, but Pynchon confines them mainly to Callisto. Once again he suggests a significance to the weather, but does not commit himself one way or the other.

Pynchon's reservations about Callisto emerge very clearly in the description of the latter's apartment, particularly in the following lines:

> Mingled with the sounds of the rain came the first tentative, querulous morning voices of the other birds, hidden in philodendrons and small fan palms: patches of scarlet, yellow and blue laced through this Rousseau-like fantasy, this hothouse jungle it had taken him seven years to weave together. Hermetically sealed, it was a tiny enclave of regularity in the city's chaos, alien to the vagaries of the weather, of national politics, of any civil disorder. (83–4)

The comparison with a painting by Douanier Rousseau is hardly necessary to suggest that the scene is a kind of artefact, a grotesquely displaced jungle which may have its own internal balance, but which is also as stylized as Rousseau's works. The emphasis on defensiveness, as if outside chaos was an aggressive force, carries with it its own ironies for Callisto's hot-house proves to be an exotic prison. Callisto is determined to shut out chaotic elements, but the one form of energy which he cannot control is sound which impinges from outside (the rain) and from below (the music). The 'leakage' poses a clear threat to Aubade's sense of order which she both personifies (even her name represents a lyrical form – a dawn song) and struggles to maintain. In fact Callisto and Aubade are melodramatists of form. They think in violently opposed extremes (anarchy versus order) and, although Callisto is ostensibly waiting for a run-down of energy (which would not be at all dramatic), he and Aubade are both arguably more anxious about the point of fracture when their hot-house would collapse into chaos. From their point of view this would be a virtual cataclysm.

Once Callisto starts dictating his memoirs it becomes clear that he is a parody of Henry Adams, specifically the author of *The Education*. Like Adams at the time of composing the book, Callisto is living in Washington. Both describe themselves in the third person; both are attempting to articulate the cultural implications of modern scientific theory; both are particularly impressed by Willard Gibbs who was, according to Adams, 'the greatest of Americans, judged by his rank in science'.[41] Adams, for a variety of temperamental and biographical reasons, adopts a passive stance (hence his use of the third person) and continually mocks his own ineffectuality. The key chapter in *The Education* as far as Pynchon's story is concerned, is 'The Virgin and the Dynamo', where two of Adams' central symbols come into confrontation. His aesthetic idealism, which Pynchon ironically hints at in Callisto's name (i.e. 'most beautiful'), gives ground before the modern embodiment of force. In trying to balance the modern scientific notion of force against religions Adams feels himself groping in labyrinths. His answer is characteristically to turn the act of writing in on itself:

> In such labyrinths, the staff is a force almost more necessary than the legs: the pen becomes a sort of blind-man's dog, to keep him from falling into the gutters. The pen works for itself, and acts like a hand, modelling the plastic material over and over again to the form that suits it best. The form is never arbitrary, but it is a sort of growth like crystallization, as any artist knows to well . . .[42]

Adams diverts the reader away from his main impulse towards final understanding and dramatizes the automatism of writing. The variety of analogies to writing conceal – but only partly – a tendency towards self-pity on Adams' part. In the last chapters of *The Education* he constantly refers to himself as aged or infirm, and there is a hint of the same melancholy when Callisto identifies his condition as 'the sad dying fall of middle age' (87). Adams calls himself 'the new Teufelsdröckh' to clarify his feelings of perplexity.[43] If uncertainty paralyzes Adams, it is fear of possible implications from the 'random factor' introduced by Gibbs' and Boltzmann's equations. Randomness is the mathematical equivalent of the chaos which terrifies Callisto. One other important parallel with Adams needs to be noted here. Struggling to understand the kinetic theory of gases, he arrives at the stark conclusion that 'Chaos was the law of nature; Order was the dream of man'.[44] Adams carries his pessimism with such urbanity that a statement such as this is never allowed to generate its full emotional impact. However, this contrast between order and chaos, dream and nature, parallels Callisto's polarities, especially that between his hot-house and the outside weather.

Perhaps Callisto's main statement in his dictation is to find in entropy a metaphor for certain social phenomena which he has observed. One example is in the increasing uniformity in American consumerism:

> He found himself . . . restating Gibbs' prediction in social terms, and envisioned a heat-death for his culture in which ideas, like heat-energy, would no longer be transferred, since each point in it would ultimately have the same quantity of energy; and intellectual motion would, accordingly, cease.
>
> (88–9)

The irony bends away from Callisto on to American society briefly and it is quite in keeping wih the closely wrought texture of this story that prime examples of the consumerism under attack should be found in Mulligan's party, namely bottles of drink, hi-fi equipment and a refrigerator. Even in his fascination with entropy Callisto is following in Adams' footsteps. In 'A Letter to American Teachers of History' (1910) Adams develops implications in Clausius' propositions and speculates that, although historians don't know physics,

> . . . they cannot help feeling curiosity to know whether Ostwald's line of reasoning would logically end in subjecting both psychical and physico-chemical energies to the natural and obvious analogy of heat, and extending the Law of Entropy over all.[45]

His argument is exactly like Callisto's in being based on an analogy and, in an essay of one year earlier – 'The Rule of Phase Applied to History', Adams had similarly predicted an end-point where the limits of human thought would be reached.[46]

In order to pinpoint what exactly is Pynchon's attitude towards Callisto and Adams it would be helpful to turn at this point to an intermediary text – Norbert Wiener's *The Human Use of Human Beings* (1950). Wiener is doing more or less what Adams and Callisto are attempting: to relate diverse fields of modern American culture to each other. But he has a great advantage over them in being primarily a scientist and mathematician. Accordingly, when discussing the notion of heat-death, he cautions: 'it is necessary to keep these cosmic values well separated from any human system of valuation'.[47] This is exactly the mistake which Adams makes in *The Education* and the essays of 1909–10, and which Callisto repeats. Their use of metaphor and analogy leads them to draw hasty inferences from badly digested scientific theory, and results in a not altogether unpleasant sense of pessimism and inertia.

The various ways in which he limits his commitment to Callisto's viewpoint suggest that Pynchon has accepted Wiener's caution. Firstly, Callisto's is only one viewpoint within the story. Secondly, the story is too humorous in tone to underwrite his apocalyptic gloom. Thirdly, Pynchon's use of musical references and form, which will be examined shortly, suggests a detachment from Callisto. And there are enough ironies to indicate that in some ways Callisto *embodies* entropy rather than examines it. His dictation ends on the verb 'cease', but it has stopped, not concluded. His dictation is a kind of monologue as if he were thinking aloud. Once the dictation has stopped we follow his line of thought in his search for 'correspondences', and in ransacking literature for parallels he once again follows Adams. He variously notes De Sade (for libertinage, perhaps), the last scene from Faulkner's *Sanctuary* where the exhausted and apathetic Temple Drake is listening to music with her father in the Jardin de Luxembourg, and Djuna Barnes' *Nightwood* again perhaps for its presentation of moral and physical decline. Decline does seem to be the theme linking these works. Callisto also pays particular attention to Stravinsky's *L'Histoire d'un Soldat* (1918) whose tango section communicates the same inter-war exhaustion:

> And how many musicians were left after Passchendaele, after the Marne? It came down in this case to seven: violin, double-bass. Clarinet, bassoon. Cornet, trombone. Tympani. Almost as if any tiny troupe of saltimbanques had set about conveying the same information as a full pit-orchestra.   (93)[48]

The neatly organized sentences of his dictation have now begun to give away to questions and fragmentary phrases as if the more Callisto hunts for meaning, the more it eludes him. This uncertainty grows with his failed attempts to recapture the spirit of pre-World War II France and his words tail off completely when the bird he has been holding finally dies: '"What has happened? Has the transfer of heat ceased to work? Is there no more . . ." He did not finish' (97–8). Verbal communication could be regarded as a kind of transfer (cf. definition 3 of 'entropy'), and as Callisto's uncertainty grows he in turn becomes more rambling and incoherent. As a means of self-explanation or as a means of communicating with Aubade, his words become useless. With the death of the bird, like Beckett's Hamm, he lapses into silence.

The passage quoted above indicates that the First World War is seen as a cultural watershed by Callisto. Stravinsky's work for him exemplifies a general feeling of exhaustion, but this feeling is stimulated exclusively by works of art. Although he pats himself on the back for being 'strong enough not to drift into the graceful decadence of an enervated fatalism' (87), Callisto seems to be suffering from a hand-me-down pessimism, an ersatz gloom without any roots in his own experience. When Aubade moves around the apartment her movements are stylized and balletic, as if she is taking part in some kind of dance. Further she describes her love-making in the following way:

> Even in the brief periods when Callisto made love to her, soaring above the bowing of taut nerves in haphazard double-stops would be the one singing string of her determination.
>
> (88)

Double-stopping on the violin was one of the noticeable features in *L'Histoire*. And in one scene (II.5) the soldier enters a room where a princess lies sleeping. He wakes her and woos her with his violin playing.[49] Unconsciously, then, Callisto and Aubade are partly miming out actions which repeat *L'Histoire* and which supply yet another reason why Callisto is 'helpless in the past' (97).

The choice of a piece of music which contains a number of then current dance rhythms (tango, waltz and ragtime) suggests a preoccupation with the Lost Generation. Callisto, like Scott Fitzgerald, went to Princeton; and he tries to put the clock back by returning to France after the war, taking with him a Henry Miller novel as a substitute Baedeker. He fails, however, to recapture the past and here we meet a common element between himself and the other 'American expatriates' who inhabit Washington, and whose fashionable cosmopolitan style Pynchon mocks in the second paragraph of the story. The epigraph from Miller who begins his narration in the Villa Borghese contrasts ironically with the Washington socialites who have reduced expatriation to posture and paraphernalia (posters, etc.). As Peter Bischoff rightly argues, Pynchon is engaging in an unequivocal parody of certain attitudes.[50]

Bischoff is the only critic to date who has spotted the stereotyped nature of the story's characters. Mulligan's party-goers use the same fashionable jargon that Pynchon mocks in the description above. Callisto is a 'romantic' in the Fitzgerald sense, and Saul and Miriam parody middle-class intellectuals who brandish slogans like 'togetherness'. Mulligan's guests, at the beginning of the story, are lying around in drunken stupors or simply sitting and listening to music. As more guests arrive, or as they wake up, lethargy gradually shifts into chaotic movement. The ironic implication of pointlessness runs throughout Pynchon's presentation of these scenes and looks forward to his satire of the whole Sick Crew in *V*. William M. Plater sees the party differently, as an attempted flight from death:

> The party is a community act in which people come together – one of the least complex manifestations of eros. However, the party is simultaneously a demonstration of the social equivalent of entropy and a transformation toward death, as the party disintegrates and disorder increases.[51]

Surprisingly, in view of this paradox, he later states that the party embodies an 'affirmation of life and union'. He suggests in effect that it is almost a sacramental act where all the willing performers come together. This sort of moralistic reading is only possible if one ignores the ironies levelled against the members of the party, which is exactly what Plater does. He misses the sarcasm at their imitation of the Lost Generation and understates the chaos and absence of communication in the party. 'Death' is a portentous word to use here, and rather too grand for the level Pynchon strikes. The party-goers are not desperately staving off dread. They are simply bored, lethargic and superficial; their main concern is filling their time, but with the least effort on their part.

Apart from its social ironies the party dramatizes one strand of meaning in 'entropy', namely that it measures the amount of energy unavailable for conversion to work in a system. Tony Tanner has described the party as a closed system, but surely this is not so since people are arriving continuously.[52] The real closed system, in intention if not in practice, must be Callisto's hot-house. As movement increases at Mulligan's party, so does its randomness. Other guests arrive and add to the bustle, the most chaotic being five sailors who imagine it is a brothel. The disorder and noise reaches climax where we could also say that the entropy within the party has approached its maximum. Mulligan's reaction to this situation is both important and surprising:

> Meatball stood and watched, scratching his stomach lazily. The way he figured, there were only about two ways he could cope: (a) lock himself in the closet and maybe eventually they would all go away, or (b) try to calm everybody down, one by one. (a) was certainly the more attractive alternative. But then he started thinking about that closet. (96)

Faced with a comparable situation at the end of 'Mortality and Mercy' Siegel just walks away, leaving the party to the tender mercies of a berserk Ojibwa. Mulligan here is tempted to do something like that. He watches the others; he too is lazy. But eventually he decides to restore order which he then proceeds to do. Partly from the sheer amount of space devoted to Mulligan's moment of decision, Pynchon is highlighting his choice. The closet offers an attractive alternative and in effect repeats on a smaller scale Callisto's retreat into a hot-house. The very fact that Mulligan can choose to restore order and does so, contradicts a superficial fatalism which the notion of entropy might create. In an examination of the relation between entropy and general culture, Rudolf Arnheim has pinpointed this superficial application, specifically to the arts:

> Surely the popular use of the notion of entropy has changed. If during the last century it served to diagnose, explain, and deplore the degradation of culture, it now provides a positive rationale for 'minimal' art and the pleasures of chaos.[53]

The intricacies of Pynchon's story demonstrate conclusively that he has no interest in minimalist art and Mulligan's final actions reverse a trend towards chaos in his party. The party anyway is neither the universe nor a microcosm and once again Pynchon is being true to scientific theory. Wiener asserts that 'in the nonisolated parts of an isolated system there will be regions in which the entropy . . . . may well be seen to decrease'.[54] One such island is the party and its entropy apparently *does* decrease.

So far we have considered the representational significance of Mulligan's party and Callisto's hot-house. The third area of meaning in 'entropy' is introduced when Saul climbs into Mulligan's apartment from the fire-escape. John Simons has pointed out that Pynchon is here parodying the biblical narrative of Paul's visit to Ephesus. *Acts* 20. 9–11 recounts how a young man named Eutychos (i.e. 'lucky') fell asleep while Paul was preaching and fell down from a loft. Paul embraced him and thereby restored him to life. He then continued his discussions until daybreak. Simons argues that

> Saul is an ironic parody of Paul in Pynchon's story, and . . . appears not as an apostle of the new Christian religion, but rather as a spokesman for the new science of decline and decay in the twentieth century.[55]

Saul parodies Paul in having had a slanging match with his wife, not a proselytizing discussion; and he saves only the book which she threw at him, not a human being.

Before examining Saul further we need to consider the broader implications of the Pauline text. It centres on a quasi-miraculous act, Paul's live-giving embrace. When we first see Mulligan and Callisto they are both asleep and embracing objects, the one an empty magnum of champagne, the other a sick bird. In other words they combine elements of Eutychos and a parody of Paul. But the embraces are the opposite of life-giving. Obviously the champagne bottle offers no possibilities and Callisto's bird finally expires. Saul himself is denied any of the stature of his biblical counterpart. His is like a 'big rag doll' and combines professional arrogance with violence. He tells Mulligan with an air of pride 'I slugged her', and obviously brings only words not *the* Word with him. Ironically, despite his claims to be a communications expert, he cannot understand why his wife flared into anger. His stumbling-block appears to be love:

> 'Tell a girl: "I love you". No trouble with two thirds of that, it's a closed circuit. Just you and she. But that nasty four-letter word in the middle, *that's* the one you have to look out for.

Ambiguity. Redundance. Irrelevance, even. Leakage. All this is noise. Noise screws up your signal, makes for disorganization in the circuit.'   (90–1)

Here the biblical ironies shade into communication theory. Paul revived Eutychos by an act of love, but this word becomes a serious problem for Saul. It is so elusive, it disturbs his 'signal' so much that it becomes a positive obscenity (a 'four-letter word'). Like Callisto and Aubade, Saul is a believer in order. He is concerned to rule out any kind of interference to technical perfection. But once again we return to a crude analogy – that between an electronic signal and a speech act. Despite his theoretical expertise, Saul has lost his argument with Miriam (about cybernetics). He himself uses a disjointed language full of slang and technical jargon and, when Mulligan casts around for something to say, he too demonstrates a very high proportion of 'noise' (i.e. hesitation-words, fillers, etc.).

Entropy grows in the conversation between the two men as their exclamations increase until finally Saul cuts off Mulligan with an abrupt 'the hell with it'. It is of course comical to witness a communications theorist break down into cliché and exclamation, and finally lapse into silence. But this episode carries ironic implications which spread through the whole story. Entropy in communications theory is a measure of the inefficiency of a signal.[56] Accordingly the more noise, or the less coherence speech-acts contain, the more their entropy will increase. In fact none of the characters in Pynchon's story demonstrates any sustained capacity to engage in dialogue. Callisto and Aubade speak in short, clipped phrases, as if they are cautiously husbanding their meaning. Mulligan's guests use short phrases containing in-jokes or jargon (like 'tea time, man'). The sailor's shouts are more noise and misapply even that, since the apartment is not, in the technical sense at least, a brothel. Apart from Mulligan's discussion with Saul, which breaks down into silence, there is only one other conversation in the story of any length. This occurs near the end where Duke puts forward a theory about modern jazz. On the face of it perfectly rational, the theory leads to absurd results when the musicians start playing silently. So, the ironies which Pynchon directs against Saul specifically, undermine yet another attempt to impose order, and suggest a broad scepticism about dialogue's capacity for meaningful communication.

In the course of his story Pynchon examines three levels of meaning in the central concept of entropy and uses a variety of ironic methods to criticize the implications or applicability of these levels. The first definition supplies a weapon for attacking the fashionable lethargy of the party guests. The third gives Pynchon an opportunity to satirize dialogue. The fourth allows him to examine Callisto's enervated intellectualism. He too is just as inert as the party guests and it is Aubade who makes the decisive gesture of smashing the window at the end. John Simons has described the story's theme as 'the supplanting of universal order by universal chaos' but this makes 'Entropy' sound like a work of cosmic proportions.[57] Pynchon never allows an apocalyptic tone to be sustained and even at the end leaves a deliberate ambiguity. By Simons' account, Aubade's final action would be a gesture of despair, but only viewed from her perspective. It could equally well be seen as a liberating gesture which has the immediate result of freeing herself and Callisto from their hot-house.

The discussion of the story so far has concentrated on relatively traditional techniques such as allusion, contrast, parallelism and narrative irony. By devoting a story to a scientific concept, and by examining different meanings, Pynchon in effect alerts the reader to the fact that he must pay attention to different ways of ordering. Indeed order could be the ultimate theme of the story. Apart from any local satirical purposes, the narrative methods examined so far tend to carry a general expectation of intelligent detached scrutiny on the reader's part. Accordingly it is not surprising that Pynchon's most extensive narrative method should stand out, particularly as another artistic medium is being applied to literature. That medium is music.

'Entropy' contains a large number of references to musicians and musical technique. It begins with information about records and proceeds with allusions to Lili Marlene, Sarah Vaughan, *Don Giovanni*, and Chet Baker and Mingus are named among others. Music, on a simple verbal level, fills the texture of the story. Two musical topics are examined in some depth. Stravinsky's *L'Histoire* has already been discussed. The second is Duke's theory arising out of Gerry Mulligan's 'Love for Sale'. In fact it is Mulligan's experimental technique which fascinates Duke. In 1952 Mulligan began using a piano-less quartet, comprising baritone saxophone, trumpet, drums and bass.[58] In Pynchon's story Duke argues that because Mulligan has cut out the piano one has to think the root chords when improvising. So far his theory sounds plausible. But then he pushes it to an extreme by arguing that ultimately one must think everything. When the quartet try to put this into practice the result is an absurd spectacle of silent 'performance' which anyway breaks down into chaos once because they get out of step, once because they are playing in different keys! Just as Callisto and Aubade unconsciously perform parts of *L'Histoire*, so the Duke di Angelis quartet follow absurdly in the steps of Gerry Mulligan's experimentalism. And once again an ideal of order (or form) has been proposed only to be found unworkable.

Apart from specific applications of musical topics, the structure of 'Entropy' draws extensively on the techniques of the fugue, a term which actually occurs in the text several times. One of the distinguishing characteristics of fugue is the use of counterpoint which in fictional terms can emerge as a rhythmic contrast.[59] The contrast is basically between the two apartments – Mulligan's and Callisto's – and the narrative moves to and fro in such a way that differences and similarities emerge clearly. For instance both Mulligan and Callisto awake from 'rest' in the same posture, but the electronic noise downstairs contrasts strongly with the natural sounds in Callisto's hot-house. Even the physical positioning of the apartments, corresponds, as Redfield and Hays point out, to the printed arrangement of musical staves.[60] Callisto, Mulligan and Saul offer us three possible voices and, after they have been introduced in turn, Pynchon is free to weave the voices together. Callisto, for instance, delivers a long monologue which contrasts sharply with the chaotic and fragmented speech of the party. But then 'noise' creeps into his ruminations as they wander further and further from his single purpose, until, like Saul, he lapses into silence. Callisto's dictation, Saul's conversation and Duke's theory provide clear equivalents of exposition, so that the different dimensions of entropy are quite literally orchestrated together. Between the various themes occur other noises from the rain outside, from the arrival of other characters, and from the record being played at the party. These correspond to the invented passages in a fugue, as well as posing a threat to Pynchon's superimposed order.

If the basic theme of the story is the contrast order/disorder, then obviously Callisto's apartment represents the first. All the elements are synchronized into harmony, a harmony which

Aubade personifies. When she is stroking a plant in the apartment, Pynchon articulates it in musical terminology:

> In the hothouse Aubade stood absently caressing the branches of a young mimosa, hearing a *motif* of sap-rising, the rough and *unresolved* anticipatory *theme* of those fragile pink blossoms which, it is said, insure fertility. That *music* rose in a tangled tracery: arabesques of order competing *fugally* with the *improvised discords* of the party downstairs, which peaked sometimes in cusps and ogees of noise. [my emphasis]   (92)

The third word takes its departure from a homophone in the preceding paragraph ('hoorhouse') which cuts across the broad contrast between harmony and discord. The two sentences actually mime out their lyrical subject through participial phrases, again contrasting with the fragments of speech in the preceding paragraph. It is as if disorder would literally stop Aubade's existence. By contrast the noise in Mulligan's party approaches a crescendo but the crescendo never comes since he reimposes a kind of order. This returns the revellers to their initial posture (prostration) and yet does not resolve the story. The party, we are told, 'trembled on the threshold of its third day' (97). The final resolution rests with Aubade. She breaks the window and, following this burst of sounds, returns to Callisto to

> wait with him until the moment of equilibrium was reached, when 37 degrees Fahrenheit should prevail both outside and inside, and forever, and the hovering, curious dominant of their separate lives should resolve into a tonic of darkness and the final absence of all motion.   (98)

As the clauses fade away in diminuendo, the ending appeals to the reader's sense of form in resolving the story, although in fact the moment of resolution is in the future, and will only occur after the work has finished, as in Eliot's *Four Quartets*. The musical metaphor cuts across various interrelated fields of sensation – of balance, temperature and light which will disappear. Above all, however, the metaphor plays on the notion of rest. Formally speaking the story has begun from rest and comes back to it at the end. In that sense it seems satisfyingly symmetrical. But, because music is a non-conceptual medium, the use of music to create form in the story does not carry with it any epistemological implications. Plater and other critics notwithstanding, the story affirms nothing.

'Entropy' examines various notions of order and disorder in such a way as to make it very difficult to locate Pynchon's own view-point. Music is of course non-verbal and so an ideal means of binding his story together without committing himself to any one view-point. Pynchon ironizes all the theories which are proposed with a bewildering thoroughness, so that at times his method appears to be purely negative. A comment made by Saul, however, suggests a way out of this dilemma. Miriam is disturbed by the way computers act like people, but Saul simply reverses the analogy and suggests that people act like computers. In a story which focuses so much on analogy and implication, Pynchon in effect suggests a caution about drawing conclusions. Callisto's intellectual enterprise forms potentially the most solemn area of subject-matter in the story and in his connection a proposition by Norbert Wiener is directly relevant. Answering the question whether the second law of thermodynamics leads to pessimism, he states that the solution

> depends on the importance we give to the universe at large, on the one hand, and to the islands of locally decreasing entropy which we find in it, on the other.[61]

In other words, it is a matter of perspective. Similarly Pynchon's story forces a relativistic view-point on to the reader, which acts against a final resolving certainty, or one definite moral direction. The various aspects of form illuminate and examine different meanings of 'entropy', while the different meanings of 'entropy' illuminate the various aspects of form.

5 'UNDER THE ROSE'

Whereas 'Entropy' remains ultimately non-committal about the applicability of its eponymous central concept, Pynchon's next story, 'Under the Rose' (1961), engages with themes which become central in both *V.* and *Gravity's Rainbow*. This semi-monologue on espionage has suffered from unjustifiable critical neglect because it was extensively revised into Chapter 3 of *V.*[62]

The story's basic plot is quite straightforward. The setting is Alexandria; the year 1898. The Fashoda crisis between Britain and France is looming on the horizon. The tale's protagonist, an English spy called Porpentine, has been waging a private combat with his German opposite number for several years. He is joined by his colleague Goodfellow and goes with him to a party at the Austrian Consulate where he meets Victoria Wren, Goodfellow's latest conquest. She is on a Cook's tour of the Nile with her father and sister. Unfortunately for Goodfellow, her favours are also being sought by one Hugh Bongo-Shaftesbury, apparently an archaeologist. Porpentine discovers quite quickly that he is in fact a German spy. They all travel by train to Cairo where Porpentine and Goodfellow 'stalk' Lord Cromer, the British Consul-General, who has been threatened with assassination. As the Fashoda crisis breaks, the key characters go to an opera performance in the Ezbekiyeh Garden. Porpentine foils (or rather confuses) the attempted assassination, with Victoria and Goodfellow pursues the German agents to Kheops. There Porpentine is shot, his two companions released.

This suggests a tale of adventure but in fact it proves to be very static. Blocks of retrospective thought constantly suspend the flow of the narrative and suggest that Pynchon is building on the character of Porpentine a meditation which extends his personal predicament outwards into history. It is perfectly appropriate for the story to begin with Porpentine in a passive posture; he is sitting outside a café smoking. He thinks repeatedly of 'them', a vague but threatening group of anonymous employees of Moldweorp, the German veteran spy. As the latter phrase passes through Porpentine's mind he catches himself up:

> It ['the veteran spy'] might have been a throwback to an earlier time, when such epithets were one reward for any proof of heroism or manhood. Or possibly because now, with a century rushing headlong to its end and with it a tradition in espionage where everything was tacitly on a gentlemanly basis, where the playing-fields of Eton had conditioned (one might say) premilitary conduct as well, the label was a way of fixing identity in this special *haut monde* before death – individual or collective – stung it to stillness forever. Porpentine himself was called *'il semplice inglese'* by those who cared.   (102)[63]

Here Pynchon uses a method of free indirect speech whereby he retains ultimate rhetorical control of such sequences (through the third person) but also conveys the immediacy of thought. In practice the distinction between narrator and character is not a very important one because Porpentine possesses the capacity to examine himself from the outside, and, even more importantly, the reader is drawn into Porpentine's predicament in a way which counters the story's apparent remoteness. As Richard Poirier has pointed out, 'we are drawn into the very process of "spying". It becomes for us more than a mere adventure; it becomes an activity of perception'.[64] In the passage Porpentine registers nostalgia for a lost time of individual heroism. His depressed sense of clinging on to outdated values is expressed in terms of a *fin de siècle* gloom. Certain clichéed labels like 'the playing-fields of Eton' are thus used ironically. No longer the totem-phrases of key social beliefs, they represent a last-ditch effort at 'fixing identify' before their referents are swept away by history. Even the Renaissance names which Pynchon attaches to the three main characters – Porpentine (i.e. porcupine), Goodfellow and Moldweorp (i.e. mole) – all help to underline their anachronistic status.

Porpentine's feeling of being superseded results in a sense of his own absurdity and helplessness, and he turns to recent history to get his bearings. The 1848 revolutions signal that 'history was being made no longer through the virtue of single princes but rather by man in the mass' (107). Here we encounter one of Pynchon's central contrasts between the Machiavellian concept of individual effective action and its modern replacement by mass action. Porpentine figures the latter to himself through the 'impersonal curves' of mathematical analysis (mathematical allusions form an important leitmotif in this story) and as he chases the Germans out to Kheops begins to doubt one of his cherished belief – that espionage has clear if tacit rules. A 'vision' of a bell-curve, i.e. the graph of normal statistical distribution, contrasts the possibility of one central guiding intelligence (Moldweorp's) with the patterns of anonymous statistical odds, a contrast which Pynchon was to develop in *Gravity's Rainbow*. Pynchon humanizes the curve into an ominous prediction of Porpentine's own death, appropriately so since the mentality he represents will have become defunct: 'Porpentine (though only half-suspecting) was being tolled down' (135). As the contrast fills

out the opposing terms would be individual against mass man,
feeling against efficiency, pragmatism against studied theory, and
so on. Porpentine resists the growing anonymity of his profession
by engaging in a running combat with Moldweorp, just as in John Le
Carré's novels George Smiley resists bureaucratization by a
personal antagonism with his Russian opposite number Karla. In
Pynchon's story Porpentine's and Moldweorp's subordinates take
on 'the roles of solicitous seconds . . . while their chiefs circled
and parried' (107). The language of duelling suggests that Pynchon
is superimposing one kind of romantic fiction on top of a quite
different unglamorous narrative mode while simultaneously
drawing attention to its inappropriateness. As we shall see
Pynchon develops these romantic allusions in a number of
directions.

Porpentine's personal duel is only one of a number of roles he
adopts. 'Under the Rose' is saturated with references to manner,
disguise and theatre. This predictable emphasis expands espionage
into a general existential predicament where surfaces have become
divorced from inner meaning, and where Porpentine feels locked
into a role endlessly performing a colonial stereotype. On the very
first page we are told that his face is 'carefully arranged'; when
Goodfellow meets him at the café he is wearing an absurd
costume (evening dress and pith helmet); and Porpentine then
goes through an impersonation of an Italian count. At this point
role-playing and games meet. A repeated metaphor for espionage
is the game (hare-and-hounds, chess, etc.) which Pynchon draws
perhaps from *Kim*, but not to understate danger so much as to
point out that it is a self-enclosed system with idealized rules.
Porpentine simultaneously recognizes the absurdity of his roles
and shifts the notion of play towards irresponsible antics to gain
psychological relief. That is one reason why he sings pieces from
Puccini's *Manon* and engages in the private make-believe of
mimicking General Gordon. But Porpentine is vulnerable. Once
he steps outside the 'zone' of espionage, as he does when he
expresses sympathy for Goodfellow's conquest and when he
shows a special feeling for Moldweorp, then he has in effect
stepped outside the game and his death becomes inevitable.

The analogies which Pynchon sets up between the story's
action and *Manon* draw attention to the role of feeling. David
Cowart has argued that Porpentine resembles Des Grieux (whose
words he sings) in falling victim to his own misguided chivalry

and that a remembered episode where Moldweorp abuses an Italian prostitute parodies the central relationship in the opera.[65] The latter point is particularly useful because it suggests that Pynchon is not drawing a single analogy and in fact the Des Grieux – Manon Lescaut connection also applies to Goodfellow's activities with Victoria Wren. In all three cases, however, the analogy does not quite fit and complicates our reading of the text. Moldweorp's behaviour is simply travesty; Goodfellow's is routine, a failure (he is impotent) and a reduction of passionate love to the level of the music-hall. Porpentine uses the opera for private manic performances; the nearest to love he gets is voyeurism as he looks through Goodfellow's hotel window, and he performs Des Grieux in full awareness that he completely lacks the latter's capacity for direct action: '. . . this chevalier has nothing to decode, no double game to play. Porpentine envied him' (128).

We encounter a similar combination of resemblance and differences in Pynchon's ironic parallels with John Buchan's *Greenmantle* (1916). Porpentine has a partner (or 'running mate' as he calls him) in Goodfellow as does Richard Hannay in Sandy or Peter Pienaar. Porpentine goes to Cairo; Hannay in disguise is ordered to go to Cairo as a German spy. Goodfellow tells Victoria Wren that the two men were in the Transvaal together, again like Hannay and Pienaar. Later in Pynchon's story some Egyptian policemen try to arrest the British agents in Cairo. At a prearranged signal they turn a gun on them and escape. This episode parallels an escape from Turkish soldiers by Pienaar and Hannay in Mesopotamia.[66] There are also broad similarities between the two works in that Hannay is pitted against the Germans in the early chapters of the novel, and also in their conversation together Goodfellow and Porpentine imitate the clipped stereotyped speech-idiom of Hannay and his helpers. These parallels mask enormous differences. Hannay is physically tough, resourceful and personifies what, in his study of novelists of empire, Alan Sandison has called an 'ideal of competence'.[67] Porpentine, on the contrary, fails as a spy. His identity is known to the Germans; he is far too introspective about his own situation; most importantly he is shot at the end of the story. In fictional terms Buchan focuses suspense on the prowess of his hero whereas it is the Fashoda crisis which creates the suspense in Pynchon's story. Buchan follows a loose plot which rests heavily on action and adventure, but the only successful action by Porpentine is to kick an Arab in the throat who is fighting with Goodfellow.

Obviously Pynchon is making no attempt to write even a pastiche of a Buchan novel. Rather the parallels remind the reader of the adventure-story genre, whether we recognize *Greenmantle* or the Brigadier Gerard stories (there is a throw-away reference to Arthur Conan Doyle in the text), in order to show qualities unavailable to Porpentine and to strengthen the story's themes. We are thus forced to note resemblances *and* differences from *Manon* and *Greenmantle* – Porpentine is more of a Prufrock than a Hannay – and in each case we realize that decisive action has given way to anxious and wearied role-playing. In the case of *Manon* Porpentine feels at several removes from the action, and is anyway imitating the theatrical; in the case of the British adventure-story all he possesses is the costume (tweeds) and the idiom.

By playing Machiavellian roles Porpentine becomes (with Goodfellow) the personification of a doomed humanism. In other words Pynchon uses the line-up between English and German spies to contrast opposing cultural values. But why, since the Fashoda crisis was between Britain and France, did Pynchon introduce *German* spies? Their presence increases the historical complexities of his story and takes us outside the boundary of the story. Porpentine is the story's protagonist but the threat of assassination focuses on Lord Cromer, the Consul-General. Cromer recognized that Germany's power was crucial in Egypt. In 1886 he wrote to Gladstone's Foreign Secretary, Lord Rosebery: 'Berlin, and not Cairo, is the real centre of gravity of Egyptian affairs'.[68] His attitude towards Germany was less neutral than this might suggest and in 1915 he published an article entitled 'The German Historians'. Here he attacked the whole concept of *Kultur*, arguing that it was based on a false elevation of the state above the individual. Pynchon's concentration on Porpentine in effect reverses this ethic. Cromer saw 1900 as a turning-point in German history (Porpentine puts it one year earlier). Cromer also attacked a false Darwinism in German historians like Treitschke which would explain an apparently incidental conversation about the Nile. Of the wilderness down the river Lepsius, a German spy named after the Egyptologist who did work at Kheops, enquires:[69]

'Doesn't the law of the wild beast prevail down there? . . .
There are no property rights, only fighting; and the victor wins
all. Glory, life, power and property, all.'
'Perhaps', Goodfellow said. 'But in Europe, you know, we are
civilized. Fortunately. Jungle-law is inadmissible.'   (117)

Lepsius here summarizes the main attitude which Cromer attacks:
a crude Darwinism, absolute war, and the principle that might
makes right. Cromer writes:

> The validity of the theory can only be admitted if human beings
> are in all respects to be assimilated to the brute creation. It
> involves a complete confusion between a law of nature and a
> 'law of life'. Animals, birds, and insects devour each other
> because they are obliged to do so in order to live, and because
> they are not restrained from doing so by any moral or intellectual
> scruples. This is the law of nature. But the 'law of life' to which
> Treitschke and his fellow-historians appeal, has been not
> ordained by Nature. It has been made by men, and, moreover,
> by bad men.[70]

This issue is alluded to in Pynchon's story, not examined. But it
forms part of the set of contrasts established between life and
death, humanity and militarism.

It is obvious that Cromer in the article quoted is launching a
profound moral attack on German *Kultur* based on the values of
Victorian liberalism and sharpened by anger over the Great War.
Pynchon, however, muffles the sources of indignation by layers
of irony which encase the character of Porpentine. The grotesque
name and depiction of Bongo-Shaftesbury, the images of the
waste land and Porpentine's memory of Moldweorp beating the
Italian prostitute give us adequate pointers to the values of the
story. Indeed, we would expect Pynchon to show a more
attenuated moralism than Lord Cromer since he is writing after
two world wars and so is correspondingly more sceptical about
the human possibilities of controlling the course of history.
Pynchon incorporates Cromer's critique into broad contrasts
between the clean and the human. The Germans are devotees of
apocalypse because it will 'purify' Europe and its dead cultures
where Porpentine is content to exist among their detritus. In this
context the final setting at Kheops takes on an ominously

emblematic force in embodying a possible consequence of Germany's puritanical militarism.

Since apocalypse is mentioned so often in the story we might wonder whether Pynchon gives the story an apocalyptic direction. It quickly becomes evident that there is a contrast between the slow pace of the story and Porpentine's and the Germans' sense of impending crisis. The story refers to a whole series of historical events (the fall of Khartoum, the Penjdeh crisis, the Jameson Raid, etc.) which *could* fit the bill of potential apocalypse but Pynchon draws on the reader's historical hindsight to suggest a receding climax. The Fashoda crisis breaks but is smothered by its distance from the story's action; Porpentine is shot but in a languid dying fall rather than a climax. Apocalypse is revealed as a state of mind which Pynchon first denies by suggesting an entropic run-down of energy (it is the 'dog-days' of 1898) and then teasingly revives at the very end of the story where Goodfellow has gone to Sarajevo to investigate rumours of assassination. The year is 1914. On a note of expectancy Pynchon closes the story.

What has been said so far about Porpentine indicates that he feels alienated from his changing profession and from history itself. Pynchon gives concrete expression to this alienation in his composition of place and in his evocation of which he was to call in *V*. 'Baedeker-land'. Porpentine and all the other major characters in the story are abroad and in the position of tourists. William Plater has argued quite rightly that the tour is crucial to Pynchon's fiction because 'it defines man's spatial and human relationship with his environment' and is a 'form of ritualized observation'.[71] Plater raises many crucial issues in his discussion which hardly mentions 'Under the Rose' even though it would directly support most of his argument. In the story Pynchon draws on certain specific aspects of tourism, partly to clarify Porpentine's predicament. Previously his faith in the rightness of his actions had 'acted as an irresistible vector aimed toward 1900. Now he could say that any itinerary, with all its doublings-back, emergency stops, and hundred-kilometer feints remained transitory . . .' (113). As he loses his sense of urgency the mathematical metaphor gives way to a touristic one. 'Itinerary' suggests a tour and certainly Porpentine is at his most relaxed in postures which are typical of a tourist – sitting in a café or in a railway carriage. But 'itinerary' also suggests a superficial contact with the terrain covered and so becomes a fitting metaphor for Porpentine's feelings of estrangement. Since he sees espionage in non-national terms, he himself is divorced from the satisfactions of national stability. So he is a kind of tourist, but without the tourist's chief aid – the guide-book. For this reason, during a mood of intense depression while talking to Victoria, Porpentine longs for a 'Baedeker of the heart', a guidebook which would offer him release from his solitude. It is the crowning irony of Porpentine's fate that the chase at the end of the story should follow one of the main tourist routes out of Cairo to Kheops.

Baedeker's 1898 guidebook to Egypt figures importantly in the way Pynchon composes the settings of the story. The action begins in the Place Mohammed Ali in Alexandria, moves by train to Cairo, lingers in the Ezbekiyeh Garden, and ends at Kheops. Pynchon is very sparing of physical detail in his descriptions. We are told, for instance, that Goodfellow is staying at the Hotel Khedival, 'seven blocks away' from the Place Mohammed Ali (104); or that Porpentine and Victoria visit a Cairo *Bierhalle* 'a few blocks north of the Ezbekiyeh Garden' (129). Apart from the fact we are dealing with a short story which must necessarily select its details stringently, Pynchon's stress on direction, on measurement by blocks, his use of a limited number of street-names actually imitates the maps in Baedeker's guide-book. The characters, like tourists, take their bearings from the two widely recognized landmarks (recognized by *Westerners*, that is) in Alexandria and Cairo. Porpentine's visits to his contacts in Cairo form a miniature tour of the city. The most intensive application of this method comes with the train journey, where Pynchon takes phrases verbatim from Baedeker's itinerary 'From Alexandria to Cairo'.[72] As Plater points out, tourism revolves around patterned movement and Pynchon here composes a particularly stylized landscape which partly reassures the reader by giving a familiar grid and coordinates and then destroys that temporary security by introducing bizarre and surreal events. The Baedeker landscape of the story functions as an analogy with the game or with Porpentine's endless performance of Des Grieux. It also resembles and grows out of espionage in offering all the characters a set of disguises and actions. It is not until Pynchon revised the story for Chapter 3 of *V.* that he underlined the illusory nature of Baedeker-land by refracting the action through all the functionaries that

Baedeker ignores (cab-man, waiter, etc.) so as to link tourism with another important theme in the novel, namely colonialism.[73]

Pynchon's use of precise historical and guidebook details have roughly the same effect as his evocation of a spy-story. They lull the reader into accepting different narrative frames of references which he then subverts. In place of striking events the peaks of this story are to be found where Pynchon introduces an incongruity which disrupts the expectations we have at any particular point. The story's narrative is further complicated by our sense of layered modes superimposed on top of each other: the journey to Kheops is a chase *and* a tour; the desert is both a waste land *and* a setting for a love-death, and so on.

There are five main points of disruption, but many other examples could be found where Pynchon jerks the reader across modes. Porpentine's 'seizure' in the Place Mohammed Ali (the first time he sings from *Manon*) grotesquely disrupts the tension in his waiting for the German spies. During a reception at the Austrian Consulate Pynchon briefly establishes a realistic episode reminiscent of E. M. Forster, where Porpentine meets Victoria Wren and family. Porpentine then meets one of 'them' (a German agent) which jolts us back to espionage, and falls down a flight of stairs which is immediately converted into theatre, a 'routine'. Similarly when Porpentine meets Bongo-Shaftesbury for the first time the encounter is a shock since he is wearing a hawk-mask of Harmakhis. The main shock of the whole story, however, takes place during the train journey to Cairo. Bongo-Shaftesbury starts discussing dolls with Victoria's sister Mildred who asks him if he has one. His answer is not what she (or the reader) expects:

> Who smiled: 'Oh yes.' And pushed back the sleeve of his coat to remove a cuff-link. He began to roll back the cuff of his shirt. Then thrust the naked underside of his forearm at the girl. Porpentine recoiled, thinking: Lord love a duck. Bongo-Shaftesbury is insane. Shiny and black against the unsunned flesh was a miniature electric switch, single-pole, double-throw, sewn into the skin. Thin silver wires ran from its terminals up the arm, disappearing under the sleeve.
> The young often show a facile acceptance of the horrible. Mildred began to shake. 'No,' she said, 'no: you are not one.'
> 'But I am,' protested Bongo-Shaftesbury, smiling, 'Mildred.

The wires run up into my brain. When the switch is closed like
this I act the way I do now. When it is thrown the other –'
    The girl shrank away. 'Papa,' she cried.
    'Everything works by electricity,' Bongo-Shaftesbury
explained, soothing. 'And it is simple, and clean.'   (121)

Pynchon brilliantly manages pace in this scene. We have just
settled down to a relaxing train-journey when this obscene, quasi-
sexual revelation occurs. The broader set of contrasts between
purity and mechanism on the one hand and humanity on the
other give the reader an explanatory frame of reference to fall
back on after this surreal shock. It is in keeping with Pynchon's
general practice on using characters to personify cultural attitudes
that Bongo-Shaftesbury should be a German agent and a cyborg,
in other words the embodiment of an inhuman efficiency. Hence
the neat cultural symbolism in Bongo-Shaftesbury shooting
Porpentine at Kheops.
    The other point where Pynchon disrupts the narrative depends
for its effects on the juxtaposition of romantic opera with
adventure in the climactic scene when the Fashoda crisis has
broken. The main characters go to a performance of *Manon* in
Cairo's Ezbekiyeh Garden. Porpentine and Goodfellow take up
their positions to watch for any attempted assassination of Lord
Cromer. Simultaneously the tension in the opera mounts and the
narrative switches to and fro between Amiens and Cairo:

The postilion horn of the diligence was heard. The coach came
rattling and creaking into the inn courtyard. Bongo-Shaftesbury
raised his pistol. Porpentine said: 'Lepsius. Next door.'
Goodfellow withdrew. The diligence bounced to a halt.
Porpentine centered his sights on Bongo-Shaftesbury, then let
the muzzle drift down and to the right until it pointed at Lord
Cromer. It occurred to him that he could end everything for
himself right now, never have to worry about Europe again. He
had a sick moment of uncertainty. Now how serious had
anyone ever been? Was aping Bongo-Shaftesbury's tactics any
less real than opposing them? Like a bloody grouse, Goodfellow
had said. Manon was helped down from the coach. Des Grieux
gaped, was transfixed, read his destiny on her eyes. Someone
was standing behind Porpentine. He glanced back, quickly in
that moment of hopeless love, and saw Moldweorp there

looking decayed, incredibly old, face set in a hideous though compassionate smile. Panicking, Porpentine turned and fired blindly . . . (132–3)

At this moment Porpentine characteristically suffers from uncertainty about himself and his whole enterprise. The alternation between action on-stage and off it suggests that the attempts to protect Cromer take secondary place to Porpentine's futile attempts to avoid his own destiny. Des Grieux reads his fate in Manon's eyes just as Porpentine 'in that moment of hopeless love' recognizes his doom in *his* Manon, Moldweorp. This episode brings completely to the surface Porpentine's despairing sense that all his actions are theatre by locating them *in* a theatre and by repeatedly referring them to the opera.

In this story Pynchon has partially returned to the method of 'Mortality and Mercy' in evoking different literary and operatic analogues which simultaneously refusing to authenticate them. Although the historical present of the story is 1898 the kind of scrutiny it enacts is modernistic. 'Mortality and Mercy', 'Entropy' and 'Under the Rose' all create remarkably dense and demanding narrative textures through allusion. By contrast Pynchon's latest story to date marks a falling off of inventive energy, a regression towards conventional realism.

6 'THE SECRET INTEGRATION'

'The Secret Integration' (1964) presents the activities of a group of young boys who live in a small West Massachusetts town somewhere between Pittsfield and Springfield. The story focuses specifically on one Tim Santara whose native intelligence is repeatedly contrasted with that of the local boy genius, Grover Snodd. The narrative opens with Tim worrying about how a wart on his finger can be removed. Similarly in *The Adventures of Tom Sawyer*, the first time Tom and Huckleberry Finn meet, they discuss methods of removing warts. The methods vary, to be sure, in both works: Huck Finn pins his faith in a dead cat, whereas Tim has to undergo fluorescent treatment. Grover knows about Indian raids and is the intellectual of the group. Similarly Tom Sawyer, this time in *The Adventures of Huckleberry Finn*, leads his cronies on raids and parades his 'learning', or rather his reading in Romantic literature, before the other children. Grover obsessively reads Tom Swift books and is the one who brings most things to the hideout just as Tom Sawyer accumulates the most 'wealth' (a tin soldier, key, chalk, etc.) from his various deals with the others. When Tim and Grover leave the latter's house they go to the hideout which is an abandoned old house that they approach by crossing an ornamental canal on a ramshackle boat. This house is the Jackson's Island of the story, the place where the children feel most liberated from parental control.

There are so many parallels with the two Twain books that Pynchon's story seems almost a pastiche at times. The children have banded themselves together into a secrety society which is planning a revolution. Of course Grover has taken over the leadership and the purpose of the relatively early gathering at his house is for the different children to report on their progress. Grover is every bit as pedantic and officious as Tom Sawyer. He holds a clipboard, ostentatiously checking off items on his list. He fusses over words like 'coordination' which none of the other children understands. More than that, Grover drills them annually for what he calls Operation Spartacus, the uprising of the slaves (i.e. children) modelled on the Kirk Douglas film. This consists of the children assaulting imaginary buildings which have been marked out on a field in chalk outline, or, with this year's advance in efficiency, with stakes and red flags from road-repair gangs. In exactly the same way Tom Sawyer invents complicated rituals of challenges, oaths, ransomes, etc. which he has culled from *Picciola*, Dumas and other sources. He leads his gang in a raid on Spaniards and Arabs, but only finds a Sunday-school picnic. In *Huckleberry Finn* Huck acts as a foil to Tom and exposes his ignorance and blind fidelity to his literary models, as in their famous exchange over the word 'ransomed':

> [Huck speaks] 'Ransomed? What's that?'
> 'I don't know. But that's what they do. I've seen it in books; and so of course that's what we've got to do.'
> 'But how can we do it if we don't know what it is?'[74]

And so the discussion goes, with tempers mounting on both sides. Huck questions Tom's dogma with a destructive and shrewd common sense. Similarly Tim asks Grover to explain the code name Operation A. The A stands, Grover tells him, for 'abattoir' or 'Armageddon' which is only a fraction less absurd than Tom Sawyer's ignorance. Tim calls him a 'showoff' and reflects: 'You didn't have to know what initials meant to drill kids' (1)[75]. Huck, of course, decides eventually that Tom's rituals are make-believe and lies, and rejects them accordingly. Tim similarly has tired of Grover's drilling in fields. Like Huck he is more practically-minded and complains: 'It just isn't that real any more' (156).

One problem in such parallels involves the perspective of Pynchon's story. He takes elements from a child's romance narrated by an adult for children (*Tom Sawyer*) and a novel which brilliantly exploits a naive child's vision in order to expose social hypocrisy, racism, and bogus romanticism (*Huckleberry Finn*). When Tom and his friends spend their first night on Jackson's Island, Twain describes it thus:

> Gradually their talk died out and drowsiness began to steal upon the eyelids of the little waifs. The pipe dropped from the fingers of the Red-handed, and he slept the sleep of the conscience-free and the weary.[76]

Here the narrator bends cloyingly over the boys as if he were a proxy parent and reassures the reader through key terms like 'waif' and 'conscience-free', but above all by exploiting the third-person narrative, that the boys will come to no harm. In stark contrast, when Huck (the 'Red-handed' in the first passage) is fleeing from his father he lands at Jackson Island, but this time without any sentimental lingering over childish innocence: 'There was a little gray in the sky, now; so I stepped into the woods and laid down for a nap before breakfast.'[77] Huck's shrewd and practical attention to natural circumstances gives enough information here. Dawn is approaching so he can afford the brief luxury of a nap. Even such an incidental detail becomes charged with drama because Huck is constantly on his guard against danger such as the river or his father. And the precarious nature of his situation is reflected in the absence of a reassuring third-person narrator.

Pynchon steers somewhere between these two extremes. He certainly avoids the sentimentality of *Tom Sawyer* and likewise never attempts the scope of *Huckleberry Finn*. Thus Tim's dissatisfaction with Grover's pseudo-revolutionary manoeuvrings takes place in a vacuum. Whereas Huck rejects Tom's romanticism along with the hypocritical claims of religion, family obedience, etc. – the values, in other words, of the shore. Again and again minor variations in perspective can be identified in Pynchon's story which show him inclining now towards *Huckleberry Finn*, now towards *Tom Sawyer*. Tim's description of Etienne is representative:

> He had gathered around him a discontented bunch the principal [of the local school], when she was yelling at them, never failed to call 'uneducable', a word none of them understood and which Grover wouldn't explain to them because it made him mad, it was like calling somebody a wop, or a nigger. Etienne's friends included the Mostly brothers, Arnold and Kermit, who sniffed airplane glue and stole mousetraps from the store . . .
>
> (150)

The sentence begins with a more or less neutral perspective which shifts, via the mysterious term 'uneducable' into Tim's. Now Pynchon is imitating Twain's use of Huck to draw attention to adult values though he is incapable of articulating a criticism of them. Grover, the self-styled mentor, does this by converting it into a term of abuse, and thereby adds one more element in the cause of imaginative openness which the story as a whole endorses. But this brief surge in seriousness lapses into children's-book humour as the following sentence picks up 'naughty' details of the Mostly brothers. Now the perspective inclines towards *Tom Sawyer*. To a certain extent Pynchon creates this wavering ambiguity by retaining a third-person narrative and yet trying to capture aspects of both Twain novels in his story.

The Twain parallels constantly give the reader the impression of a shadow text lying behind Pynchon's. In the earlier stories allusions to other literature become part of their very rhetoric. Now Pynchon seems to engage in a derivative mimicry which relates to another problematical area of the story – its security. 'The Secret Integration' contains a gratuitous amount of realistic details about children, events and places which do not figure in the actual narrative. These details build up a cumulative cosy sense of a safe community which pulls against the story's racial theme. Even though Pynchon explicitly denies safety in the concluding sentence the boys all go home to bed, back to a domestic security worthy of *Tom Sawyer* which virtually dismisses any more weighty concerns.

A coloured family (the Barringtons) has recently moved into Mingeborough (Tim's home town) and a question mark hangs over the story as to whether they will be accepted or not. A clear sign of an answer is given when Tim surprises his mother on the telephone:

> She'd been dialing with one hand and holding the other in front of her in a tight, pale fist. There was a look on her face Tim had never seen before. A little – what do you call it, nervous? scared? – he didn't know. If she saw him there she gave no sign, though he'd made noise enough. The receiver stopped buzzing, and somebody answered.
>
> 'You niggers,' his mother spat out suddenly, 'dirty niggers, get out of this town, go back to Pittsfield. Get out before you get in real trouble.' Then she hung up fast. The hand that was in a fist had been shaking, and now her other hand, once it let go of the receiver, started shaking a little too. She turned swiftly, as if she'd smelled him like a deer; caught Tim looking at her in astonishment.
>
> 'Oh, you,' she said, beginning to smile, except for her eyes.
>
> 'What were you doing?' Tim said, which wasn't what he'd meant to ask.
>
> 'Oh, playing a joke, Tim,' she said, 'a practical joke.'
>
> Tim shrugged and went on out the back door. 'I'm going out,' he told her, without looking back. He knew she wouldn't give him any trouble now about it [going out], because he'd caught her. (147)

Pynchon's management of perspective here is masterly. Tim tentatively tries to define his mother's expression but cannot. The verb 'spat' catches the physical suddenness of her ways of speaking, and at the same time carries connotations of disgust which Tim misses. The other physical details reinforce this suggestion of extreme tension. Her hands are shaking, she 'smells' Tim like a deer scenting danger. Once again Pynchon hints at guilt through manner and confirms it through the unnatural divorce of her eyes from her general facial expression. Momentarily the child–parent roles are reversed. Tim catches his mother doing something which he interprets as simply naughty, but which a broader adult perspective would take as shameful. The crowning irony in the whole passage is that she explains her behaviour in the same terms that the children use, i.e. as a practical joke. Tim's shrug is ambiguous, but at least partly sceptical, perhaps because he misses the all-important element of play in her expression.

Of course, although Tim literally shrugs the incident off, its memory lingers throughout the rest of the story to re-surface, startlingly when Carl Barrington, Tim and the others are walking back home from their hide-out. A garbage truck rushes past them and alerts them that all is not well. When they arrive at the Barringtons' house they find garbage spread all over the front lawn, some of which Tim immediately identifies as his own family's. While they are picking it up Mrs. Barrington comes to the door and screams at them. Once again adult behaviour strikes Tim as mysterious; he tells her 'we're on your side' (191), but to no avail. Pynchon is here dealing with a sensitive topical issue of the mid-1960s. So important was an integrated housing policy that the 1966 Civil Rights Bill included extensive proposals to enforce it.[78] Pynchon's choice of location in the Berkshires is highly strategic and in scenes like the one quoted above he establishes a clear ironic distinction between an adult and a child's perspectives.

The problem here is that Pynchon devotes so much attention to the boys' games (their manufacture of sodium bombs, attempts to 'sabotage' the railway, etc.) that the racial theme is virtually smothered. They go to an abandoned Gilded Age mansion whose labyrinthine layout attracts their imagination. Making their way to this house becomes ceremonious and thrillingly dangerous: 'the route to the hideout was thus like the way into a reefed and perilous harbour' (164). Pynchon skilfully energizes the objects in the house as they react on the boys' imagination. The sheer details of place, fanciful 'memories' of previous inhabitants contrast the boys' play with the suburban monotony of their surroundings. Briefly then Pynchon touches on themes he has already explored in 'Low-lands'.

The first two sections of the story (set in Grover's tree-house and the old mansion) and the conclusion where the boys return home frame two retrospective sections, in the first of which Tim remembers going with another boy to a hotel to act as counsellors to a coloured musician suffering from alcoholic withdrawal.

McAfee (the musician) has called the local chapter of Alcoholics Anonymous for help and predictably interprets it as a racial put-down that they send him two children. In this long and somewhat rambling part of the story he tells the boys of his loneliness which Tim only really glimpses once he tries to telephone a former girlfriend of McAfee's:

> . . . Tim's foot felt the edge of a certain abyss which he had been walking close to. . . . He looked over it, got afraid, and shied away, but not before learning something unpleasant about the night . . .   (183)

Although Pynchon registers McAfee's loneliness convincingly it is difficult to accept that Tim actually *learns* much because he is insulated by his own ignorance and the comforts of home. Pynchon attributes a change in awareness to the boy whereas in scenes like this he is more important to supply the reader with eyes, as when he witnesses the dumping of garbage on the Barringtons' front lawn. Pynchon tacitly leaves the racially aware reader to draw his own conclusions.

When Carl's name is first mentioned, Pynchon's narrative gloss – 'He meant Carl Barrington, a colored kid they knew' (145) – cuts right through the adult taboos about racial contact. This simple, matter-of-fact statement accepts differences among the boys as a natural thing and Pynchon unobtrusively hints at the racial mixture of the other boys' families through their names. They range from French (Cherdlu) to English (Slothrop) and Italian (Passarella); and Grover, who acts to a certain extent as a moral guide to the boys, has impressed on them the abusive nature of words like 'wop' and 'nigger'. Accordingly, when Tim arrives at Grover's house, he tells him that 'she used that word again' (152), which both associates a sense of shame with a key term of abuse, but also once again momentarily reverses the parent–child relationship. It is as if Tim and Grover are two parents comparing notes about children who have just learned to swear. The fact that Carl behaves just like any other member of the group and is accepted as such offers an integration which undermines the parents' prejudices – hence the story's title. The fact, however, that it is children who are doing the integrating offsets the political weight of their action because the story's ironies depend largely on their ignorance of racial issues. For the story to succeed Pynchon would need to strike a firmer balance between the children's imagination (which dominates the second section) and the racial details (which dominate the retrospective sections). His uncertainties about perspective and how to apportion emphasis lead to a bizarre conclusion where Pynchon suggests that Carl was a composite image assembled in the children's minds; he 'had been put together out of phrases, images, possibilities that grownups had somehow turned away from' (192). This grossly offends our sense of reality because for Pynchon's two themes to work out he must come across as actual (for there to be a real racial 'problem') *and* a figure who captures the boys' imagination. The uncertainty at the end tilts the balance towards the latter (it is significant that he goes back to the hideout) and the racial issue evaporates into fancy. Given the obvious weaknesses of the story it is surprising that Pynchon should revive details from it in *Gravity's Rainbow*.

2

V.

1 THE WHOLE SICK CREW AND THE NOVEL'S PRESENT

When Pynchon's first novel, *V.*, appeared in 1963 it was greeted
with puzzlement, or dismissed as a confusing practical joke by the
reviewers. It was described variously as an 'allegorical bedlam', 'a
wearisome joke' and a novel weighted down with much 'learned
lumber', 'a kind of sick museum of prevailing literary styles'.[1]
There were a few serious readings probably in reaction against
the sheer breadth of the book as well as its humour. Like *In Our
Time* and *U.S.A.* it intercalates sections within a linear narrative
set in 1956 in order to broaden the scope of that narrative (see
schema). The two main sequences which alternate with each
other and thus establish one of the novel's rhythms, are the latter
which centres on a character called Benny Profane and takes place
mainly in New York, and a series of historical chapters which
spread from 1898 to 1943. The historical sections are linked by the
search of one Herbert Stencil for a mysterious figure called V.,
and the novel's chronology is as follows:

Chapter
1 Christmas Eve 1955: Profane in
   Norfolk, travels to New York.
2 Early 1956: The Whole Sick Crew.   Stencil in Mallorca (1946)
3   Egypt, 1898.
4 Early 1956: Esther's nose job.   Schoenmaker   in   France
                                             (1918).
5 Profane hunting alligators.   Fairing's Journal (1934).
6 February to mid-April: Profane
   with the Mendozas.
7 Stencil meets Eigenvalue.   Florence, 1899.
8 April: various episodes.
9   South-west Africa, 1922 and
                                             1904.
10 Early Summer to August.
11   Malta, 1939 and 1940–3.
12 August–September.
13 Late September: preparations to
    leave for Malta.

71

There has been a tacit agreement among critics that the historical chapters tend to be richer and more varied that those set in 1956, predictably in a novel which demonstrates the absurdity and monotony of contemporary life. Nevertheless, Benny Profane's narrative has a very important part to play in establishing the novel's themes. His sudden appearance in the first chapter without preamble or much reference to his past implies that Profane only has an existence in the present. His drifting from one casual job to another and from one equally casual liaison to another, together with the prominence of parties in his experience suggests that Pynchon is drawing on 1950s novelists like John Clellon Holmes or Chandler Brossard to set up a freewheeling narrative where characters' risks, experiments and the moment-by-moment excitement of their lives contrasts with domestic sobriety. Pynchon himself makes this kind of contrast early in the novel when he attacks the stereotyped behaviour of girls from Long Island suburbia. Within the terms of this ironic attack Profane should appear comically unconventional and indeed Pynchon's fascination with chance fights and escapades partly initiated by Profane's naval buddy, Big Bodine, persists to the very end of the novel.

Profane's role in the novel is by no means as clearcut as these details might suggest. In fact, there is an uncertainty of perspective towards him which can be seen from the way Pynchon describes one of the many drinking sessions in Chapter 1 where Profane and his friends are present: 'Try to squeeze a water-melon into a small tumbler some time when your reflexes are not so good. It is next to impossible.'[2] Pynchon's momentary adoption of the second person draws the reader into the circle of Profane's naval cronies and involves him in the tensions between them. At issue here is how much emotional life is attributed to Profane. Later in the novel he is credited with an innate sympathy for bums and derelicts, and repeatedly demonstrates a nostalgia for the Depression when he was born. These feelings are uncontrolled and lead nowhere. They are examples of what Richard Poirier calls 'an uncertain pathos' surrounding Profane, one which pulls against an external view of him as a figure rather than character.[3] Pynchon's uncertainty whether to view Profane from the outside or from a position nearer to conventional characterization blurs what would otherwise be an ironically crisp depiction. In the heading to the first chapter Pynchon attaches two labels to him – schlemihl and yo-yo – which both suggest a 'flat' or truncated character. The term 'schlemihl' is associated mainly with Jewish–American fiction and means, according to Leo Rosten, 'a clumsy, butterfingered, all thumbs, gauche type'.[4] It sums up Profane's belief that objects are in conspiracy against him, a comic version of the paranoia we meet repeatedly in the historical sections, a belief which is demonstrated in two passages of comic accidents and in a number of other slapstick episodes such as an attempt at sex on a pool table which goes wrong, leaving Profane on the floor, the pool balls streaming onto his stomach. His drift into and out of such episodes resembles a cartoon or stylized comedy where the audience is freed to laugh by the distancing absurdity of events. In other words, the less sense we have of Profane as a person in these situations the more comic he becomes, and this relates very closely to the term 'schlemihl'. Unlike its application in the fiction of say Malamud or Bellow, Profane himself is using 'schlemihl' as a self-protective label which further reduces his responsiveness towards complete passivity.[5] Contrasting himself with Randolph Scott, Profane reflects: 'a schemihl, that was hardly a man: somebody who lies back and takes it from objects, like any passive woman' (288/268). Sure enough, the passivity comes out in his liaisons where he uses his schlemihl-label to evade involvement, sometimes on surprisingly conventional, sometimes on anti-conventional grounds.

By adopting this label Profane deliberately tries to minimize his own humanity and reduce himself to an amoeba-like passivity. The second label of yo-yo draws our attention to movement as one of Profane's determinants. His basic premise is that nothing has any reason and thus 'happens' to pass through Norfolk, Virginia at the beginning of the novel. He chooses an employment agency by the crease his erection makes in the *Times*. In short, Profane is an absurd figure because he is so much at the mercy of chance. He makes a minimal effort to resist this by travelling backwards and forwards on the Times Square–Grand Central shuttle in New York, one of the examples of yo-yoing. This clearly reveals the difference between Profane and a Beat protagonist like Sal Paradise who sets off for the West in the confident hope that he will find happiness in a particular place or with a particular friend (Dean Moriarity). The road thus becomes a metaphor of possibility although the hope becomes more and more difficult to sustain as Sol crosses and re-crosses the continent. The only sense in which Profane goes on the road (Kerouac's title is referred to in Chapter 1) is to work on a repair gang.[6] Since Profane has no goal he has no direction and hence yo-yoes on the New York shuttle and later on the Staten Island Ferry. Pynchon is careful to point out that his dress is exactly the same at the end of the novel as at the beginning, thereby suggesting that he has not changed at all. Profane represents an attenuated and lethargic version of Beat mobility reduced absurdly to moving in order to fill the monotony of life. Thus it is quite appropriate for him to run as it were off the page into darkness at the end of the novel.

Profane performs an important function in *V.* as a connector, in relating characters to each other and in revealing themes. In Chapter 1 he sees one of his buddies revving a motorbike in the middle of the night; this reminds him of a girl called Rachel Owlglass who is having an 'affair' with her M.G.; his memory makes yet another jump back to a crazed Brazilian who was obsessed with a machine-gun. Ostensibly, the connections are made through memory but in fact they are purely structural associations and tell us scarcely anything of Profane himself. Rather, they shed early light on the transference of feeling on to inanimate objects which Pynchon suggests is one of the defining characteristics of modern life. Profane scarcely glimpses this general factor just as he misses the significance of his repeated nightmare of a street: 'The lights gleamed unflickering on hydrants; manhole covers which lay around in the street. There were neon signs scattered here and there, spelling out words he wouldn't remember when he woke' (39/30). In such an urban novel, it is not surprising that the street should become an emblem of threatening anonymity. Profane fears his own disassembly in this street. Pynchon is probably drawing here on Eliot's poetry (e.g. 'Rhapsody on a Windy Night') and on the paintings of Giorgio di Chirico which use strange lighting and perspective to create an atmosphere of brooding threat in street scenes.[7] The street reappears constantly throughout *V.* as an embodiment of urban anomie or as a setting for violence.

Profane introduces a group of New York characters known collectively as the Whole Sick Crew who all participate in a common lethargy. Fergus Mixolydian, 'the laziest living creature in New York' (56/45) has connected his TV set to his forearm so that he has become an extension of it. Slab is a self-styled Catatonic Expressionist painter who imitates the declining years of Monet by painting endless variations of one subject – Cheese Danishes (he has reached number 35!). Pynchon dismisses their pretended avant-gardism as 'an exhausted impersonation of poverty, rebellion and artistic "soul"' (56/46) and reinforces this attack with destructive criticisms from other characters on the edge of the group. Their criteria is reflected by the comparatively static series of portraits Pynchon creates; even when they do move the motion is repetitive and monotonous from party to party. Apart from the intrinsic absurdity of the Crew's pursuits they also emerge as self-deceived because they are so heavily involved in the network of consumerism – Raoul writes pulp TV scripts, Mafia Winsome (a possible parody of Ayn Rand) writes best-sellers and so on.

The names of the Crew and the other minor contemporary characters demonstrate their absurdity. They suggest the personification of a function (Stencil, Schoenmaker the cosmetic surgeon, etc.), or involve the characters in commercial materials or products (Teflon, Chiclitz, etc.). The names might reflect the characteristic of their owners (Slab suggesting inertia) or glance at pop culture (Benny meaning a benzedrine pill). As Terry Caeser has pointed out, Pynchon seems to parody the very act of naming, making it virtually impossible to believe that there is an identity behind them.[8] The general tendency of these grotesque names is to push all the characters back into their environment so that they become animated extensions of their surroundings. Once this norm is established it is their signs of humanity that startle the reader not their absence.

These characters' dialogue strengthens our cumulative impression of atrophied humanity. Pynchon probably took Slab's name from *Philosophical Investigations* where Wittgenstein hypothesizes a minimal language between a builder and his assistant which would consist of nouns like 'block' or 'slab'.[9] At one party two members of the Crew utter trendy monosyllables like 'man' and 'scene' and later in the novel Pynchon develops the allusion to Wittgenstein to sum up the Crew's conversations as variations on a fixed (and very limited) number of items 'depending on how you arranged the building blocks at your disposal' (297/277). In all areas of their life (artistic, love-making or conversational) they move within a closed area of possibilities. The only options open to them are repetition or permutations of the already familiar, both of which will carry them nearer towards ultimate inertia.

The pretensions of the Crew to be artistic form part of a larger unconscious impersonation which reflects how strong a hold the media have taken over characters. Early in the novel, we are told 'American movies had given them stereotypes all' (14/6), and sure enough, one of Profane's naval cronies Pappy Hod imitates a film gangster; two other characters fight according to the style of a Western saloon brawl; and two policemen appear briefly who take 'Dragnet' as their model. And so the list could go on. Pynchon is particularly shrewd at demonstrating the ways in which films, advertisements and popular art-forms can invade and dominate characters. The Crew are the ultimate examples of this process because they do not appear to possess any authentic identity of their own. Lying behind this general situation stands, as I suggested earlier, consumerism. At one point Roony Winsome, a New York record agent, reflects angrily on the current Davy Crockett craze which is sweeping the country and thereby casting a bogus glamour over 'a foul-mouthed louseridden boozehound' (219/203). Here the contrast between the truth and the image projected by the advertisers is clear enough. Even in the cases of Mafia's self-delusion and Rachel's 'love' for her M.G. consumerism is playing its part. The popular success of Mafia's novels leads her to imagine that her doctrine of Heroic Love is realizable; and Rachel's submission to the promotion of speed leads to a bizarre transference of feeling. Even Pig Bodine, normally the personification of careless vitality to Profane, suddenly becomes sinister when astride his motorbike; his head becomes a 'sphere of dead black' (22/13). Blackness, the inanimate and death are repeatedly linked in *V.*, as in the three girls who Profane calls in Little Italy. They resemble automata, 'all lipstick and shiny-machined breast- and buttock-surfaces'. (139/126).

Pynchon diagnoses two tendencies in his contemporary characters. Just as Nathanael West's Hollywood hangers-on reduce themselves to routines – become as it were pure roles – so Pynchon's New Yorkers reduce themselves to objects. Secondly, they engage in a constant mimicry of the images projected by the American media. Examining the growing influence of advertising on American life, Daniel J. Boorstin has argued that there is more involved in the process than growing superficiality:

> Rather these things express a world where the image, more interesting than its original, has become the original. The shadow has become the substance. Advertising men, industrial designers, and packaging engineers are not deceivers of the public. They are simply acolytes of the image.[10]

Pynchon follows Boorstin in presenting a topsy-turvy world where media images dominate the consumer imagination and prescribe styles of behaviour rather than simply reflecting them. For Boorstin the original has been lost; for Pynchon the real has become smothered in layers of representation.

Pynchon takes the specific example of cosmetic surgery to demonstrate an individual's conformity to the stereotyped images promoted by the media. The surgeon, Shale Schoenmaker, was originally a romantic idealist hero-worshipping such First World War pilots as Evan Godolphin who reappears in the historical sections of *V*. Godolphin crashes and in a surge of love for humanity Schoenmaker conceives a mission to improve graft surgery. Between then and 1956, some shift occurs in this purpose which Pynchon is careful not to dramatize as corruption. Nevertheless, consumerism has taken over his original humane impulse and he defends his job on the grounds of supply and demand. *V.* describes in great detail an operation he performs on Esther Harvitz, another member of the Crew who, like Marilyn Monroe, has decided that her nose is too far from the WASP retroussé stereotype to be tolerable. Schoenmaker's model while working on her is, symbolically, a mould. Pynchon stresses the violence of the operation and also its bizarre sexuality. The doctor appeals to her 'gently, like a lover'; his sponge-strokes are caressing; the scalpel sets up a copulatory rhythm; and the running metaphor enables Pynchon to make outrageous puns on terms like 'hump'. It is difficult to see Esther as a victim here because, like the other New Yorkers, she is co-operating so wholeheartedly with the process. Schoenmaker turns the sexual metaphor on its head and begins an affair with her by pretending it is another operation, thereby confirming in every sense one character's vision of New York as a chain of 'screwers and screwees' (49/38).

The absurd names, the targets of Pynchon's irony and his detailed depiction of Esther's willing submission to violence suggest a situation where humanity and the environment are constantly overlapping. The text of the New York chapters is filled with reference to consumer-articles and media products so that humanity is reduced to a matter of fleeting remembrances. Characters constantly attenuate into mechanistic processes or into promoted images, and the activity which embodies this mechanism is party-going. We have already seen the party become a set-piece in Pynchon's stories where it enacts the slide towards disorder. In *V.* his emphasis has shifted rather on to monotony. The first party in New York is described in terms of a familiar pattern: 'he would play his guitar. . . . The lights in the living room would go out one by one, Schoenberg's quartets (complete) would go on the record player/changer, and repeat, and repeat . . .' (57/46). The insistent 'would . . . would . . . would' sequence underlines the predictability of the party as if it is unwinding towards some point of equilibrium. Certainly parties figure again and again in the 1956 chapters and they never carry any connotations of festivity.

Pynchon's repeated comparisons of human to mechanical processes and his sardonic demonstration how inanimate objects smother characters and reduce them to items in the general environment all suggest a gradual atrophy or prosthesis of humanity. During the historical chapters, Herbert Stencil at one point wonders what the figure V. would be like if brought up to date and imagines a sophisticated robot. Robots have already been introduced as a possible culmination of this process through a job Profane gets as a night-guard with a company which uses automata to simulate car accidents. The two under his care are called SHROUD, a kind of grotesque *memento mori* consisting of transparent plastic limbs built around a human skeleton, and SHOCK which contains foam vinyl flesh. One night to his astonishment Profane finds himself having a conversation with SHROUD who performs the role of a mock-sibyll, prophesying that humanity will become automata.[11]

"What do you mean, we'll be like you and SHOCK someday? You mean dead?"

Am I dead? If I am that's what I mean.
"If you aren't what are you?"
Nearly what you are. None of you have very far to go.

(286/267)

The absence of speech marks for SHROUD's words, the general absurdity of the situation of the fact that the automaton is transparent make it ridiculous for Profane to attribute life or an 'inside' to it, and surrounds the whole event with brilliantly controlled ambiguity. SHROUD's 'message' centres on a comparison between a scrapyard and the pile of corpses from concentration camps, in other words is partly a warning about humans' treatment of each other, but the humour of the situation prevents this warning from ever becoming too solemn. In effect SHROUD makes explicit a series of recurring metaphors linking the human and mechanical (Stencil, for instance, calls the Crew a 'machine'), and challenges the presumption (particularly ironic in Profane of all people) that man is superior to a machine. In spite of the scene's absurdity a challenge is also thrown out to the reader to take Pynchon's mechanistic metaphors more literally than just rhetoric. Profane's two conversations with SHROUD are juxtaposed with an example of mechanistic process (a Crew party), examples of man's vulnerability before the inanimate (a list of natural disasters taken from the 1957 World Almanac) and a brief section where a character compares the workings of the brain with a flip-flop circuit. These examples alone should be enough to warn us not to treat the SHROUD episode either as pure comedy or as an episode in isolation from its context.[12]

SHROUD startles Profane by comparing human beings to scrapped cars, to the detritus of the consumer circuit, and consumerism also provides the link between the general New York context and some of the most bizarre episodes in the novel. The first job which Profane gets in that city is as a member of a squad set up by the City Council to hunt alligators in the sewers. Pynchon is here drawing on a city legend which dates back to 1935, but originates the sequence in Macy's (who sold the baby alligators as pets; when the pets were unwanted they were flushed into the sewers) to set up a perspective on the creatures as objects.[13] The alligator-hunts burlesque three things: American war movies, American hunt narratives, and missionary colonialism. The squad-leader builds up a fantasy of warfare (his members

wear arm-bands and report to an operational HQ) which infects
the rest of his group even though they recognize that it is fantasy.
Secondly, unlike classic hunt-narratives such as *Moby-Dick*, 'The
Bear', or *The Old Man and the Sea*, Profane is not operating in open
nature but in the very opposite setting. There is no question of
individual prowess because they are working for the Council:

> They worked in teams of two. One held a flashlight, the other
> carried a 12-gauge repeating shotgun. Zeitsuss [the squad
> leader] was aware that most hunters regard use of this weapon
> like anglers feel about dynamiting fish; but he was not looking
> for write-ups in Field and Stream.   (113/101)

The throw-away reference to a fashionable hunting journal makes
it clear that the myth of individual confrontation of nature is
simply not available. Walden Pond has become a tourist resort
and the only way in which Profane can 'go west' is by dying, as
the punning title of Chapter 5 suggests. The nature myth is only
available through parody.

Inset into the hunt-narrative is the story of a certain Father
Fairing (to reappear in the Epilogue) who is harried by an
apocalyptic vision of the city being taken over by rats and so
descends into the sewers to convert them. Absurd enough at the
beginning, his quest becomes even more ridiculous when he is
outwitted in theological argument by a rat called Ignatius, falls in
love with another rat called Veronica, and even takes to eating his
subjects when they are slow to convert. Passing allusions to *Heart
of Darkness* reinforce the suggestion that this section offers a
bizzarely displaced parody of colonialism. As such it has more
relevance to the historical chapters of *V.* which also make use of
textual uncertainty. Profane quotes passages from Father Fairing's
journal which, we are told, is kept in the Vatican Library. Such
paradoxes will arise during Stencil's quest for *V.* and will
inevitably bring his methods into question.

The novel as a whole works through absurd images, parody
and burlesque. Both in the contemporary and the historical
sections Pynchon carefully demonstrates the self-mystification
and what Richard Poirier calls the 'local ignorance' of his
characters.[14] Although this can occasionally produce a rather
olympian narrative tone Pynchon establishes his detachment quite
successfully. It is when he tries to find relief from the prevailing

absurdity of modern life by attributing emotional weight to his characters that the results can be awkward and embarrassing. One particular character who stands apart from the Crew is a black saxophone player called McClintick Sphere. Sphere is closely modelled on Ornette Coleman, not to parody him as Stanley Edgar Hyman suggests, but to develop his stature.[15] His origin in Fort Worth, method and line-up all parallel Coleman's, as does the fact that he is playing at the V-note (modelled on the Five-Spot where Coleman began performing in 1959). In his novel *Go* (1952) John Clellon Holmes explains the importance of jazz for the post-war generation:

> In this modern jazz, they heard something rebel and nameless that spoke for them, and their lives knew a gospel for the first time. It was more than a music; it became an attitude towards life, a way of walking, a language and a costume . . .[16]

Jazz in Holmes' and Kerouac's fiction creates solidarity by binding together its enthusiasts. In *V.*, however, Pynchon presents Sphere as an isolated man of skill who contrasts very strongly with the Crew. The first section to describe his playing uses a technically precise vocabulary to mock his audience's ineffectual efforts 'to dig'. Sphere's artistic stature matches the substantiality of a relationship he forms with Paola Maijstral who ironically disguises herself as a black prostitute called Ruby. When she tells Sphere the truth about herself he under-reacts and formulates a general principle which has been much quoted by critics: 'Love with your mouth shut, help without breaking your ass or publicising it: keep cool, but care' (365–6/342–3). Richard Poirier offers the following comment on this passage: 'This is the stoical resolve of an embattled underground. . . . But the phrasing, especially coming from a spokesman so ludicrously named, asks to be dismissed as banal . . .'.[17] The general issue raised here is what sort of affirmation is possible in such an ironic novel. Sphere is strangely isolated from the rest of the New York characters, a figure without a context, even though his relationship with Paola is an importantly positive one. Also, and this is true for the novel as a whole, gestures of warmth or humanity take precedence over any theoretical statements. Thus Sphere remains an authentically positive character when he is enacting his love for Paola, but immediately becomes suspect when he generalizes his behaviour into a statement, one which is ironically echoed by SHROUD to Profane only a few pages later.

A particular difficulty arises from making a statement about *love* which Pynchon established as a dominant theme in an early scene which takes place in a Norfolk bar – the Sailor's Grave. To celebrate Christmas, the barmaid Beatrice declares a 'Suck Hour' where the customers fight for access to beer spouting from foam-rubber breast-shaped pumps. This grotesque image telescopes together the profane, prosthetics and a travesty of femininity. Beatrice's name ironically contrasts her with her romantic counterpart and introduces a whole series of examples of debased or deflected love. Like Gaddis' drifters in *The Recognitions* the Crew form casual liaisons and drop them as easily. Love becomes distorted through the various substitutions characters find: Esther secure in her surgery, Mafia Winsome practising her stereotyped code of Heroic Love, Paola disguised as Ruby, Rachel caressing her M.G., and so on. In the case of Benny, women become an extension of his misfortune; 'women had always happened to Profane the schlemihl like accidents' (134/121). While he remains passive, they try to enlist him in roles of their own devising – as protector (Paola) or erotic sparring partner (Mafia) – and from roles there is no escape. Rachel, as befits the owner of an employment agency, publicizes her 'views' with embarrassing piety and gains no exemption from Pynchon's irony. In a novel where things either run down or stay the same the consequences of Esther's relationships (she leaves to get an abortion in Cuba) and of Fina Mendoza's rejection by Profane (she is gang-raped) remind the reader of a constant juxtaposition of sex and either violence or monotony. To confirm the latter Profane forms yet another casual relationship with a girl called Brenda Wigglesworth and runs out of the novel. *V.* is a novel of absences and any mention of love is bound to strain against Pynchon's grotesque humour.

As if he recognized that the prevailing context of irony rendered even direct editorial comment difficult, Pynchon disperses narrative insights among his characters and simultaneously mocks those insights to drain off their solemnity. So when Rachel criticizes Benny for being afraid of love she sheds light on his behaviour but the early image of her caressing her car undermines the authority of her statements. Similarly Roony Winsome offers a definitive summing-up of the Whole Sick Crew, concludes:

'anybody who continues to live in a subculture so demonstrably sick has no right to call himself well' (361/338), and accordingly tries to throw himself out of the nearest window. At this point the narrative suddenly jerks into slapstick when Winsome falls onto a fire-escape and is then grabbed by Pig Bodine. There is probably an element of self-protection in these tactics as if Pynchon wants to make comments but wants also to minimize his own claims to narrative authority. In fact his point of view at times seems to be that of a rather old-fashioned moralist. The grotesque behaviour of his New York characters, their absurd names and roles, only seem absurd if we expect the human and the natural. The muffled indignation which lies beneath Pynchon's portrayal of Esther's 'nose job' grows out of an implicit belief that media images should not distort an individual's sense of beauty. The sharper sarcasm against Mafia's fiction of Heroic Love clearly attacks another kind of self-deception, and so we could continue. In many of the contemporary sections of *V.* Pynchon's ironies work from a notional viewpoint of individuality even though he simultaneously demonstrates again and again why this individuality can no longer be achieved. The result can seem paradoxical. F. J. Hoffman, for instance, asserts that the novel cuts the ground from under its own feet because 'one of its principal faults is that it makes fun of the reason why it makes fun of everything else'.[18] This puts the matter far too simply. *V.* is an absurdist novel which specializes in negative effects, in demonstrating what has decayed in modern man. In order to make its own effects possible Pynchon adopts a symbolic external viewpoint and an elaborate narrative structure which constantly gives the reader the impression that Pynchon is speaking from the viewpoint of history itself. Since the historial sections all gradually converge on the present we shall see that their local themes and methods will authenticate Pynchon's presentation of contemporary life as absurd.

2   THE HISTORICAL SECTIONS

The second main line of action in *V.* describes the efforts of one Herbert Stencil to track down a mysterious figure called V. Stencil's search sets up the historical chapters of this novel which tend to be comparatively self-contained but which also overlap into the New York chapters. Stencil's hunt for information takes place on the edge of the Whole Sick Crew and his path crosses that of Profane as if Pynchon was partly imitating the criss-crossing of Bloom and Stephen in *Ulysses*. One of the dangers in describing Stencil is of over-humanizing him. Before the war he was a drifter just like Profane, until he was galvanized into action by his father's journals. The fact that he is the 'century's child' suggests that he is functioning as a representative of modern man in search of meaning. Denis de Rougemont who, as we shall see, exerted an important influence on *V.*, sees the search as basic to western man's nature: 'the quest is our form of existence' and as such is endless.[19] Jung's work *Modern Man in Search of a Soul* is referred to in connection with Stencil only to be dismissed as 'Rusty Spoon talk', i.e. an intellectually pretentious description worthy of the Crew. From the very beginning Pynchon stresses the absurdity of Stencil's quest. His habit of referring to himself in the third person becomes a ridiculous mannerism or possibly a symptom of paranoia.[20] Stencil's conspiratorial mentality is mocked when he is wounded in the buttock by pellets from Profane's shot-gun and pats himself on the back for having escaped from a nameless 'them'. Similarly his conversation with the 'soul-dentist' Dudley Eigenvalue at the beginning of Chapter 7 offers a cautionary warning about inferring a purpose where none might exist. Even Eigenvalue's name – 'its own value' – contrasts with Stencil's which suggests the personification of a procrustean process. Eigenvalue tells him roundly: ' "In a world such as you inhabit, Mr. Stencil, any cluster of phenomena can be a conspiracy" ' (154/140). Stencil's mentality will recur in the historical sections of *V.* and possibly reflects on one particular aspect of the Suez crisis – Dulles' foreign policy. Pynchon in short subjects Stencil's search to a constant barrage of irony and ridicule from sophisticated intellectual criticism (Eigenvalue) to slapstick (his wounding), comic imagery ('clownish Stencil capering along behind V.: 61–2/50) and outright dismissal as 'mad'. His incorrigible solemnity and single-mindedness makes Stencil into the fool of his own obsession, an obsession which he sedulously protects by circular logic. When asked why he is doing the search, he answers 'why not?'; and when asked what his motive is, replies 'the motive is part of the quarry (386/362). This statement particularly reveals that Stencil's quest is really a principle of motion and, far from aiming at an ultimate goal, Stencil becomes terrified at the thought of finally identifying V., ending his quest, and lapsing back into inertia. As Mark Siegel rightly puts it, Stencil's search is an 'anti-quest' and he is an anti-hero in the sense that his identity is constantly attenuating into the various characters in the historical chapters.[21]

Following Pynchon's own lead in a narrative comment, several critics have found parallels between Stencil's quest and Henry Adams' autobiography but these parallels need to be treated with considerable caution.[22] *The Education of Henry Adams* describes the efforts of an individual to get his bearings among the bewildering historical and intellectual cross-currents of modern life. Adams' use of the third-person to describe himself is a wry admission that he had always been unconsciously at the mercy of larger forces. In 'The Dynamo and the Virgin' Adams both contrasts two symbols of power and hints at a continuity between them; Diana is the animated dynamo. The crucial passage which relates his search for the Virgin's power reads as follows:

> . . . the historian's business was to follow the track to the energy; to find where it came from and where it went to; its complex source and shifting channels; its values, equivalents, conversions.[23]

In *Mont St. Michel and Chartres* he begins this search, broadening Venus into the female principle, but in *The Education* Adams' sense of difficulty in achieving certainty results in a constant ironic awareness of his own limitations. While Stencil mimics Adams' tracking activities and while it is obvious that *V.* owes a debt to Adams' version of the Virgin, *The Education* presents itself as a text to be parodied much less than *The White Goddess*, as we shall see, where an ironic self-awareness is conspicuously absent. Indeed, as Don Hausdorff points out, Stencil's *father* resembles Adams' detached sceptical stance much more than his son.[24] *The Education*'s honest acceptance of doubt and problematic valuing of the self amid competing intellectual doctrines would make this work rather congenial to Pynchon's stance in *V.*

The sheer absurdity of Stencil's activities suggests a different kind of source altogether, Nabokov's *The Real Life of Sebastian Knight* (1941).[25] The narrator of this novel, called simply V, sets out with Stencil's recklessness and determination to write the definitive biography of his half-brother Sebastian Knight. Again like Stencil, he travels widely (to Cambridge, Berlin, Paris, etc.) in search of clues, both questers making use of the vocabulary of detective fiction (one of the Crew describes Stencil's search as 'all quite mysterious and Dashiell Hammettlike': 127/114). Both claim to be objective but both make actually arbitrary assumptions about their material. Nabokov's V begins to wonder whether he is just indulging in fantasy, but stifles his doubts:

> . . . my quest has developed its own magic and logic, and though I sometimes cannot help believing that it had gradually grown into a dream, that quest, using the pattern of reality for the weaving of its own fantasies, I am forced to recognise that I was being led right . . .[26]

The final shift into the passive voice gives away the narrator's self-delusion from his sense of pattern. Also, just as Stencil retraces V's movements in a bizarre kind of mimicry, so V takes on Sebastian Knight's identity. Both seekers are indulging in masquerade – Knight in a solitary performance of his subject, and Stencil, as befits a 'quick-change artist', through a series of impersonations. As Richard Poirier points out, Nabokov parodies the way his narrator acts out a stereotyped literary form, the definitive biography.[27] Stencil too is in effect performing his allegiance to detective-stories and spy-thrillers despite Eigenvalue's brusque condemnation: 'You're a bad detective and a worse spy' (153/139).

At this point we need to distinguish between the possible influences on *V.. Sebastian Knight* offered Pynchon a parodic model whereas Adams' autobiography and particularly *The White Goddess* offered him parodic butts. Both the latter works and *The Golden Bough* are mentioned in *V.* but Pynchon had already to a certain extent disposed of Adams' pessimism in 'Entropy'. In *V.* he turns his attention mainly to parodying Graves' study by presenting mythic allusion in modern secular contexts in order to remind the reader that myth is now only available as a kind of detritus. *The Golden Bough, From Ritual to Romance* (famous for Eliot's application of its doctrine in *The Waste Land*), and *The White Goddess* all apply evolutionary analysis to myth and religion. Graves, for instance, sets out to show the primeval origins of 'the language of poetic myth' and the persistence of this language into modern poetry.[28] His study is thus about continuity and has a clear moral purpose in trying to revitalize the spiritual outside any forms of institutionalized religion. It very quickly becomes evident that Stencil is not producing any firm evidence and certainly nothing of a spiritually affirmative nature, but, even more important, he unconsciously parodies Graves' actual method. Stencil starts his search in Majorca in 1946, which was where Graves worked on *The White Goddess*. Stencil's search begins from a sudden fascination with a passage in his father's journals; Graves experienced 'a sudden overwhelming obsession'. Both are concerned with tracing metamorphoses and both with mapping out their subjects' movements. Both use initial letters as clues and Graves even mentions the V-shape briefly. Again like Stencil, Graves contrasts his own 'poetical' method with the Grecian logical mode of thought, referring approvingly to Joyce at one point.[29]

Stencil's quest then parodies mythography, and the failure to recognize this purpose vitiates an early attempt by Paul Fahy to analyse myth in his novel. He usefully points out a number of allusions to Graves (and to Frazer) but then concludes that the mythology of *The White Goddess* is 'entirely consistent' with Pynchon's use of the V-symbol.[30] It is not clear what 'consistent' can mean here. Certainly Pynchon borrows enough details from Graves for *V.* to resemble the White Goddess but his parodic borrowing prevents myth from becoming an area exempt from the besetting faults of the present – absurdity, decline, inanimacy, etc. Stencil's search parodies the mythic journey and the retracing of a mythical figure degenerates into a comically frantic pursuit of clues. The proliferation of V-shapes mocks the search for analogues and resemblances, and mocks also the very notion of metamorphosis. The further Stencil pursues his search, the less sure he is what sex V. has or even whether it is person and not a thing or a place.

Before going any further with Stencil's quest in general some account is necessary of the historical chapters of the novel, i.e. those associated particularly with the search for V. and which are set in earlier periods. A chapter-by-chapter discussion will reveal the astonishing variety of tone and effects which Pynchon manages, a variety which is scarcely glimpsed by general discussions of the quest or the identity of V. This method of proceeding is also closer to the experience of reading the novel in that we experience the local richness of these chapters before we try to interrelate them.

(a) 'In which Stencil, a quick-change artist, does eight impersonations'

Chapter 3 of *V.* presents a radically altered form of the story 'Under the Rose'; the latter probably formed part of the original manuscript of the novel.[31] In the story we saw Pynchon making extensive use of the Baedeker guidebook to Egypt to compose the landscape which was stylized into a system of coordinates within which the tourist took his bearings from the nearest museum, hotel, station or bank. Later Pynchon draws out the implications in such a composition:

> This is a curious country, populated only by a breed called "tourists". Its landscape is one of inanimate monuments and buildings; near-inanimate barmen, taxi-drivers, bellhops, guides: . . . More than this it is two-dimensional, as is the Street, as are the pages and maps of those little red handbooks. (408–9/384)

Baedekerland now emerges as a self-contained system which, William Plater argues, 'offers Pynchon a model for the way in which his characters can discover their world'. He continues:

> . . . the tour can take place anywhere because once the tourist confronts the discrepancy between illusion and observation, even one's own home can become alien territory and he a stranger in it.[32]

He is certainly right to insist that Pynchon uses the notion of tourism broadly to articulate the illusion of contact with alien hands. Not that the illusion is confined to foreign countries. When Esther rides near Central Park on a bus she thrills at the thought of the dangers she has 'braved', ignoring the fact that the bus insulates her from all but a visual contact with the place. Momentarily she becomes just as much a tourist as Porpentine travelling by train to Cairo.

The Baedeker ethos inevitably carries colonialistic implications in the way that all functionaries within the system blur into an anonymous background mass; become, in Pynchon's terms, 'near inanimate'. The main revisions to 'Under the Rose' reverse that process by filtering the narrative through the eyes of a waiter, factotum, cadger, train-conductor, cab-driver, mountebank and waitress. Pynchon brings these characters out of anonymity by giving them names, dreams and memories of their own. Ironically, the very qualities which humanize them – Waldetar the conductor's nostalgia for Portugal, Gebrail the cab-driver's weakness for fatalistic rhetoric, and so on – also fragments the narrative and makes it virtually impossible to understand without some knowledge of the short story. Partly this is a matter of reduced information, partly a result of the varied reactions of the reflectors to Porpentine and Goodfellow. They are taken for music-hall entertainers, street-fighters, thieves or simply fakes.

These interpretations all pull in the direction of theatrical performance and impersonation. Daniel Boorstin reveals one irony in that 'Baedeker actually instructed the tourist how to dress and how to act the role of a decent, respectable, tolerant member of his own country'.[33] Being a tourist thus consisted of imitating one's national stereotype. Boorstin then quotes Baedeker on the English custom of wearing tweeds and his admonition not to be noisy in public. Porpentine is dressed correctly but jerks bizarrely out of role when he begins to sing from *Manon* in the central square of Alexandria. Following Boorstin's argument we could say that by being a spy he is impersonating an impersonation. Similarly Maxwell Rowley-Bugge, the third reflector, has had to leave England and change his name because of a 'weakness' for young girls.[34] Add to this the general disparity between functionaries' roles and their true feelings and we have a remarkably complex collection of performers. The chapter title leads us to expect impersonations and the refractive method draws repeated attention to role playing.

Inevitably the change in method attentuates the historical dimension of the chapter. The reduction of information and the shift from reflector to reflector muffles the rise in tension as the Fashoda crisis breaks. It becomes much more difficult for the reader to piece together a 'situation' out of the cryptic fragments of conversation which are overheard. In place of the final chase out to the pyramids Pynchon now has Porpentine shot in the theatre where *Manon* is playing. A visual vantage-point is fixed at the end of a corridor and, as in *L'Annee Dernière à' Marienbad*, a 'voix neutre et monotone' recounts the action.[35] The absence of sound, the immobility of the camera-eye perspective and the absence of names stylizes this section and tests the reader's interpretative faculties which have already been called on by the fragmentation of most of this chapter.

'Under the Rose' was ironically apocalyptic in tone and its conclusion jumped from one crisis – Fashoda – to another, Sarajevo in 1914. In *V.* Pynchon has shifted the emphasis on to fatalism and death, particularly through the symbolism of the desert. Tony Tanner has rightly drawn attention to the various dead landscapes of the novel and relates them to the theme of entropic decay.[36] In other words the landscapes comment metaphorically on western culture and one of the strongest wasteland images in *V.* is the desert. Particularly in the context of Egypt where human settlement seems precarious, and, as we shall see, in the South West African section the desert carries obvious connotations of death. Gebrail the cab-driver performs an important rhetorical function here in linking a vision of the desert swamping all life to the dead materials of Cairo which he sees in terms of stone, metal, iron and glass. Gebrail's nihilistic gloom ('Nothing was coming, nothing was already here': 85/73) excludes apocalyptic panic and looks forward to the mysterious land of Vheissu in the new historical section. Gebrail's preoccupation with death also relates to a new leitmotif of disease which is introduced through Porpentine's bad case of sunburn. His peeling face is described as 'gangrenous' and 'like leprosy'. Disease, the inanimate desert and city, and the human inanimate (Bongo-Shaftesbury) all converge on death and that is why the shooting of Porpentine makes such an appropriate conclusion to the chapter.

The last revision which should be mentioned is the readjustment of characters. Porpentine now takes a far less central role since his antagonist Moldweorp has been dropped altogether, and accordingly the allusions to *Manon* sink from a major theme to a private peculiarity of Porpentine. Victoria Wren becomes more prominent, being changed from a mere ingenue to a more complex figure. She is explicitly linked with sexuality and the loss of her supposed virginity to Goodfellow is made ambiguous by her resemblance to Maxwell's Alice a remarkably unvirginal young girl. Since Victoria is the first avatar of *V.* it is important that she should take a more prominent part in the action.

(b) **'She hangs on the western wall'**

The second historical section of *V.* takes place in Florence in 1899 and, whereas Chapter 3 presents multiple perspectives on a single action, now offers the reader multiple lines of action which criss-cross and overlap. Young Evan Godolphin, who we know will change Schoenmaker's life, has gone to Italy to meet his father after years of separation. His father, an explorer, has discovered a mysterious land called Vheissu and gets embroiled in the activities of the British secret service who are partly interested in Venezuela after the 1895 border dispute. At the same time a certain Signor Mantissa and his associates are planning to steal 'The Birth of Venus' from the Uffizi. One of Mantissa's helpers, the Gaucho, has organized the Venezuelan nationalists in Florence into a group called the Figli di Machiavelli and is planning a march on the Venezuelan consulate. Pynchon makes it impossible to keep these narrative strands separate by constantly weaving backwards and forwards between them. Indeed much of the slapstick humour in this section grows out of the confusion between the various actions. As if to underline this multiplicity V-words suddenly proliferate bewilderingly, words which Pynchon capitalizes so as to catch the reader's eye. On only one page we find Via, Ponte Vecchio, Vaporetto and Visitor's Guide. The fact that this happens so early in the V-sequence increases our suspicions of Stencil's quest which have already been aroused by the chapter's preamble – Stencil's conversation with Dudley Eigenvalue.

The theme of tourism continues here through Evan Godolphin's arrival in Florence and through the general plotting of the action which centres on at least one prominent tourist attraction – the Uffizi Gallery. The layout of the streets receives constant and precise attention to orchestrate characters' movements, their planning of an escape route and the Venezuelan march. As in Chapter 3, a facsimile German bierkeller is used as one of the meeting points. The setting of this chapter is of course a Renaissance city and Pynchon uses two Renaissance artefacts to reveal the discontinuity between past and present – 'The Birth of Venus' and *The Prince*.

Signor Mantissa wants to steal Botticelli's painting from sheer love. Pynchon describes him as an artefact which shades back into recent Italian history:

His eyes were streaked and rimmed with the pinkness of what seemed to be years of lamenting. Sunlight, bouncing off the Arno, off the fronts of shops, fractured into spectra by the falling rain, seemed to tangle or lodge in his blond hair,

eyebrows, mustache, turning that face to a mask of unaccessible
ecstacy, contradicting the sorrowing and weary eyeholes.

(159/145)

This painterly description transforms Mantissa into one of
Botticelli's characters who, according to Pater, was fascinated by
'a sense of displacement or loss about them – the wistfulness of
exiles . . . which runs throughout all his varied work with a
sentiment of ineffable melancholy'.[37] Mantissa's Pateresque view of
the painting contrasts comically with the Gaucho's who only sees
a puzzling fat blonde. The painting contrasts yet again with
Victoria Wren who now reappears with a number of conquests that
make her, as the narrator dryly puts it, a 'young lady of enterprise'
(166/151). 'The Birth of Venus' thus becomes what David Cowart
calls an 'ironic emblem' of V. at the beginning of her career.[38]

'The Birth of Venus' is an enigmatic painting; is Venus
concealing herself from shame, or – witness her smile – so as to
entice her admirers? Similarly, the second Renaissance work
introduced here, *The Prince*, balances between two different political
possibilities. The key passage for our purposes reads:

> So, as a prince is forced to know how to act like a beast, he
> should learn from the fox and the lion . . . one must be a fox in
> order to recognise traps, and a lion to frighten off wolves . . .
> [But then, he adds, in modern times] those who have known
> best how to imitate the fox have come off best.[39]

Mantissa, whose name means 'a worthless addition' sees himself
as the fox, cunning but immobilized by the reversals of fortune.
His opposite number, the Gaucho, proudly and endlessly declares
that he is the man of action and takes as his chosen text the final
chapter of *The Prince* where Machiavelli calls for a strong ruler to
unite Italy. The one character emerges as a parody aesthete, the
other as a personification of violence and bombast. The Gaucho
believes in virtù, which is glossed in 'Under the Rose' as the
individual's capacity to affect history. To Victoria Wren this means
in practice, skill and efficiency to the Gaucho an early form of the
Führer (it is an important detail that he has German blood). The
fact that these two works provide such different reactions suggests
how remote they are from 1899. 'We are not, any of us, in the
Renaissance at all' (201/185), Evan Godolphin says at one point.

The Renaissance is reduced to a visual back-drop to the action or a mere façade, the most bizarre example being a factory for making Renaissance musical instruments which is in fact used by the Italian secret police.

The ambiguities which had begun around Victoria now multiply even further. We see her praying in church but never associate her with spirituality; she wears white but is far from innocent, and she watches a rioter being bayoneted without any signs of emotion. One object in particular focuses this ambiguity – a comb which she wears depicting five crucified British soldiers. Graves describes 'The Birth of Venus' as an 'exact icon' of the goddess's cult and on the same page notes that a gold comb is one of her appurtenances.[40] Pynchon draws our attention to Victoria's comb but denies that it is a religious object. It is rather a tourist gew-gaw which she picked up in a bazaar and which becomes a secular icon of her association with violence and death.

Tourism also provides a link with the most enigmatic location in this chapter – a mysterious land in the African interior called Vheissu. Godolphin senior has discovered it, but here again there are ambiguities. The bright shifting colours give him the impression of being 'inside a madman's kaleidoscope' (170/155). The absence of records coupled with his fading memory make him wonder whether he dreamt the country. For him Vheissu contrasts with the surface contacts of the tourists he observes in Florence. Godolphin is seized by a perverse transcendental urge to penetrate beneath Vheissu's glittering surface. He first personifies the country in a female Queequeg, tattooed enigmatically from head to toe, but satisfaction with that image quickly gives way to a frenzied desire to discover what lies beneath, 'to flay that tattooing to a heap of red, purple and green debris, leave the veins and ligaments raw and quivering and open at last to your eyes and your touch' (171/156). It is a startlingly brutal transformation of the impulse to explore and one which anticipates the ritualized cruelty of the South-West Africa section. Melvyn New sees this image as central: 'Godolphin expresses a sadistic sexuality that is one of Pynchon's dominant images for European colonialism.'[41] It is of course a *negative* image which brings no insights, just as Godolphin's expedition to the South Pole reveals to him a monkey embedded in the ice. It is ironic that he had to go to a wasteland to have a 'revelation' poised between melodrama and absurdity.

Vheissu, the Antarctic and other information in this chapter is converted by the characters into the stuff of espionage. The fact that Pynchon narrates all the strands of action in the same way collapses them together into a collective depiction of a certain kind of conspiratorial mentality. The chapter thus presents a farcical spy-thriller where the characters address each other through cloak-and-dagger clichés such as 'there is something afoot . . . bigger than a single country' (177/161). In fact one of the implicit sources of absurdity in this chapter is the repeated efforts which characters make to act out melodramatic roles. Pynchon deflates the intensity of these efforts by constantly shifting the tone of the narrative so that it never settles into one familiar mode. One brief example will make this clear. Young Godolphin thinks that he is participating in a thriller but this only becomes serious when he is arrested by the police. At the police-station threat swings back to farce when his name is mistakenly entered as Gadrulfi. Once written down it sticks by the logic of bureaucracy, and becomes all the more sinister because, this time by conspiratorial logic it must be an alias. The closed carriages, secret messages, interrogations and rendezvous supply Pynchon with targets for a subversive humour which increases the general confusion by punning (could 'Gaucho' mean 'of the left'?), slapstick, displacement (a Gaucho in *Florence*?), bathos and farce. The supeme absurdity is the plot to steal the Botticelli by hiding it in a hollowed Judas-tree. Cumbersome and farcical as it is, this scheme makes an implicit ironic comment on all the other examples of conspiracy in this section. The circular logic and tendency to reduce everything to information, the currency of espionage, looks forward to the role paranoia will play in *Lot 49* and *Gravity's Rainbow*.

(c) 'Mondaugen's Story'

One theme which is already discernible in the historical sections of *V.* is the rise to totalitarianism and violence, which is partly signalled by references to Germany. Similarly tourism rarely appears separate from power politics or colonialism. 'Mondaugen's Story' in that sense confronts the violence which is peripheral to the Egyptian chapter and, whereas 'She hangs on the western wall' dramatizes the absurd way in which individuals act on preconceived historical patterns, we now see the cruelty and slaughter which can result from such a mentality. Pynchon's choice of South-West Africa is thus an unfamiliar example of the theme of colonialism and one which grows into a major interest in *Gravity's Rainbow*.

The two main dates which this chapter focuses on are 1904 and 1922. In 1904, as a result of cattle-thefts and general bad treatment, the Herero tribe rebelled against the German authorities. The then governor Major Leutwein was replaced by General Lothar van Trotha who issued a *Vernichtungs Befehl* (extermination order) which resulted in the slaughter of four-fifths of the tribe. Following their defeat the survivors were gathered in concentration camps at Lüderitzbucht, Shark Island and Swakopmund, and forced to work on harbour or railway construction. Hopes that the natives would receive better treatment under the Union came to nothing and in 1922 Abraham Morris, the Bondelswaartz leader, returned illegally from exile and an attempt to arrest him led to a tribal uprising. The Union authorities massacred these rebels with machine guns and bombs dropped from aeroplanes 'for the first time in history', as the government report on the uprising noted.[42]

Whereas in the preceeding chapter of *V.* Pynchon presented suspicions and half-myths, he is now scrupulously careful to take his details from two sources – a blue book on German atrocities and the Union government report on the 1922 rebellion.[43] Many of the descriptions of natives being beaten or killed are taken directly, often verbatim, from these reports, as are the figures of native deaths. The latter are presented in the same neutral and objective language as is the list of disasters given in Chapter 10. The care with which Pynchon uses his historical sources and the accuracy of these figures makes it clear that he is creating a fiction around historical data, but in a way which respects the authenticity of this data. There is no ambiguity at all about the basic events, and these are in turn fitted into a broader historical sequence. There is a very strong continuity between 1904 and 1922 because the Germans are constantly present in a position of racial superiority. The similar weaponry of the German and Union soldiers blurs the distinction between them. Also Mondaugen and the other European settlers withdraw into a villa which parodies the ineffectuality of the League of Nations. Pynchon clearly relates the native slaughter of 1904 to the extermination of the Jews ('this is only 1 per cent of six million, but still pretty good': 245/277 – v. Appendix) and colonialism persists as a live issue into 1922 because a German character expresses the hopes of Nazi irredentism.[44]

Pynchon introduces the reader to this unfamiliar area through the eyes of an innocent outsider, Kurt Mondaugen, whose name (literally 'moon-eyes') indicates his function as a visual register. Mondaugen's ignorance parallels that of the reader and the narrative partly enacts his and our learning of historical facts. Mondaugen also reveals the sheer strangeness of the landscape, which is yet another wasteland. The huge spaces, strange light and proximity the Kalahari ('that vast death') make it a positive threat which dwarfs the human figure. Signs of life are scarce and across this wilderness sounds the mocking cry of the strand wolf, a kind of scavenging hyena. This is a landscape where death is constantly present and offers an appropriate context to mass killing.

Mondaugen's ostensible reason for being in South-West Africa is to do research on some mysterious radio signals. His equipment is absurdly bulky, breaks down and, to crown it all, Mondaugen is accused of being a Union spy. A German character called Weissmann believes that the signals form a code and at the end of the chapter proudly announces that the 'message' spells 'Kurt Mondaugen' in anagram and 'Die Welt ist alles was der Fall ist'. This sentence – 'The world is all that the case is' – is the opening statement of Wittgenstein's *Tractatus* which appeared in 1922. In other words this bizarre synchronicity mocks both Weissmann's preoccupation with plots and the reader's desire to form connections. Mondaugen's comment, 'I've heard that somewhere else' (278/259), nudges the reader who will at any rate hear it again in a seduction-song from Mafia which weaves lyrical games around the terms of symbolic logic. Critics unfortunately have not always recognized Pynchon's ironic joke against the conspiratorial mentality and Stencil's obsession with codes, and have looked for hidden meanings here. William Plater has even erected a whole theory of Wittgenstein's doctrinal importance on the flimsy basis of this allusion.[45]

The affair of Mondaugen's electronic researches is a local side-issue to this chapter, however. The narrative works by an inward progression towards dream rather similar to the plot of 'Low-Lands'. The first clear sign of this progression comes when Mondaugen takes refuge in the villa of a settler called Foppl. In yet another version of a hot-house, this time drawing on Poe, the guests celebrate an endless *Fasching*, the festival of feasting and carnival which takes place in the days before Ash-Wednesday.[46] Like the Whole Sick Crew they close themselves off from experience by the mindless activity of a party, with the difference that the natives are now half-mythologized into demonic forces. By association Mondaugen dreams of a Depression party in a beer-hall where a cat is being roasted on a fire. Paul Fahy notes that the ritual detail comes from *The Golden Bough* and suggests that this dream 'seems mythically to prophesy some new Dark Age in Europe'.[47] Certainly it retains the form of a boisterous ritual, but one emptied of all significance beyond cruelty. This is reinforced by the grotesque physical atrophy of those present:

> Smoke hung like winter fog in the beer hall, changing the massed weaving of bodies to a more writhing perhaps of damned in some underworld. Faces all had the same curious whiteness: concave cheeks, highlighted temples, bone of the starved corpse there just under the skin.   (244/226)

Throughout this chapter Pynchon makes extensive use of the symbolism of black and white. Blackness, predictably since the dominant perspective is European and Protestant, carries racial and spiritual connotations of damnation, whereas whiteness is associated with disease, bones and death.

In such a context love is distorted into sado-masochism which we encounter voyeuristically through the scenes glimpsed by Mondaugen: Vera Meroving (another avatar of V.) beating Weissmann, Foppl beating a native, and so on. The labyrinthine structure of the villa, the way people appear and disappear, the strange accelerations and decelerations of the action render these visions dreamlike. Mondaugen's dream-images blur into blocks of memory-images which make the boundary to his psyche very uncertain. He loses a clear sense of when he is awake and when asleep, and then falls ill, hallucinating hyenas and jackals in the house. 'Waking' from a long passage describing Foppl's experiences with his horse Firelily, Mondaugen finds 1904 brought grotesquely up to date when Hedwig Vogelsang (yet another form of V.?) enters his room riding a native whom she calls Firelily.

These sections make the core of Mondaugen's story and enact the compulsions of a common dream. As delegate to the departed

Von Trotha Foppl assumes authority over his guests and over Mondaugen's psyche, bending both back to 1904. He forces the guests to dress according to the earlier period, and addresses the native he is beating as a loving parent. Colonialism and sado-masochism here merge in the notion of submission, but the guiding impulse seems to be a nostalgia so strong that it breaks contact with the present. Foppl's villa is symbolically surrounded by a kind of moat. Pynchon retains the third-person for all the sections of this chapter and thereby blurs the transition points from dream to memory. We seem to gain access to Foppl's memory through Mondaugen's experience, and the latter's dreams are invaded by figures from the villa. The progression inwards from landscape to villa (an embodiment of German nostalgia), sado-masochistic ritual, dream and memory could thus be seen in terms of power. Mondaugen is caught up in a common purposes as were the German soldiers of 1904. A metaphorical leitmotif of machinery hints at this submission to authority and the spurious liberation from responsibility which went with that submission. Although he is absorbed into the group it is significant that Mondaugen makes a gesture of rejection by leaving the villa at the end of the chapter.

At the deepest level of his memories Foppl uses an idiom which fits all deaths into a fated pattern of events. This argument from design licenses him to commit further massacres since he can hide morally behind jargonistic phrases such as 'operational sympathy'. The main body of these memories is devoted to his relationship with a Herero girl called Sarah, named ironically after the biblical type of conjugal fidelity. A battle of wills takes place between them, he using his boot, sjambok and penis to force her into submission. After being raped by the other members of his platoon, she commits suicide by walking into the sea. Foppl sees this as the culmination of a process over which he has no control and which takes us back into the landscape itself:

> . . . a sun with no shape, a beach alien as the moon's antartic, restless concubines in barbed wire, salt mists, alkaline earth, the Benguela Current that would never cease bringing sand to raise the harbor floor, the inertia of rock, the frailty of flesh, the structural unreliability of thorns; the unheard whimper of a dying woman; the frightening but necessary cry of the strand wolf in the fog.   (274/255)

This catalogue brilliantly captures the non-humanized, alien nature of the landscape, but makes racist assumptions in its linkages. Foppl separates 'humanity' (i.e. Germans or Europeans) from an environment which includes rock, prisoners and the materials used for the concentration camps (thorns). Implicitly he sees all these from a distance, just as Foppl's guests watch the massacre of the natives from the villa as if it were a private entertainment. Pynchon follows McLuhan in stressing how visual tourism is and here extends it simplications of moral non-involvement. When at the very end of the chapter Mondaugen rests his face against the scarred back of a native this slight gesture represents at least a minimal human contact.

This chapter dramatically relates the theme of the inanimate to political totalitarianism and sexual neurosis. Its method is of recession into images of its own collective past. The panoramic method of *V.* does not really give Pynchon enough opportunities to pursue these weighty issues and for that reason he will revive the south-west material in *Gravity's Rainbow*, setting up lines of historical and fictional continuity with the rise of fascism.

(d) 'Confessions of Fausto Maijstral'

The fourth historical section of *V.* makes a very important departure from the earlier chapters in that Paolo Maijstral gives Stencil her father's Confessions which concentrate on the Axis' siege of Malta. For the first time he is presented with a ready-made text, whereas all the three earlier chapters have undergone a process of 'Stencilizing'. Pynchon indicates the subjective distortion which might have crept in through the preamble to Chapter 3 which is based on fleeting comments in Stencil père's journal. These comments each give the 'seed of a dossier' around which Stencil builds his inferences, just as the reader infers a continuous narrative in spite of the fragmenting perspectives. The conversation with Eigenvalue supplies an important warning against conspiracy-theories. 'Mondaugen's Story' has no preamble but contains a unique interruption in mid-chapter which draws attention to the tendentious accuracy of the conversations and which reminds us that the narrative has been channelled through Mondaugen (but after 34 years) to Stencil and then to Eigenvalue.

Fausto's Confessions consist partly of quotation from and partly commentary on his own journals, thus avoiding the need for external glosses. Because Fausto makes commentary on his own literary style an integral part of his Confessions they have a unique importance in *V*. He divides his life into four segments taking as their dividing points the birth of his daughter, the worst day of air-raids and the death of his wife. In the last, i.e. present phase Fausto has inherited a 'physically and spiritually broken world' (307/286), a stagnant period where he sees through all the shapes we project on to experience. He dismisses these as fictions. His starting-point is thus total scepticism which explains why he gets his bearings through a clinically factual description of his room and why he begins by defining himself in various ways. His notion of successive identities is related by William Plater to 'a principle of communication theory formulated by George Herbert Mead that the self emerges in the act of communication by becoming an object to itself'.[48] This begins to reveal the differences between Fausto and Stencil. Demonstrating a modernistic formal awareness, Fausto recognizes both the artificiality and the necessity of suspending the transience of his experience so as to write his Confessions. By his formal rigour he earns the right to refer to himself in the third person whereas Stencil's practice is more compulsive and suspect. Fausto's alternating quotations and commentary set up a double perspective of events in Malta which, as in 'Mondaugen's Story', captures the immediacy of past events while examining the idioms of expression. He is particularly alert to condemn excessive rhetoric and any signs of 'retreat' (a favourite term of condemnation here), quoting, for instance, this passage after an air-raid: '. . . one in this God-favoured plot of sweet Mediterranean earth, one in whatever temple or sewer or catacomb's darkness is ours, by fate or historical writhings or still by the will of God' (311/290). The allusion to John of Gaunt's speech from *Richard II* (Shakespeare is an important early influence on Fausto), the rhythmic accumulation of resonant phrases will contrast later with the starker, more jagged notation of impressions. The notion of the suffering earth will give way to 'rockhood' but, although we are invited to condemn the style of the passage, certain key features (allusion to the earth, to God, etc.) lodge in our memory and feed the themes of this chapter.

During his commentary Fausto raises a number of important issues which relate beyond his Confessions to the novel as a whole. His notion of identity-phases questions clear continuity and explains why Pynchon refers to characters several times as being in fugue, i.e. of adopting roles quite divorced from their earlier personality, and also relates to the discontinuity created by intercalating the chapters of *V.*. Fausto defines more clearly Benny Profane's dream of the alienating street and generalizes it as the characteristic nightmare of the twentieth century. Even more important is the way he approaches this image: 'A street we are put at the wrong end of, for reasons best known to the agents who put us there, if there are agents. But a street we must walk' (324/303). His caution not to project a human agency on to events relates to his scepticism towards an over-humanized history and refers outwards to the various explanations of what are often purely natural phenomena.

Fausto's geometrical description of his room and his general scepticism towards traditional literary procedures resemble some of Alain Robbe-Grillet's theories. In the famous essay 'Nature, Humanisme, Tragédie' he makes a prolonged plea for us to recognize the non-human in nature and attacks the anthropomorphism which creeps into the use of metaphors. One of his key statements runs thus: 'La metaphore, qui est censée n'exprimer qu'une comparaison sans arrière-pensée, introduit en fait une communication souterraine, un mouvement de sympathie (or d'antipathie) qui est sa veritable raison d'être.'[49] Robbe-Grillet repeatedly attacks the spurious 'solidarité' which metaphors create between man and his inanimate context. We have already seen the pressure exerted on characters by an alien and largely inanimate landscape in Egypt and in the scrubland of south-west Africa. Foppl's party is as much a withdrawal from a threatening land as much as from a native rebellion. Fausto would seem to go along with Robbe-Grillet when he states that 'metaphor has no value apart from its function; . . . it is a device, an artifice . . . Fausto's kind [i.e. poets] are alone with the task of living in a universe of things which simply are, and cloaking that innate mindlessness with comfortable and pious metaphor' (326/305). Like Robbe-Grillet he phrases his statement in terms of truth and falsehood but arrives at a position diametrically opposite to the other writer's. Metaphor takes on a positive existential value from its consequences for human action. Thus to see human endurance in terms of 'rockhood' might be a cliché, but it could enable Malta to survive the air-raids. For all his rigour, Fausto cannot get away from metaphor – what else is 'cloaking' in the passage quoted? – and paradoxically the 'lies' which poets tell come to have greater value than the opposite possibility. In effect Fausto clings on to the traditional role of the poet as one gifted with privileged insight but reverses it into a liability since the poet has to carry the burden of reality. It would be dangerous to attribute too much authority to Fausto's statements on metaphor. Rather they sensitize the reader beforehand to the rich style which Fausto will use in describing his love for Elena, Paola's mother.

Immediately after the passage on metaphors follows a poem which plays on the term 'transcendental' by limiting it exclusively to a mathematical meaning. This joke effectively distinguishes Fausto's later journals from one of the texts which interested him in his youth – Di Chirico's *Hebdomeros* (1929). At one point in this novel ('a series of anecdotes or reminiscences') Hebdomeros advises his followers: 'What is needed is *discovery*, for in discovering things you make life possible in the sense that you reconcile it with its mother *Eternity*.'[50] Fausto symbolically rejects this transcendence in refusing the priestly vocation, and uses allusions to T. S. Eliot's poetry to heighten his reactions to the present. We have already seen that Eliot exerted an important influence in Pynchon's short stories. Similarly throughout *V.* allusions regularly appear in order to sharpen the sense of spiritual absence in the modern world; wasteland images, the deadly automation of city life and evocations of monotony all owe their debt to Eliot.[51] Fausto makes explicit this influence and partly dismisses it as a matter of attitudinizing. But this is not the end of the allusions to Eliot. They help Fausto to articulate the sequence of his reactions which sink from florid rhetoric to the inanimate and then rise back to life. At the lowest point in this curve Fausto's fellow-poet Dnubietna produces a pastiche of the symbolist lyric which opens 'Burnt Norton' II:

> Motes of rock's dust
> Caught among corpses of carob trees;
> Atoms of iron
> Swirl above the dead forge
> On that cormorant side of the moon.
>   (320/299–300)

The stress on inanimate objects (rock and iron) and their linkage with death marks a certain stage in Fausto's experience. The most important image here is of the carob tree, sacred to Mara, the tutelary goddess of Malta, but here just one more dead object. References to the carob tree form an imagistic theme in this chapter, a metaphor of at least physical fullness. Here, however, the metaphor has as it were lost its referent while retaining its special status as a significant object. Throughout this chapter contrasting images of Malta present it either as a place of stone (a rock, inert and linked with death) or as a mythic source of life, a place of fertility. The latter possibility makes the island more amenable to human life and therefore far less alienating than say the desert wastes of south-west Africa.

Fausto's Confessions centre on two crucial experiences: the Axis air-raids which are dominated by references to rock and stone, and his love for Elena Xemxi which is articulated through images of vegetation. The vitality of the one thus counteracts the centrality of death in the other. Their love-relationship should be seen against the emerging symbolic status of Malta in the novel. Paola calls the island 'a cradle of life' and Fausto points out that its name is a feminine noun and that its culture is matriarchal. One significance of the island then is its embodiment of fertility as enacted specifically in the love between Fausto and Elena. At the beginning of their romance he dramatizes his commitment through images which blend together the natural and spiritual; he will 'break open this small pod of a heart and offer in communion the St. John's bread I have cherished . . .' (312/291). We constantly associate Elena with growing things, with a literal pastoral context of azaleas and orange-blossom.

This section of the Confessions is virtually unique in V. because the term 'love' can be used and enacted without trace of embarrassment. This does not mean that Fausto nostalgically idealizes the relationship. On the contrary the longest scene between him and Elena concentrates on pain and fear. Wandering around Valletta after an air-raid they find themselves in a small park. Here their carefree joy slides into something more threatening. Each tries, with mounting desperation, to break down the barriers of self and manage some kind of communion. All they can manage in fact is a painful mimicry of sexual coupling:

Her nails, broken from burying the dead, had been digging into the bare part of my arm where the shirt was rolled up. Pressure and pain increased, our heads lolled slowly like the

> heads of puppets toward a meeting of eyes. . . . My own nails
> fastened in reply and we became twinned, symmetric, sharing
> pain . . .   (336/315)

Shortly after this Elena is killed by a bomb, but the very intimacy
of parts of the Confessions in addressing Paola suggests that Fausto
has retained a hold on life.

Life and death are contrasted in this chapter through two
different forms of Christianity – Catholicism and the Protestant
Manichaeism personified in the Bad Priest (yet another form of
V.) whose other-worldly spiritualism undermines the continuities
of Maltese life. This sinister figure is constantly associated with
death and dies itself in one of the most grotesque scenes of the
whole novel. Fausto finds the Bad Priest in a cellar being literally
dismantled by a group of children. The iconic images associated
with V. (the wideawake hat, clockwork eye, comb, etc.) merge
with artificial limbs and teeth so that the figure only retains a
ghastly resemblance of humanity. Paul Fahy has shown how
virtually each detail comes from *The White Goddess*, except that all
these objects are secularized into prosthetics.[52] The scene mimes
out the progressive emptying of spiritual significance from this
figure, a process which has been going on in earlier chapters and
which now culminates in its death. Pynchon's grotesque imagery
here resembles West's burlesque of the rags-to-riches myth in *A
Cool Million* where Lemuel Pitkin loses his teeth, and an eye, etc.
as a result of an endless series of confidence tricks; or, alternatively,
a closer analogue could be found in Swift's poem 'A Beautiful
Young Nymph Going to Bed', where the squalour of the girl's
artificial hair, eye and teeth erodes the idealism in the title. Swift
satirizes urban notions of beauty in his nymph's unveiling.
Pynchon uses similar details of physical immediacy to depict the
extinction of a mythic principle in an act which at times resembles
a sacrifice, at times a rape.

(e) 'V. in love'

The penultimate historical section disrupts the chronological
sequence of the earlier chapters and jumps back to Paris in 1913.
Two narrative threads are interwoven: the preparation and
opening night of an experimental ballet, and V.'s love-affair with
the prima ballerina. Over these actions hang lowering yellowish

clouds compared to a 'halo of plague' oppressing the city. Throughout the whole section Pynchon repeatedly draws attention to the claustrophobic heat which reflects a general languor in most of the characters. The continuity between weather and character emerges pointedly through the description of two women at a party:

> The black hair seemed to float like a drowned corpse's hair against the cerise tunic. The entire room and the bodies inside it . . . the scattered Hosts, the black furniture, were all bathed in an exhausted yellow light, filtered through rain clouds which refused to burst.   (403/378)

The opening glance at Millais' painting of Ophelia cleverly links death with the immobility of this scene. Black is a dominant colour throughout the chapter, partly for its connotations of modish satanism. Even the light itself here seems to partake of the general exhaustion registered by the characters. The whole of Paris thus resembles one huge hot-house, a place of stagnation where relief is sought from boredom through satanism and sexual deviation.

The central character who embodies particular aspects of this decadence is the ballerina Mélanie l'Heuremaudit. Pynchon presents a psychological sequence here whereby Mélanie, as a result of sexual 'games' with her father has developed a narcissistic desire to be watched by father-substitutes. We see this in a scene where she indulges in a sexual mime of 'dancing' with a painter's dummy, and in a dream where her father winds her up as if she were an automaton. In a sense this is literally what she has become. Her eyes are described as dead and, in keeping with Freud's explanation of narcissism, she has withdrawn her feelings into a private world of fixation.[53] She has thus become a kind of psychological hot-house, as hinted at in the name of her family home – Serre Chaude.

Part of Mélanie's falling-way from humanity involves a revulsion towards her own body. She only feels calm and able to admire her beauty once she has donned a costume. V. similarly, whose atrophied humanity is reflected in her attenuation from Victoria to an initial, also has black eyes and is the owner of a dress shop. This is more than a mere job; it hints at her moral status since, as one character notes, 'it was her clothes, her accessories which determined her' (400/375). For Mélanie clothes seem to be even more than this, and offer her a prosthetic substitute for her own skin. We constantly see her in juxtaposition to things; indeed, she is given the nickname La Jarretière (i.e. the garter), and the so-called love between her and V. finds its expression in an imitation of the inanimate: 'V. on the pouf, watching Mélanie on the bed; Mélanie watching herself in the mirror; the mirror-image perhaps contemplating V. from time to time' (409/385). Pynchon describes the scene as a 'still life' although the French term *nature morte* would more aptly express the proximity of love and death.

The thematic linkage of love and death is of course familiar to us, but how are we meant to react to V.'s love-affair? The character who stands nearest to the narrative perspective, Itague, interprets Mélanie for us in Freudian terms, so clearly we are not invited to unravel the intricacies of her psyche. Pynchon's stress on the visual and the fact that psycho-analysis is referred to explicitly makes us take up a detached attitude towards her. It is always a very difficult matter deciding how much humanity a Pynchon character possesses and, although we gain access to Mélanie's dreams and fantasies, she nevertheless remains a figure, an object to be arranged by her producer or by V. Mary Allen has accused Pynchon of sexist bias in mocking the relationship but the charge is unjustifiable because Pynchon presents it within a context of a general transference of humanity on to the inanimate.[54] The love-relationship does not receive special treatment but is rather presented, like the satanic party and ballet *première*, as a phenomenon. Pynchon is particularly careful not to over-moralize their lesbianism, or even to over-define it.

The ballet where Mélanie performs is also characterized by the presence of the inanimate. German-made automata are to take part, and it too will unite a notional love with violence, the central action being a rape. David Cowart has shown that this section almost becomes a miniature *roman à clef*, so closely does Pynchon follow the actual *première* of The Rite of Spring. Stravinsky records in his *Autobiography* that his original image for this work was 'a solemn pagan rite' where a young girl dances herself to death 'to propitiate the God of Spring' and Nijinsky's wife notes that it was set in the primitive period of Russian nature-worship.'[55] The operas Pynchon uses regularly link love and death and The Rite of Spring is no exception. It combines solemnity with death, but with a death which has a transcendent value. At the climax of the ballet in the novel Mélanie is lifted aloft on a pole in a similar act of sacrifice. This particular act relates back to the mythic significance of Victoria Wren's name, the wren being described in *The Golden Bough* as 'the Lady of Heaven's hen'.[56] Frazer notes the custom of hunting the wren which is killed and then carried aloft on the end of a pole. Pynchon here conflates Frazer and Stravinsky to produce a work which travesties both and which contains neither mythic meaning, solemnity nor transcendence. It simply breaks down into chaos. At the crucial moment when Mélanie is lifted on the pole, impaled on her crutch, it is discovered that the protective device has been left off. The result is a gruesome death. Mélanie dies in a multiple travesty of the sexual act, mythic elevation and romantic apotheosis. She dies in a grotesque *Liebestod* where the act of death and the act of love have literally become one.

It is appropriate to the love–death theme that the chapter ending with the death of V. should be juxtaposed to that dealing with V. in love. With the latter chapter the historical sequence of the novel almost comes to an end and perhaps for this reason the chapter contains more authoritative summings-up than any other. Itague has already been mentioned as an extension of the general perspective, and he supplies important comments on the theme of decadence. The narrator also explicitly identifies Mélanie's lover as V. and reinforces the continuity with earlier chapters. The love–death theme is generalized and the peculiar state of 'Baedekerland' defined. The frequency with which critics quote these explanatory passages testifies to their apparent applicability to the novel as a whole, and yet Pynchon is careful not to make them too categorical. He surrounds them with textual ambiguity. Notice, for instance, the way in which uncertainties creep into the account of V.'s love. Mélanie's narcissism is explained and then the narrator adds with a shrugging refusal to be anything other than tentative: 'such may have been the case with Mélanie, *though who could say*' (407/382: emphasis added). V.'s hidden motives are similarly hypothesized and then dismissed. The reader himself is brought into the love–death theme as if it were contagious: 'we all get involved to an extent in the politics of slow dying' (410/386), and the narrator further complicates the issue by speculating about V.'s possible reactions to the process of dehumanization she was participating in. In a whole range of ways Pynchon renders this section so self-involved that he almost seems to be trying to distract the reader away from the explanations to examine the text itself. He is thus careful to blur the identity of the narrator into Itague (one observer), Stencil (whose day-dreams are quoted) and Porcépic – the composer who acted as V.'s confidant and transmitted the story to Stencil. So at the same time as clarifying his themes, Pynchon also sheds doubt on their authenticity by surrounding the comments with hypotheses and speculations.

At the beginning of this chapter death is figured through *fin de siècle* images and love is immobilized into static self-regard. Pynchon's pastiche of the Decadence supplies historical precedents for the Whole Sick Crew's aesthetic inertia and the chapter comes to a logically fatal climax. Mélanie has been in love with the inanimate and mimicked the animate; it is therefore in a sense only a marginal change for her literally to become a dead object.

(f) 'Epilogue'

The epilogue both reinforces the symbolic importance of Malta in the novel as origin and potential end of western culture (in the Suez crisis) and also brings back together Stencil's father and V. (this time under the name of Veronica Manganese) during some disturbances on Malta in 1919. Stencil père thus emerges here as much more humane than he did in the Florence episode. Veronica Manganese is predictably less human than Victoria but not quite as remote and threatening as the Bad Priest. As with the other historical sections, linkages multiply. A remarkably cunning Father Fairing appears who seems to have little or no connection with his obsessed namesake in the New York sewers. Even the atmosphere of espionage is essentially a post-war recapitulation of the Florence chapter, this time almost filtered through Stencil's consciousness.

Although he is notionally a British secret agent, Stencil preserves a detached and ironically sceptical attitude to political events which is usually a sign of intelligence in Pynchon's fiction. His specific scepticism about the Peace of Versailles is of course borne out by our historical hindsight, but he also – in marked contrast to his son – expresses reservations about his methods of gathering and interpreting information. As in Florence he rejects a conspiratorial interpretation of situations – and this stance is endorsed by a line of pentecostal references which ridicule the persistence of apocalyptic fears. So impossibly difficult does it seem to Stencil to understand any given situation that he has a solipsistic nightmare of wandering through the nervous system of a brain. This image of being trapped in a labyrinth constantly 'chasing dead ends' could stand as a representation of one possible reading of the novel. It is a hint to the reader as well as a step towards calmness when Stencil accepts the part contingency plays in the June disturbances:

> Who knows how many thousand accidents – a variation in the weather, the availability of a ship, the failure of a crop – brought all these people, with their separate dreams and worries, here to this island and arranged them into this alignment? Any Situation takes shape from events much lower than the merely human.   (483/455)

Although this insight leads Stencil towards suicidal despair, it helps to explain why, for instance, Pynchon inserts into one of the New York sections a list of disasters. Here he is thrusting contingency onto the reader's attention. Similarly in the epilogue he arranges a list of grievances taken directly from the government report on the 1919 disturbances, which are separated typographically by indicator-hands so that sheer variety of grievance is revealed.[57] Stencil consciously stops himself from grouping them into a conspiracy and thereby distinguishes himself from his superiors who are determined to see the nationalist Dr. E. Mizzi as a 'bogey-man'.

Stencil's perception of contemporary politics gives him a disturbing sense of helplessness and this triggers off a professionally damaging wave of nostalgia. Unlike Porpentine in 'Under the Rose', a display of feeling does not lead to Stencil's death, but it does lead him to dismiss Fausto Maijstral's father from being an informer after a plea from his pregnant wife. Stencil can find no intellectual justification for his own action here. It is simply one of the very rare, and curiously old-fashioned gestures of humanity in the novel.

Nostalgia also characterizes the mythic allusions of this chapter, and includes even the boat, a xebec with Astarte as figurehead, in which Stencil comes to Malta. Astarte, identified in Graves and Frazer with the moon-goddess and Venus, blurs into Mara, the goddess of Malta. Stencil's captain, Mehmet, narrates an inset story of how she lifted the Grand Siege of 1565 by working miracles. Although Mehmet hedges round the story with some uncertainty, the miracles represent essentially an act of power which, being set in the past, contrasts strongly with any modern mythic references. The latter are always secular, made in a profane context, to the traces and relics of mythology. V. herself not only has no power, but gradually collapses into total inanimateness and passivity. Mehmet prefaces his story with a fantasy-image he claims to have seen through a time-warp, of a man painting an abandoned sailing ship. Tony Tanner sees this as an entropic emblem of the novel itself, embodying both decline and futility.[58] Before we attribute too much authority to this image, however, we should note that Mehmet is a remarkably *cheerful* prophet of doom and that Stencil's non-sequential notion of contingency carries more weight in this chapter.

The crucial question with the epilogue, and one which binds all its themes together, is in what way the chapter concludes the novel. *V.* begins and ends with references to ships and the sea; Norfolk dockyard leads ultimately to Malta of 1919, under naval colonial control. The beginning and end in that sense seem symmetrical, but we cannot sustain such a neat explanation for long. Our sense of the novel's closure is inevitably reduced by the fact that the epilogue takes place in the past. The growing crisis of Suez together with individual characters' expressions of crisis builds up into a suggestion of imminence which collapses in the epilogue since the June disturbances are such a minor affair, and easily controlled. It is as if Pynchon colludes with his reader's historical knowledge that the Suez crisis will break and then pass. The possibility of Armageddon which hovers constantly in the background of *V.* thus remains firmly in that background by Pynchon's refusal to give a climactic ending. Indeed the fact that the epilogue covers roughly February to June, 1919 places it shortly before D'Annunzio's establishment of the Regency of Carnaro in Fiume where V. was present.[59] The reader is thus located within a historical continuum by his knowledge that events will take place in the novel *after* the epilogue. Pynchon plays off the materials of the chapter against the formal expectations of an epilogue (closure, resolution, summing-up), just as the thematic density of other chapters contradicts their mock-picaresque titles. After Pynchon has recounted the last stages of the June disturbances he dismisses them as a 'minor eddy' in Malta's history. The sea at this point becomes a local

metaphor for history and one way in which we could explain
Stencil's death in a water-spout is that his fate has confirmed his
fears about the individual's disappearing role in history, in that he
is assimilated into the sea. His death slightly resembles the
conclusion to *Moby-Dick* with the two differences that he dies as
the result of a chance phenomenon killed by the very contingency
he glimpsed; and also that this time there is no survivor's
epilogue. The very fact that Stencil *dies* gives an impression of
finality but the end only resembles a conclusion because many
issues are left open and his son's search is continuing.

3 INTERCONNECTIONS

In *V.* Pynchon appears to be following the practice of *Ulysses* by
localizing techniques in certain chapters and then undermining
the impression of self-containment by a complex system of cross-
references. Even the New York sections are caught up in this
thematic lattice so that the reader cannot treat them in isolation.
We now need to ask whether there is any logic to the sequence of
the historical chapters. Does Stencil offer us any guidance here?
Enough examples should have been given at the beginning of this
chapter of how Pynchon constantly discredits and ridicules
Stencil's activities, so that we can scarcely take him as an
interpretative model. All of the historical chapters possess a
richness broader than anything he recognizes because his V-
search blinkers him to such a limited range of possibilities. A
particularly blatant example of how Stencil constantly misses the
point comes at the end of Fausto's Confessions where the only
thing which fascinates Stencil is a brief mention of his father.
Stencil's incorrigible tendency to think in conspiratorial patterns is
repeatedly mocked, as is his allegiance to naive chronological
sequence. Pynchon's arrangement of the chapters clearly destroys
that expectation by splitting the time of chapter 9 between 1922
and 1904, and by moving backwards and forwards within the
sequence. If we try to reorder these chapters we run the risk of
'Stencilizing' events and damage the way in which Pynchon plays
off historical time against novelistic chronology.

There have been two main attempts to rationalize the order of
the historical chapters of *V*. The first by Max Schulz develops his
premise that 'each is a parody of a different frame of reference by

which our knowledge of experience is recorded'.[60] He argues that chapter 3 shows the uninvolved eye-witness, chapter 7 the inadvertent participant, chapter 9 personal remembrance, chapter 11 a journal record and the epilogue a contriver of events. There are several problems here, however. In chapter 7 there is so much fragmentation of the action that it is impossible to say who is participating *inadvertently*, and who not. In chapter 9 Mondaugen could just as easily be described as an inadvertent participant, as having a personal memory of events. And Fausto demonstrates so much scepticism towards his journal that the chapter can scarcely be called *parodic*. Richard Patteson, like Schulz, sees the point of the sequence to be an epistemic variation of narrative technique in order to examine various ways of perceiving. His description is more accurate partly because he drops the notion of parody and reinforces his account by thematic linkages, arguing that V. is a 'metaphor for the connection that makes any meaning . . . possible'. Patteson suggests that the varieties of technique trace out a gradual process of interiorization which calls into question their efficacy. The chapter which does not fit neatly into this sequence is 'V. in Love' (chapter 14) which Patteson rationalizes as follows: 'Pynchon almost seems to place this most conventional chapter near the end of the novel to test just how greatly the reader's perception has been altered.'[61] This is not special pleading, but rather an honest admission that any account of order in this novel must be approximate.

Clearly one of the ways in which Pynchon unifies this novel is thematically and one of its strongest themes is the repeated identification of love and death. This has been examined by a number of critics, notably David Cowart, but a more recent article by L. V. Groves has made an important contribution to the understanding of *V.* by locating the influence of Denis de Rougemont in this novel. She quotes the following passage from the latter's *Love in the Western World*: 'Happy love has no history. Romance only comes into existence where love is fatal, frowned upon and doomed by life itself', and demonstrates how central is 'a thematic identification of erotic passion with separation and death'.[62] By drawing our attention to De Rougemont's history of the myth of erotic passion Groves makes it possible to see, for instance, how strategic are Pynchon's references to western works of romance – to *Tristan* (Tristan's sword appears as a puddle of beer), to *Romeo and Juliet* (in a rock n' roll song), *Don Giovanni* and so on. The great lovers of western culture are reduced to the banal ingredients of pop culture or to casual liaisons. The love-death theme also explains the first bizarre scene of the novel where Profane enters a bar called The Sailor's Grave (death) and where a barmaid called Beatrice (love) has installed breast-shaped beer taps which the customers suck every payday (ritual). This scene alerts the reader to a seemingly endless series of distortions which love undergoes throughout the novel from inward search (Stencil) through surgical submission (Esther) and sado–masochism (Foppl's villa) to narcissism (Mélanie). In one way or another love stands firmly at the thematic centre of *V*.

One aspect of De Rougemont's account which Groves scarcely mentions is his emphasis on the secrecy of the romantic myth and the way it exerts its powers over us unconsciously. Also, even though the myth has as it were become secularized, it still shows itself in modern life: . . . 'from mystical love down to the love interest of Hollywood films, there is only a long decadence . . . and yet all the time it has remained the same myth'.[63] Since the myth is still exerting its influence over us, albeit in debased forms, there is considerable urgency in attacking these manifestations. De Rougemont's stress on the secret power of the myth relates bizarrely to Stencil's sense of conspiracies and to the surface-depth contrast at the very end of the novel (the calm surface of the sea gives no glimpse of what it hides beneath). The contemporary traces of the romantic myth offer what De Rougemont presents as examples of either self-mystification or a deception created by the 'image-makers' in the media and advertising agencies. By rendering many of his characters grotesque Pynchon forces us to consider them as phenomena at the same time as we register their self-absorption in their own activities. Thus the switch devised by Fergus Mixolydian for connecting his body to his TV set is obviously fantastic on the level of realism, but by its sheer strangeness it draws our attention to his reversal of the notion that media are extensions of human faculties. This and other examples suggest that Pynchon's grotesque humour in this novel performs a demystifying function, startling us into consideration of its main themes. The process of reading the novel is thus far more demanding than Edward Mendelson suggests. To participate in its decadence, he argues,

'you have only to become passive'.[64] The alienating effect of
Pynchon's humour in fact demands a positive engagement with
the text.

Mythic decadence proves to be inseparable from a corresponding
decline in religion which, as Tony Tanner notes, 'usually takes
the form of yearning or a sense of absence', and he notes that
'communion' appears in *V.* as a travesty of or substitute for Holy
Communion.[65] At one point during his hunt for alligators Profane
feels to be on the verge of a revelation ('surely the alligator would
receive the gift of tongues': 122/110). In Cairo the cab-driver
Gebrail similarly wonders if he will receive a sign from God. But
there are no revelations in *V.* Profane waits for nothing and then
blasts the alligator with his shotgun; Gebrail sees only the
hindquarters of a horse ('a poor horse's ass'). Even when a Puerto
Rican girl breaks up a street-fight the religious language is
deliberately ludicrous:

> The air turned summer-mild, a boy's choir on a brilliant mauve
> cloud came floating over from the direction of Canal Street
> singing O Salutaris Hostia; . . . Fina was borne up by a swarm
> of pneumatically fat, darling cherubs, to hover over the sudden
> peace she'd created, beaming, serene.   (144–5/131)

As in the description of Bloom's mock-ascension at the end of the
'Cyclops' section of *Ulysses*, Pynchon's language destroys its own
image as it progresses. The bathos of juxtaposing a street name
with the Catholic anthem and of 'swarm' and 'pneumatically'
deflates the religious tone into a collocation of absurdly concrete
images. Fina, described ironically as 'St. Fina of the Playboys',
turns out to be just the opposite of saintly when she takes part in
group sex at the end of the chapter. Religion, like love, has been
reduced to bizarre traces which Pynchon indicates ironically. The
repeated references to the wind reflect this process because
Pynchon in effect dismantles the conventional religious metaphor
he refers to in 'Entropy' (breath–spirit–pneuma, etc.) and restores
it to literal physical meaning. The wind which blows repeatedly
through the novel reminds us of spiritual absence in resembling a
metaphor without its referent.

Apart from love and death the other theme broad enough to
include most of the novel's episodes is that of entropic decline.
'Every situation', writes Tony Tanner, 'reveals some new aspect

of decay and decline, some move further into chaos or nearer death'.[66] 'Decline', 'decay' and 'decadence' are indeed repeated terms in the novel which build up a cumulative impression of a process at work. Assuming that V. is a female figure we can observe a gradual replacement of bodily organs with inanimate substitutes which, Groves argues, shows her revulsion from physical life.[67] Counterpointed against this decline towards the inanimate, totalitarian politics rise in tandem with violence. Tanner shrewdly points out the connection between these processes in that people tend to use others as mere objects – witness, for instance, the anonymous statistics of the German slaughter in South-West Africa.[68] Just as Pynchon complicates any linear sequence of decline by shuffling his chapters chronologically, so also the relationships between Paola and Sphere, Fausto and Elena, and Fausto's parents imply that love is not a totally lost possibility. The various patterns which the novel forms offer one stay of order against entropy, however ambiguous their meanings might be, and the sheer exuberance with which Pynchon constantly produces ever more startling examples of decay prevents any easy slide into gloom. His repeated use of surprise-effects suggests that his text is open and unpredictable and thereby contrasts it with any kind of irreversible determined process.

At this point we seem to have reached paradox. Pynchon is both suggesting a process and contradicting it. At many points in the novel we appear to be caught between alternative possibilities. Take Stencil, for instance. His activities tempt the reader into similar exercises of inference and decoding, but then Pynchon's ironies discredit this approach. Profane then seems to offer the only alternative of mindless drift – what Pynchon will later call 'anti-paranoia'. Must the reader choose between Stencil and Profane, the hot-house or the street? This pairing of possibilities is represented graphically when Victoria Wren stands at the intersection between two roads in Florence. The initial of the novel's title teases the reader into trying to locate an identity behind it, but 'V' can also be the logical symbol for alternative. Between these two extremes of randomness and total order a third possibility is raised, ironically by Stencil's father. His experience in British intelligence has convinced him that any situation is composed of cross-purposes which intersect at a particular time. The notion of cross-purposes can include the actions of Nature since, as he reflects, 'any Situation takes shape from events much lower than the merely human' (483/455); and it enables Stencil to reconcile a belief in order with contingency. Pynchon more or less forces the reader of *V.* to a similar conclusion by introducing some repetitions which simply confuse. Why should Mehmet repeat Stencil's description of V. to Profane ('Disguise is one of her attributes')? Why should Stencil and his companion on Majorca, and Foppl's guests both be described as 'the last gods on earth'?[69] Such parallels lead nowhere. They rather induce uncertainty in the reader, because one thing comes to resemble another. The proliferation of significances for V. from a whole range of characters through place-names, the shadow of a street-lamp, spread thighs, victory sign, etc. mocks the reader's search for certainty over the novel's title. Just as Pynchon's characters are firmly embedded in their historical contexts so the welter of descriptive detail and the multiple meanings of V. immerse the reader in the text and create a margin of confusion or uncertainty. Characters' sense of history is incorporated within the flux of events. Similarly the reader's sense of the text is complicated so as to make a clear overview well nigh impossible. We glimpse possible processes which seem all the more ominous because they cannot be firmly grasped. As we shall see, this uncertainty plays a crucial role in Pynchon's next two novels.

3
The Crying of Lot 49

1 QUEST AND ILLUSION

Although published only three years after *V.*, *The Crying of Lot 49* (1966) makes a staggering contrast with the earlier novel.[1] It is less than a quarter its length, it appears to possess a simple linear plot, and it covers both a short time-span and a very specific local area – Southern California. The novel's perspective throughout stays close to that of its protagonist Mrs. Oedipa Maas although, as we shall see, this method presents Pynchon with certain formal difficulties. Oedipa is named as co-executor for a dead real-estate tycoon and former lover – Pierce Inverarity – and during her investigations into his estate stumbles across an underground postal network whose roots lie in Renaissance Europe. Whereas in *V.* Stencil personified an absurdly blinkered activity, Oedipa is much closer to a conventional fictional character because Pynchon grants her more awareness. Stencil's quest is absurd from the beginning; Oedipa's moves from normality into strangeness and, unlike Stencil, she realizes how a plethora of information constantly sidetracks her from a simple search. Although both novels use a quest pattern Oedipa reacts much more than Stencil and discovers one of the central paradoxes of the novel, a paradox pointed out by Norbert Wiener: that although the United States has the most highly developed communications media in the world, information is nevertheless guarded with the utmost secrecy by small groups.[2]

The instructions from Inverarity's lawyers set Oedipa in motion, jerk her out of her routine life as a Californian housewife, an existence divided between cooking, visits to her local supermarket and Tupperware parties.[3] She stops off at a motel in the Los Angeles suburb of San Narciso where she meets her co-executor, an ex-actor called Metzger. During an evening of television Inverarity rapidly fades out of the novel as a person and attenuates into a disembodied principle of power or ownership. Oedipa's naively simple efforts to remember him as a person give way to

117

Metzger's comments on various TV advertisements which reveal glimpses of Inverarity's deals and investments. Indeed we could say one of Metzger's main roles in the novel is to alert Oedipa to Inverarity as a force. Once he has done this a characteristic rhythm establishes itself whereby Oedipa is led towards the conclusion that it is all invented. This would always be a risky reaction in reading Pynchon, especially here where a second block of information follows from the same source (Mike Fallopian) on the rise of the US government mail monopoly. True to his agrarian decentralist prejudices Fallopian sees the establishment of the monopoly as a 'parable of power' rather than a progress of reform although this is not an issue which the reader is called on to decide. It is rather an assault on the reader's assumptions of truth by a principle of juxtaposition. If one block of information is plausible then might not the adjoining one be also? His history of the mail service rather draws our attention to the postal system in itself, his information coinciding with Oedipa's first glimpse of the underground mail in action. Shortly after this she hears yet another story, this time of a deal to sell the bones of dead American GIs to a cigarette company for conversion into filters. Here, as with all the other information she receives, there is a sting in the tail in that a connection always exists with Inverarity. He had shares in the filter business, a large collection of postage stamps, and Peter Pinguid finishes his life also as a California real estate speculator. The proliferation of these connections causes panic to rise in Oedipa and raises enormous problems of understanding for her.

Whatever memories she might have of their affair, Inverarity poses a threat to Oedipa from the very beginning of the novel. The metaphors of enclosure which conclude Chapter 1 function as a prelude to her increasing vulnerability to what she discovers around her. While she and Metzger watch a film on the television where Metzger acted, they play strip Botticelli as Oedipa tries to guess what the film's outcome will be. Not only does she fail to predict its ending but the distinction between film and reality collapses. Pynchon concludes the chapter with a triple climax combining sex, film (the young Metzger is electrocuted) and pop music (a group called the Paranoids have been serenading them and finally blow all the fuses in the motel). This climax punningly dramatizes the way in which the media have now 'penetrated'

Oedipa, impregnated her with the desire to see how they relate to each other.[4] The scene in the motel is thus a comic but crucially important preliminary stage to Oedipa's search where the multiple layers of protective clothing are stripped away and where the self is revealed as being in unavoidable contact with its own technological environment. More is involved than the willed atrophy of humanity which characterizes the Whole Sick Crew. The self emerges as constantly open to incursions from its technological environment, a process which threatens anonymity. Oedipa's moment of terror when she fails to find her reflection in a broken mirror looks forward to the later stages of the novel where the disturbing implications of her own isolation are becoming clearer. Mirrors function ambiguously in *Lot 49*. On the one hand they suggest the closed system of narcissism; on the other they at least provide a visual self-image.

We can see this process of penetrating Oedipa's defence at work in Pynchon's brilliant mock-Jacobean melodrama, 'The Courier's Tragedy', which Oedipa goes to see in pursuit of information. This pastiche draws details from a range of Jacobean tragedies and weaves them into a surprisingly plausible whole. Oedipa goes to see the play to verify a resemblance with the story of the GIs' bones and yet, because she must sit through the whole play, she cannot simply verify the resemblance. She must take in new information. The same happens throughout the novel. The more connections Oedipa makes, the more information she receives, hence *further* connections have to be made, and so on. Pynchon keeps the novel moving at a fast pace so that it becomes proportionally more difficult for Oedipa to organize the information she receives.

'The Courier's Tragedy' follows Jacobean melodrama in several important general aspects which all bear directly on the novel.[5] Firstly it evokes an atmosphere of conspiracy growing out of the machinations between two Italian states, an atmosphere which forces the virtuous pretender Niccolo to masquerade as a Thurn and Taxis courier simply to stay alive. Within such an atmosphere surfaces are deceptive as when, in *The Duchess of Malfi*, Antonio says of the Cardinal that 'What appears in him mirth is merely outside.'[6] Oedipa similarly tries to see through appearances and becomes seized with a panic that mounts towards paranoia later in the novel. Pynchon also imitates the complexities of Jacobean plots which grow out of a web of interests or revenge themes. The equivalent in the novel of this intricacy is the network of Inverarity's interests which intersect at many points with what becomes known as the Tristero system. 'The Courier's Tragedy' contains the obligatory variety of tortures, maiming and violent deaths which carry a number of oblique tongue-in-cheek comments from Pynchon about the lurid taste of Jacobean audiences.

'The Courier's Tragedy' contains many allusions to religion which prove to have a significance for the novel as a whole. Here again Pynchon is faithfully following Jacobean practice where appeals for divine justice usually develop a shrillness from the inscrutability or tardiness of retribution. Jacobean drama abounds in the vocabulary of damnation, of negative spirituality, as when Vindice in *The Revenger's Tragedy* rails against the superannuated lechery of the Duke: 'O that marrowless age/would stuff the hollow bones with damn'd desires,/And 'stead of heat kindle infernal fires.'[7] Pynchon does not evoke helplessness in his religious references so much as simply blocks or inverts them. Thus an image of Saint Narcissus is poisoned and used as an instrument of murder; the evil illegitimate son is called Pasquale (i.e. paschal); a secondary character called Ercole tears out another character's tongue, impales it on a rapier, sets fire to it and brandishes it aloft as a parody of Pentecost; and, as if that wasn't enough, a cardinal is forced to parody the eucharist with blood and flesh from his own mutilated body. Since these events occur during a summary where we are constantly aware of Pynchon's ironic narrative voice, they seem comically lurid, and yet the linkages with other parts of the novel give them an added significance in retrospect. Saint Narcissus on the one hand relates to Pynchon's use of the Narcissus myth (in the name San Narciso for instance), on the other – since as Bishop of Jerusalem he changed water into oil for liturgical unction – his name joints with the references to Pentecost and the Eucharist as miracles. They link thematically, if negatively (since they are parodic or inverted miracles), to the various hints of impending revelation later in the novel.

One figure missing from 'The Courier's Tragedy' who we might expect from the Jacobean genre is the vulnerable female character who is subjected to cruelty, often of a sexual nature. The predicament of, among others, Castiza and Castabella in Tourneur's tragedies, Vittoria Corombona and the Duchess of

Malfi has led Robert Ornstein to state that 'though good usually triumphs and evil is destroyed at the close of Jacobean tragedy, we are made to feel how vulnerable are the walls . . . which seek to check or contain the uncivilized fury of civilized man'.[8] If we specify that the walls are of a tower and substitute 'information' for Ornstein's 'fury' we have come close to Oedipa's predicament. Her vertiginous fear of being at the centre of a monstrous hoax, her panic-stricken sense that Inverarity might have bequeathed her the role of comic butt, internalize her feelings of horror. Although Oedipa's fears never reach the exaggerated horror of the characters within the play we can see them beginning to move in that direction when she discusses the performance with the director Randolf Driblette. She jumps to the conclusion that others have been enquiring about the play with 'cold corpse fingers of grue on her skin',[9] as if she has become infected with the play's own vocabulary. In one sense Oedipa's fears are all the stronger from their vagueness and from her inability to define a clear antagonist.

'The Courier's Tragedy' then sheds light on the subsequent tone of *Lot 49* and on Oedipa's predicament, as well as referring to some of the novel's themes. It also mimics the process of the novel in beginning with one subject (the scheming of claimants to two Italian states) and sliding into another; by the fourth act a sinister counterforce is beginning to emerge – 'Those who, sworn/To punctual vendetta never sleep' (48/50) – who reveal themselves on stage as sinister black-dressed figures. These are the Tristero. Similarly the novel begins ostensibly as an investigation into Inverarity's estate and also moves on to the Tristero. Later in the novel Oedipa adopts the play's melodramatic 'they' to denominate the forces she feels at work against her. The play may even be an application of Norbert Wiener's comparison between the mania for information in the USA and USSR with Renaissance Venice as 'nothing but the old Italian cloak-and-dagger melodrama presented on a larger scale'.[10] In other words Jacobean melodrama supplies Pynchon with a means of dramatizing Cold War paranoia in offering him conspiratorial patterns to mimic.

One last significance of 'The Courier's Tragedy' should be considered, namely its reflexive reference to the process of reading Pynchon's novel. Edward Mendelson has suggested that there is an analogy between Oedipa witnessing the play and the reader apprehending the novel.[11] We could apply this analogy, for instance, to Pynchon's method of presenting the play. During his summary Pynchon constantly shifts comically from Jacobean vocabulary to jarringly modern colloquialisms ('The Duke . . . is in his apartment busy knocking off a piece', etc.) which inevitably distance the reader from the play. Pynchon sets up an illusory security in the reader here, mimicking Oedipa's passively spectatorial attitude, and yet the subsequent relevance of allusions within the play make it clear that Pynchon's humour acts as a dramatic irony. It further has the effect of denying the reader anything like direct access to the play. Indeed it brings into question the ontological status of the play, since Driblette modestly insists to Oedipa that it only exists in his head and that his role is 'to give the spirit flesh'. A series of transformations take place in the play which also draw attention to its own text. A group of soldiers are killed and their bodies dumped in a lake; subsequently their bones are salvaged, converted into charcoal and then into ink. The evil Duke Angelo uses this ink in his communications and writes a letter which strangely reappears in the last act as a confession of all his crimes. The dead soldiers have thus been converted into words, assumed into the text, but the text itself proves to be mobile. Edward Mendelson sees the latter transformation as a 'miracle' but this is surely a solemn reaction to what is, initially at least, a comical violation of probability.

Oedipa's conversation with Driblette raises the question of the play's identity. He admits that he had introduced conspiratorial looks between the characters as well as the appearance of the Tristero assassins on stage, which innovations are perfectly consistent with his sense of the text as a score. Oedipa, however, sees the play as a text and this sets her off on one avenue of investigation. Backstage at the theatre she sees tattered multiple copies of the script, made from a paperback edition which has disappeared. So Oedipa has to travel to a used book store to find her own copy and verify the lines mentioning the name of the Tristero. She discovers a pencilled reference to a textual variation and that the paperback edition has been taken from a larger hardback edition which was published in Berkeley. So Oedipa dutifully travels to Berkeley, pays for the latter and collects her copy from a warehouse in Oakland. But then she discovers that the hardback edition does not contain the lines she wants, so now she is thrown back on to the editor, Emory Bortz, who, it transpires, teaches English in San Narciso. Pynchon has already brought into question the nature of the play; now he questions the text which proves to be impossible to locate geographically or epistemologically. Oedipa's journey takes her in a circle back to San Narciso, and in a circle again since she has gone from one individual (Driblette) to two editions and back to an individual (Bortz). Pynchon's wickedly accurate mimicry of textual variants in Bortz's edition indicates once and for all that Oedipa is not going to find the textual stability she longs for.

How does all this relate to the process of reading *Lot 49*? We have already seen how *V.* examines its own procedures in Fausto's Confessions and raises one possible way of being read in Stencil's V-quest. Oedipa's conversation with Driblette performs a similar function. He tells her bluntly 'It isn't literature, it doesn't mean anything' (52/54), but we discover subsequently that this is not the case. It *does* mean something within the structure of the novel as a whole. Then Driblette attacks Oedipa's obsession with the text: 'You guys, you're like the Puritans are about the Bible. So hung up with words, words.' This is not a warning to the reader against interpretation – all of Pynchon's fiction aims to stimulate thought – so much as a warning to Oedipa of the addictive nature of her search. In that sense Driblette's role counters Metzger's. Metzger whets Oedipa's appetite for discovery; Driblette tries to block it, but this does not give him any privileged status. He is not Pynchon's spokesman since his warnings are offset with grandiose (or perhaps just theatrical) claims to be a demi-god. He brings the play into being, he asserts; he is 'the projector at the planetarium', a solipsistic image which Oedipa takes over for her own use later in the novel.

The humour surrounding Oedipa's search for the ultimate text of 'The Courier's Tragedy', the transformations within the play and Driblette's obvious desire not to satisfy Oedipa's curiosity all nudge the reader not to expect too much certainty within the novel. Thomas Schaub is surely right to take uncertainty as one of Pynchon's major premises and his refusal to satisfy, for instance, the desire for a final resolution is made abundantly clear in the last lines of the novel where Oedipa settles back in her seat at an auction to await the crying of Lot 49.[12] Instead of resolving the narrative Pynchon places Oedipa in an audience and by repeating the novel's title throws the reader back into the text. By this stage in the novel it has become clear that Oedipa's search for a text, which is frustrated by her inability to separate the play from its author, editor and producer, is a comically exaggerated imitation of the reader's own potential anxieties in making sense of the novel.

Inevitably these anxieties resolve to a large extent around information since Pynchon takes a constant delight in teasing the reader towards crucial revelations and then denying them. About half-way through the novel Oedipa visits Berkeley campus and reflects how different her own youth was 'along another pattern of track, another string of decisions taken, switches closed' (71/76). The railway metaphor here articulates her sense of options which have since closed, but it could also sum up the way in which information proliferates during the novel. The starting-point is predictably Inverarity whose stamp collection alerts Oedipa into noticing a misprint on a letter from her husband and then into realizing the existence of an underground postal system. Mike Fallopian plays a key role in this by introducing a historical dimension into the information although his account of how the Peter Pinguid Society began characteristically straddles fact and fiction by naming figures such as Admiral Popov or the Confederate gunboats. Fallopian's rational tone increases the plausibility of his account, as does the reader's recognition that confrontations between the USA and Russia have taken place. Thus the story combines plausibility with blatant fiction (the name of Pinguid, for instance) in a way which involves the reader in Oedipa's desire to verify, and the sequence of stories and information which she receives is carefully calculated to keep her and the reader guessing. On the one hand we can certainly not dismiss them as fiction; on the other we cannot finally resolve their accuracy.

It would be tempting to dismiss the Peter Pinguid story as absurd, but then Fallopian is also working on a history of the US mail monopoly and Pynchon cites the dates of acts of Congress which created it. The very fact of placing a historical emphasis on a means of communication is similarly an authentic method, specifically the creation of Harold A. Innis whose works Pynchon could have encountered through his reading of Marshall McLuhan. Innis' most famous work, *Empire and Communications* (1951), appraises European civilization through the history of papyrus, parchment, paper and printing. He repeatedly emphasizes how means of communication give power, noting, for example, Augustus' introduction of a state post to unify and control the Roman Empire. Monopoly is one of Innis' themes and it is consistent with this general approach that Pynchon should include references to one postal monopoly (the American) and then redirect his attention to another – the Thurn and Taxis system.

Oedipa's line of enquiry from Inverarity's stamp collection splits into a historical investigation and a contemporary one when she tries to uncover more about the underground postal system. A second line of enquiry opens up when she visits Fangoso Lagoons (one of Inverarity's many concerns) and hears how a company of American troops were cut off by Germans near Lago di Pietà and gradually wiped out. So far it seems plausible, but then we learn that an ex-GI had used his Mafia connections to salvage the soldiers' bones and ship them to America where they were subsequently used in making cigarette filters, yet another of Inverarity's concerns. So we have come back in a loop to this seemingly unavoidable source. Furthermore, Oedipa sees 'The Courier's Tragedy' after this story which makes the massacre within the play seem all the more possible. And yet Oedipa's source for the GI story is one Manny Di Presso, by no means the most outrageous name in the novel, whose fear of pursuit by the Mafia and apparent paranoia (a term we will meet again) strains against his stay. To further compound the uncertainty the pull against Di Presso's credibility is countered in the last chapter by a confrontation at the same lake recounted in a seventeenth-century travel narrative.

It would even be too orderly to suggest that Pynchon alternates certainty with doubt. In virtually every piece of information he blends the two together and denies both Oedipa and the reader the time to sort out the information – sorting, in various senses, is the book's true subject – by moving us rapidly on to the next events. Similarly we can distinguish approximate lines of enquiry which Oedipa pursues: she follows up the references to WASTE (the underground system), the text of 'The Courier's Tragedy', and the history of the Thurn and Taxis postal monopoly. But this list is by no means exhaustive and in chapters 3–5 the avenues cross over each other in a way which ironizes the superficial linearity of the plot-sequence. The chronological sequence of events proves to explain nothing, partly because it includes a proportion of sheer chance and partly because the texture of the events is so complex. Pynchon indicates this complexity by using recurrent images of networks or labyrinths – the layout of San Narciso, the map of Fangoso Lagoons which Oedipa sees on the television, Driblette's eyes or even the huge office at Yoyodyne where Oedipa gets lost, an anxiety-image visually and tonally similar to the huge layout of desks in the film version of *The Trial*.

It is at Yoyodyne that Oedipa meets Stanley Koteks whose name and whose membership in WASTE comically hint at the possible futility of Oedipa's search. Koteks' insistence that WASTE is an acronym, i.e. that like V. it must stand for something else, does not obliterate the hint but only adds yet another alternative for Oedipa to consider. Genghis Cohen, the philatelist who Oedipa consults over Inverarity's stamp-collection, discovers that many of them are forgeries which once again reflects on Oedipa's whole undertaking since the stamps like 'The Courier's Tragedy' have become a text which she must scrutinize in closer and closer detail. The proliferation of sightings of the muted horn which links the former Tristero system to the present underground reaches a climax in chapter 5 when Oedipa makes a nocturnal journey around San Francisco but it occurs in far too varied contexts for Oedipa to be able to examine or organize them. This journey around San Francisco immediately precedes the sudden ending of references to a contemporary organization. As Edward Mendelson points out, from then onwards the Tristero becomes a matter of the past and of history.[13] It would, however, be a mistake to conclude that the last chapter relaxes any of Pynchon's earlier stress on ambiguity and uncertainty. Oedipa's search for the accurate text of 'The Courier's Tragedy' has had to be delayed until this late stage in affairs when she finally tracks down the editor, Professor Bortz. He tells her that the lines she quotes are from an obscene parody in the Vatican library, in other words from a kind of textual forgery which has been gratuitously decorated with pornographic woodcuts; and that is the end of one avenue of enquiry, or so it seems.

Pynchon blocks one source but opens another through a travel narrative by another Renaissance figure, Dr Diocletian Blobb. In the central section of this chapter Pynchon returns to his bewildering mixture of fact and fantasy, this time naming far more texts than he has done before. He quotes from Blobb's *Peregrinations* which David Cowart has compared to Thomas

Coryat's *Crudities*, a possible source for Webster; but then refers vaguely to 'obscure philatelic journals'.[14] He then indicates a footnote to Motley's *Rise of the Dutch Republic* which was almost certainly one of his sources for historical data, although the footnote itself does not exist. Now textual sources of information proliferate ranging from a pamphlet on anarchism through old stamp catalogues to a typescript sent to Cohen 'supposed to be a translation of an article from the 1865 issue of the famous *Bibliotheque des Timbrephiles* of Jean-Baptiste Moëns' (119/129). The hint of doubt ('*supposed* to be') offsets the temporary 'authority' Pynchon gives this text by quoting it, and obscures a tactic which Pynchon is following, namely, to insert fictitious references into historical texts. The footnote in Motley does not exist and Moëns' monograph on Thurn and Taxis stamps of 1880 adds little to our understanding of the historical issues involved beyond confirming that the monopoly grew out numerous mergers and family quarrels.[15] Text leads into text in a way which explains retrospectively why, when she first meets the stamp-dealer Genghis Cohen, Oedipa sees him 'framed in a long succession or train of doorways, room after room receding in the general direction of Santa Monica' (65/68). This vision comments metaphorically on the way texts and sources recede into each other apparently without end, stretching towards resolution but never reaching it.

With the help of Bortz, Cohen and the California library system Oedipa assembles a composite explanation of how the Tristero organization began. Manfred Puetz and Thomas Schaub have both examined Pynchon's historical summary here and demonstrated that it is accurate, concluding that he took most of his information from E. W. Puttkammer's *The Princes of Thurn and Taxis* (1938). Schaub argues ingeniously that the history of Thurn and Taxis by analogy implies that the growth of the Tristero is equally plausible, but there are important details which reinforce doubt.[16] The founding figure of the Tristero is '*perhaps* a madman, *perhaps* an honest rebel, *according to some* only a con artist' (110/119: my emphasis). Pynchon's rhetoric changes from the definite to the tentative at this crucial point and then blurs the account by multiplying possible interpretations. Bortz, for instance, sees the Tristero as a kind of mirror-image of the legal monopoly; hence their icons of a muted horn and dead badger modify and mimic the post-horn on the Thurn and Taxis coat of arms and the pieces of badger-fur which their couriers originally wore. Furthermore Bortz even invents a character called Konrad who allegedly fired the Tristero with enthusiasm for controlling the Holy Roman Empire and hypothesizes that the Tristero could even have been responsible for the French Revolution. Ironically it is Oedipa who questions these assumptions so that when Pynchon quotes the alleged Moëns text and states that it read 'like another of Bortz's costume dramas' (119/129), he is narratively endorsing a degree of scepticism which Oedipa does hold.

There is nothing new in a novelist trying to blur the distinction between history and fiction; that dates back at least to Walter Scott who used it as a strategy to increase the authenticity of his fiction. Pynchon in *Lot 49* is blurring the boundaries of his text, however, not simply to draw attention to its own fictiveness, but to indicate ambiguities and gaps in history itself. In this way he denies the reader a reliable standpoint outside the text. He repeatedly introduces metaphors, allusions or characters which comment on Oedipa's search in a way which raises doubts and uncertainties. As Barth does in *The Sot-weed Factor*, Pynchon juxtaposes historical references with reminders of the novel's status as artefact so that the reader's sense of history and of fiction are brought into maximum confrontation. Oedipa's growing inability to stabilize 'The Courier's Tragedy' textually and find conclusive evidence about the Tristero thus mimes out the reader's difficulty in apprehending Pynchon's text. Just before the end of the novel Bortz challenges Oedipa to look up the Moëns text and verify once and for all that its information is correct, and the challenge extends to the reader, especially the reader who naively persists in hoping for final resolution. Partly from sheer fatigue Oedipa does not take up the challenge, on the other hand she does go to the stamp auction to discover who the mysterious new dealer is. Frank Kermode has pointed out that Oedipa's predicament consists of being caught between fear of the absence of order and of a total but malevolent order.[17] Similarly in *V.* Stencil is obsessed by total continuity whereas the reader, by the very nature of the book's structure, is directed to accept local and provisional continuities. In *Lot 49* Pynchon's perspective is detached enough from Oedipa's to question her sources and assumptions, but too close to give an alternative overview. His weaving backwards and forwards between fact and fiction attacks the reader's sense of probability. The more surprising events turn out to be true, the more the reader's sense of possibility within the text and outside it is broadened.

2 OEDIPA'S JOURNEY TOWARDS PARANOIA

Lot 49 is unique among Pynchon's novels in focusing so closely on one central protagonist. Pynchon uses a narrative rhetoric similar to that of Henry James's later works where the reader is confined at any point to one consciousness, but a consciousness articulated in the third person, as if Pynchon were looking over Oedipa's shoulder. Chapter 3, for instance, begins as follows:

> Things then did not delay in turning curious. If one object behind her discovery of what she was to label the Tristero system or often only The Tristero (as if it might be something's secret title) were to bring to an end her encapsulation in her tower, then that night's infidelity with Metzger would logically be the starting point for it; logically. That's what would come to haunt her most, perhaps: the way it fitted, logically, together. As if (as she'd guessed that first minute in San Narciso) there were revelation in progress all around her
> (29/28)

The most noticeable characteristic of this paragraph is that Pynchon constantly draws back from attributing too definite an awareness to Oedipa. The Jamesian periphrastic tenses ('was to label', 'would come to haunt', etc.) suggest a knowledge of subsequent events – Pynchon is not tying himself rigidly to the moment – and yet the tone of the passage reflects Oedipa's early sense of puzzlement, rather like Alice in Wonderland, as the first sentence hints. *Lot 49* deals in hypotheses based on tantalizing evidence. The repeatedly tentative nature of its narrative comments 'if . . . as if', etc.) reveals traces of the detective-story genre which underlies the novel, and which some critics have taken as its model.[18] One of the main differences, however, lies in the degrees of uncertainty. In the detective story there is a pattern to locate behind events. In *Lot 49* there is uncertainty to the very end about whether a pattern exists at all.

This sort of prose style simultaneously proposes interpretations and at the same time refuses to validate them. The conditional clauses relate to another device which Pynchon uses extensively throughout the novel, namely, the balancing of alternatives against each other. Thomas Schaub has commented on this rhetoric specifically in connection with Oedipa's much-quoted 'epiphany' as she is coming into San Narciso and argues that 'this style generates a tension between the opposing worlds it implicates and joins (suburban swirl: sacred text), and it is this stylistic tension that positions characters and reader alike at the interface between opposite views of the same event'.[19] This 'interface' could be interpreted variously as a point between presence and absence, as an excluded middle, or as a point between the rigid alternatives of binary mathematics.[20] At this stage in his writing Pynchon can indicate stylistically this in-between state but it is not until *Gravity's Rainbow* that he develops his interest in probability-theory to conceptualize the area between zero and one. Not only does this either/or rhetoric render ambiguous local events but it also posits alternative resolutions to the novel, neither of which, as Molly Hite points out, can be realized.[21] Indeed the very possibility of resolution is brought into question. The prospect of a final discovery ensures momentum in the narrative but the narrative stops on the very brink of that last revolution.

This general rhetoric characteristic of the novel sheds important light on one particularly contentious issue – the status of the religious and transcendental references which run throughout *Lot 49*. Edward Mendelson has put the case most forcibly for their positive value. He argues that spiritual language is applied to Oedipa in a much clearer way than to any other character, notes Pynchon's use of the term 'hierophany' from Mircea Eliade, and sees parodies of Pentecost at the end of the novel and in the play. He states quite categorically that 'religious meaning is itself the central issue of the plot'.[22] In contrast Schaub has pointed out the important element of doubt and uncertainty in Pynchon's sacred terminology which teasingly gestures towards another realm without categorically asserting its reality. We could take Schaub's argument a step further by suggesting that the religious allusions in *Lot 49* are either parodic or paired with a profane meaning which constantly deflates the possibility of the spiritual. Thus when Oedipa contemplates the streets of San Narciso it is 'as if, on some other frequency, or out of the eye of some whirlwind rotating too slow for her heated skin even to feel the centrifugal coolness of, words were being spoken' (15/13). Here the secular reference strains against the spiritual one so that we could say *either* that the spiritual allusion charges the secular one with more potential significance than normal, *or* that the secular phrase prevents the spiritual one from being too affirmative. When Oedipa sees a map of Fangoso Lagoons she experiences 'some promise of hierophany', but only a promise and the loose syntax similarly jumbles together sacred and profane in a non-committal way: 'printed circuit, gently curving streets, private access to the water, Book of the Dead . . .' (28/18). Equally non-committal is the title Pynchon gave to the first part of the novel when it was published separately – 'The world (This One), The Flesh (Mrs. Oedipa Maas) and the Testament of Pierce Inverarity'.[23]

Mendelson performed an important critical service in drawing attention to the novel's spiritual allusions, but it needs to be pointed out that a main source of irony in *Lot 49* is that it constantly heads for a revelation which never comes. This raises further sources of ambiguity and anxiety for Oedipa since she is forced to wonder whether she fails to gain access to the spiritual because she is incapable or because there is nothing there. Certainly the prevailing ironic and sceptical temper would set up a context inhospitable to the spiritual. Thus in every case of spiritual allusion we need to be on the alert for anything that will undercut it. Immediately after her epiphany in San Narciso Oedipa wonders whether her husband sees his studio in a religious way, but this is only a fanciful and inconclusive speculation; when Oedipa first sees the muted posthorn she calls it a hieroglyph (i.e. a potentially sacred sign), although it occurs in the most profane of contexts – on the walls of a ladies' toilet. We have already noted the religious parodies in 'The Courier's Tragedy'. The naming of Mr. Thoth who Oedipa sees in an old people's home offers yet another mockery of the sacred. Thoth was the lord of ritual and magic; according to Harold Innis, 'he represented creation by utterance and production by thought and utterance', but the rambling old man Oedipa speaks to offers anything but enlightenment.[24] In Revelation 1.7 we are told of Jesus that 'he cometh with clouds' and Pynchon inverts this image by using the Californian smog as a metaphorical counter to the supposedly impending revelation with all its stress on vision.

Many of the religious allusions in *Lot 49* focus on Pentecost, hence one significance to the book's title (the most obvious secular allusion would be to the California gold-rush). In Acts II immediately after the miracle of speaking with tongues Peter quotes from the prophet Joel of what will happen in the last days. Firstly he declares 'your young men shall see visions and your old men shall dream dreams' (vs. 17) but Oedipa never quite manages a vision and Thoth's dreams are confused by TV cartoons. Joel also prophesies that 'the sun shall be turned into darkness' (vs. 28) which finds novelistic expression in Oedipa's depression and isolation at night. It is a promise that 'whosoever shall call on the name of the Lord shall be saved' (vs. 21) but Pynchon secularizes this completely into mere exclamation. One of the signs of religious hope in the Book of Joel is that the trumpet will be blown in Zion but then the Tristero sign blocks this symbolism by muting the horn. The miracles of Pentecost revolve around the Resurrection and Oedipa has indeed the ambition to give life to Inverarity's estate, but without success. True she is taught about miracles by a Mexican friend of hers called significantly Jesus who she meets at night in San Francisco and yet once again the circumstances of the meeting (in a Mexican 'greasy spoon') pull against its value as spiritual instruction. After the pentecostal descent of the Holy Ghost Peter heals a lame man by faith and explicitly refuses to give him money. Oedipa is denied any such healing powers and when she tries to help a derelict the only method she can think of is to give money.

This series of spiritual inversions reaches its peak at the end of the novel where 49 suggest the eve of Pentecost. Indeed the last thing noted in The Acts before Pentecost is the fact that the apostles are choosing a replacement for Judas *by lots*. Imminence has been one of the key characters of *Lot 49* and when the auctioneer spreads his arms it seems to Oedipa that once again he is on the verge of revelation: 'Passerine spread his arms in a gesture that seemed to belong to the priesthood of some remote culture; perhaps to a descending angel' (127/138). By now the tentativeness of the analogy should be familiar and Pynchon has anyway poked facetious fun at the notion of revelation. Oedipa tells Cohen that his fly is open and in the next sentence wonders what to do 'when the bidder revealed himself'. Slight suggestions of threat (from the black-suited dealers) and imprisonment (the lock of the door snaps shut) anyway offset what element of hope might be present. In this scene and others Pynchon uses religious parody to mock the earnestness of Oedipa's search. Seeking the Word she finds only words.

Before we leave these spiritual allusions two more points need to be made. The first is that an alternative counter to the sacred might be death as well as profane irony. *Lot 49* begins with a death; the TV film revolved around death in battle; the story of the Lago di Pietà concerns bones; Driblette commits suicide after producing a play which specializes in lurid killings; Cohen makes wine from dandelions picked in the East San Narciso cemetery; and so on. The number of references to death far outweighs that of spiritual allusions and they vary from new items (a monk immolating himself in Vietnam) to historical events (the massacre of Wells Fargo men on the site of Fangoso Lagoons).[25] Predictably all these deaths are linked through the colour of black and woven firstly into Oedipa's sense of being threatened by the Tristero and then later her harrowing sense of being isolated in a void. References to the 'dark Angel', the shadow and spectral voices are no more categorical than the allusions to the hierophany and articulate crises of fear in Oedipa's search. Since there is a broad and gradual shift away from comedy during the novel it is quite appropriate that references to death should gain their maximum impact near the end.

If the references to death relate to Oedipa's fears and depression we could also argue conversely that the positive spiritual allusions suggest hope to her. Once she has been sensitized Oedipa begins to see her environment in transcendental terms. Inverarity's stamps become windows on other worlds and San Narciso becomes charged with hidden meaning as a visual grid. Like Emerson, Thoreau and Melville Oedipa comes to see her environment as a kind of text which she struggles to read. She develops an exhilaratingly sharp sense of how even the most trivial things can be charged with potential meaning. Thus in her 'moment' at San Narciso, the most striking example of a general tendency, the layout of the houses forces itself on her ('sprang at her') with a totally new clarity. Her sharpened visual sense of place then leads on to references to a 'hieroglyphic sense of concealed meaning' and implies that meaning here is not so much a matter of another realm as a direct result of Oedipa's new concentration of attention.

Oedipa develops a new capacity to see things afresh. As a housewife she is a figure of conventionality locked in trivial suburban rituals and yet one process which the novel enacts is the progressive opening out of her awareness of America. The repeated use of the term 'revelation' could thus be taken in a non-transcendental sense, to refer to her discovery of a California (and hence an America) which she did not know existed. Throughout the novel Oedipa shows a wide-eyed reaction to what is happening around her. Since the narrative takes her into unfamiliar contexts she resembles a tourist at times, especially in San Francisco. When she visits Berkeley campus she feels dislocated because the political protests seem to have little or no connection with her own university days. She gives the reader his eyes and thereby becomes a medium herself, but without suffering dehumanization. Her recurrent response is one of bewilderment, hence her name; for the sphinx she has to confront is her whole environment.[26] Pynchon strikes a delicate balance between charting the enlargement of her awareness and enacting the epistemic bewilderment caused by the deluge of information to which she is subjected. Oedipa thus becomes a heightened paradigm of man's vulnerability to his own systems of information. Even in her dealings with other characters Oedipa almost becomes converted into a means: for Mucho a sympathetic ear, for Hilarius a guinea-pig, for Metzger a sexual convenience, and so on. Most of her experiences prove to be betrayals of one kind or another and the fact that other characters try to exploit her links them analogically with the effects of media.

Oedipa is in many ways an average person with a certain amount of resilience coming from her common sense. Indeed her 'ignorant' objections to many of the propositions foisted on her consistently have more intellectual weight than she realizes. However this common sense and her mannerism of talking to herself to convert events into humour prove to be inadequate defences against the assaults of information. In the crucial chapter 5 when Oedipa travels round San Francisco by night taking imaginative possession of the city she has become attenuated into disembodied eyes and ears, perceiving the rich diversity of the urban life which surrounds her. Here the attenuation of self can be exhilarating but usually Oedipa's isolation is charged with fear. The object of this fear is the loss of self which she witnesses in her husband and which is hinted at in what happens to her name. She 'adopts' that of Arnold Snarb, is distorted into Edna Mosh by Mucho for technological expediency and even passes herself off as Grace Bortz. At first Oedipa's insights refresh her but then they have a physically debilitating effect. She is immobilized, suffers pains and insomnia, imagines she hears voices and finally comes to the brink of nervous collapse. It is significant in the last chapter that Oedipa consciously avoids following up leads because she is afraid that the proliferation of revelations might swamp her ego and destroy her. Similarly the one possibility that she has delayed admitting – that she may be the victim of a gigantic hoax – is linked with the inevitability of her death, i.e. once again the destruction of the self. Almost the last image Oedipa encapsulates these fears in spatial terms: 'She stood between the public booth and the rented car, in the night, her isolation complete, and tried to face towards the sea. But she'd lost her bearings. She turned pivoting on one stacked heel, could find no mountains either' (122/133). This is a total inversion of her only vision of San Narciso which is now a darkened expanse within Oedipa has become totally disorientated.

In Oedipa Pynchon enacts the self's difficulties in ordering its contemporary environment. Much of the novel's early humour grows out of the environment's unnerving tendency to startle her, and the novel's later tone becomes more sombre as Oedipa's efforts to order her experiences take their physical toll. Other characters in *Lot 49* are usually defined through an overriding obsession and yet they might be sources of information for Oedipa, hence her urgency to communicate with them; but faces turn out to be masks and eyes threaten. Oedipa resorts to sunshades as a defensive reflex to this threat. The terminology of revelation traditionally draws on extensions to seeing but the harder Oedipa strains to see – metaphorically and literally – the more obstacles there are to her vision whether in lacquer-spray haze, steam or darkness. If events take on a sinister order – then the opposite possibility of total *dis*order is equally terrifying.

The fear that everything is connected takes Oedipa towards the psychotic state of paranoia, although Pynchon is clearly not interested in delving deeply into her psychology. Paranoia emerges in *Lot 49* as an organizational possibility and, M. R. Siegel has shown that it functions in *Gravity's Rainbow* as a basic principle of ordering.[27] Long before Oedipa begins to register panic Pynchon draws attention to paranoia in a humorous way. At Echo Courts Oedipa meets a pop group called the Paranoids; in Fallopian's history of the US mail she meets a conspiratorial theory of history; Di Presso's deal with the bones is a criminal conspiracy involving the Mafia; and 'The Courier's Tragedy' builds up an atmosphere of plotting and counter-plotting. This emphasis follows on consistently from Pynchon's depiction of the conspiratorial mentality in *V.* where he ironically exposes its capacity to mould historical events according to a predetermined pattern. Now paranoia grows out of a sequence of coincidences towards the point where Oedipa feels herself trapped in a logical spiral. Near the end of the novel she surveys the possibilities of what is happening to her: 'Change your name to Miles, Dean, Serge, and/or Leonard, baby, she advised her reflection in the half-light of that afternoon's vanity mirror. Either way, they'll call it paranoia. They' (117/128). The whole paragraph is riddled with alternatives which resolve into four possibilities: either the underground network exists, or she is hallucinating it; or she is the victim of an elaborate plot, or just fantasying it in her madness. Oedipa posits hypothetical observers of her actions ('they'), but suddenly realizes that the pronoun links them to equally hypothetical malign agencies which she has feared are at work isolating her. The only way she could escape from paranoia would be to communicate meaning fully with those beyond her predicament who might diagnose her illness, but she also realizes that *if* there is a conspiracy calling it paranoia could be yet another malevolent act. In other words Oedipa loses any means of verifying her predicament and can only address her own reflection in the mirror. In his now classic account of political paranoia Richard Hofstadter has commented that 'this enemy seems to be on many counts a projection of the self: both the ideal and the unacceptable aspects of the self are attributed to him'.[28] If we associate the Tristero with blackness and the shadow, who first appears as a radio character but then takes on more sinister weight, Pynchon could be using the term 'shadow' in a Jungian sense as the dark, anarchic side of the self.[29] Oedipa is after all a conventional and orderly figure whereas the Tristero comes to represent the spirit of opposition and revolt so that she could be grappling with a projection of her own repressions in the paragraph discussed above which implies as much in her Narcissus-like posture. Solipsism is clearly an issue raised by a painting to which Pynchon refers enigmatically in this novel.

3 THE NOVEL'S MEDIA

In the Florence chapter of *V.* Pynchon uses Botticelli's 'The Birth of Venus' and Machiavelli's *The Prince* as open texts on to which characters can project their varying interpretations. In *Lot 49* the equivalent texts are 'The Courier's Tragedy' and a painting by the Spanish exile Remedios Varo. Pynchon further indicates that the novel can offer multiple significances by repeatedly using two key words with varying meaning – 'lot' and 'horn'. 'Lot' can signify in this context a saleable portion of land, parking area or item in an auction as well as destiny and, perhaps most relevant of all, simply plurality. 'Horn' is more complex since its meanings range from a biblical emblem of power through a musical or postal instrument to the more profane telephone or, as 'horny', sexually aroused. Pynchon uses the word with all these shades of meaning and yet Oedipa's recurring uncertainty suggests also that she is on the horns of a dilemma. As we have seen, even the syntax indicates that she recognizes contrasting possibilities without being able to choose. The hardback edition of Wharfinger's plays carries a gloss that there is 'no clear meaning for the word *trystero*' (70/75), an important indication of uncertainty, which again comments ironically on Oedipa's search. If he follows the textual hints closely the reader will be as sensitized as Oedipa except that he will note for instance more meanings to 'horn' than she can since Pynchon constantly reminds us by his verbal dexterity that he is articulating the narrative and hence creating a verbal texture larger than Oedipa's consciousness.

The Remedios Varo painting in question is 'Bordando el Manto Terrestre' ('Embroidering the Tapestry of this World') which Oedipa remembers having seen in Mexico with Inverarity during their affair (Plate 1). The painting is introduced via an analogy with Rapunzel with Inverarity playing the prince who liberates her. Oedipa thus figures her own situation in terms of enclosure (perhaps by someone else – Rapunzel is shut in by a witch); it is an image which rationalizes her own pensiveness into a passive waiting for deliverance. The painting increases this sense because it depicts four girls shut in the top of a tower embroidering a huge tapestry which spills out of the tower and which contains scenes from this world. It is a key moment for Oedipa when she sees the painting and she is moved to tears by the realization that her self-image was fanciful and that she is held in place by 'magic,

Plate 1 'Bordando el Manto Terrestre' by Remedios Varo

Plate 2   James Clerk Maxwell

anonymous and malignant' (13/11). Although the realization is potentially melodramatic Oedipa has significantly exchanged a metaphor of confinement for one of openness (fields of force) which looks forward to her receptivity towards insights later in the novel. David Cowart has discussed this and other relevant paintings by Varo through the theme of solipsism, arguing that 'she doubts external reality altogether' as a result of seeing 'Bordando el Manto Terrestre'.[30] If it is doubt she feels, it is a liberating doubt and the first step in Oedipa's sloughing off her suburban attitudes. Inverarity makes a poor 'knight of deliverance' just as Oedipa makes a rather self-deceived 'captive maiden', references which help to drain off solemnity from her quest before it gets under way, and denies possible analogies with say, Tennyson's 'The Lady of Shalott'. Yet Cowart is right to raise the issue of solipsism since this recurs through Oedipa's image of herself as the projector in a planetarium, her repeated and anxious looks at herself in mirrors and through a question she jots down in her notebook – '*Shall I project a world?*' (60/63).

The most important thing about the Varo painting is that, like 'The Courier's Tragedy', its significance goes beyond what Oedipa perceives so that it makes reference to broader aspects of the novel. The tower, for instance, is surrounded by thin clouds which find alternative expression in California's smog-haze. The four girls are presided over by a sinister hooded figure in black who looks forward to the mysterious figures in the play. By a strange coincidence in the background of the tower a figure (also in black) is playing a long instrument which slightly resembles a kind of horn. And lastly the painting depicts the tower convexly which exaggerates the space lying behind it; perhaps for this reason Pynchon states that the girls are 'seeking hopelessly to fill the void' (13/10). The picture thus presents an image of futility which makes anticipatory comment on Oedipa's attempts to put boundaries on her information which, it seems, expands and proliferates endlessly.

It should be evident by now that *Lot 49* constantly draws attention to its own means in a way which makes it impossible to attempt any kind of crude illusionist division between form and content. The novel as a whole imitates, the various information Oedipa receives by incorporating within itself important elements of ambiguity, uncertainty and coincidence. Of all the possible influences on Pynchon Marshall McLuhan's *Understanding Media*

(1964) seems the most immediate. Pynchon mentions McLuhan in a letter to Thomas F. Hirsch of 1968 and this text is the most obviously applicable to *Lot 49* which is absolutely saturated with references to media (v. Appendix). It begins with a letter and develops a concern with the postal system; it makes extensive use of means of communication – roads, telephone, radio, TV, etc. Indeed, as Thomas Schaub points out, sooner or later *everything* becomes media for Oedipa.[31] This harmonizes completely with one of McLuhan's most basic and most contentious assertions, namely that 'the "message" of any medium or technology is the change of scale or pace or pattern that it introduces into human affairs'.[32] By considering media as a whole he can dovetail content into means so that he arrives at a special and opaque sense of communication summed up in his slogan 'the medium is the message'. In other words McLuhan has virtually argued the notion of content out of existence.

Apart from the novel's allusions to itself there are plenty of points in *Lot 49* which demonstrate that Pynchon is applying McLuhan's basic premise. At the beginning of chapter 3, for instance, Oedipa receives a letter from her husband Mucho. As she fears it is 'newless', that is, it has no content; but then she looks at the outside and notices that its franking contains a misprint. This is only a detail, but it is a crucial one since it suggests that Pynchon is drawing attention to communication as an act or process rather than as a quantity (information or content) which is transferred from place to place. In the bar where Oedipa meets Mike Fallopian the latter gets a letter from a friend which is full of banalities. Once again there is no content. The value of the letter is as a gesture, that Fallopian's friend should be collaborating with others in their underground mail-system in a communal act of withdrawal from the normal processes of American society.

The fact that Pynchon uses McLuhan does not of course necessarily mean that he endorses all his propositions. In the two examples given above the first acts as part of Oedipa's sensitivity towards her California environment which is defined here in terms of communication media. And, as Pynchon has noted elsewhere, 'Los Angeles, more than any other city, belongs to the mass media'.[33] In the second example, however, Pynchon does not lose sight of content and the fact that nothing is communicated ironically offsets the value of the act. McLuhan himself veers from pessimism to optimism throughout *Understanding Media*. On the one hand he argues that 'were we to accept fully and directly every shock to our various structures of awareness, we would soon be nervous wrecks'; on the other, 'the computer . . . promises by technology a Pentecostal condition of universal understanding and unity'.[34] Pynchon is particularly sceptical about this Pentecostal rhetoric which he actually uses in *Lot 49*, but without asserting any clear value, and his narrative confirms the more gloomy of McLuhan's assertions since Oedipa does become a nervous wreck under the pressure of the information which bombards her. McLuhan insists again and again that his reader should gain awareness of the media although this awareness is alternately a threat and a source of exhilaration. Pynchon enacts the same kind of process by presenting familiar materials in startling combinations and contexts, and indicates the ambiguous value of the process through Oedipa's shifting emotional predicament.

In describing the effects of the media on man McLuhan uses the Narcissus myth to show how an individual can convert himself into a closed circuit. He applies the mythic figure, via the etymologically cognate term 'narcosis', to the average individual's unconsciousness of the media: 'It is this continuous embrace of our own technology in daily use that puts us in the Narcissus role of subliminal awareness and numbness in relation to these images of ourselves.' Pynchon takes up this analogy by having Oedipa go to a motel called Echo Courts in San Narciso, a parallel which Schaub has noted.[35] Pynchon enacts Oedipa's emergence from this state of numbness partly by a growth in awareness where none was present and partly as a stripping away of defences. Her tower noted earlier metaphorically extends her own skin and marks an appropriate starting-point for both strands of the narrative.

McLuhan's use of the Narcissus myth depends partly on etymology and Pynchon takes up a further sense of 'narcosis' which relates directly to a culture where drugs are in widespread use. Oedipa's psychiatrist, Dr. Hilarius, is a bizarre combination of Timothy Leary and Josef Mengele. One specific area of topical allusion comes from the fact that Hilarius, like Leary, is experimenting with hallucinogenic drugs such as psilocybin and LSD. Leary had a close connection with California, taking his Ph.D. at Berkeley and working at Oakland. Hilarius is running an organization called *Die Brücke* – the bridge inward – which he wants Oedipa to join, but drugs for Oedipa have value only as potential metaphors; she imagines the road to Echo Court as a hypodermic needle inserted into a Los Angeles freeway. She never considers drugs because she is afraid of losing control over herself and in this respect contrasts quite strongly with her husband.

Mucho enacts Oedipa's experiences in reverse, moving from sensitivity to numbness. His earliest mentioned job was as a used car salesman where he totally contradicted the stereotype. He sees the cars in McLuhanesque terms as metal extensions of their owners and hence could not help seeing the cars' rubbish as a residue of the owners' lives:

> . . . motorized, metal extensions of themselves, of their families and what their whole lives must be like, out there so naked for anybody, a stranger like himself, to look at, frame cockeyed, rusty underneath, fender repainted in a shade just off enough to depress the value . . . (8/4)

Pynchon brilliantly evokes the life lying behind this debris through a concentration of attention which is of a piece with the novel as a whole. Rubbish miraculously becomes charged with significance as the syntax edges away from simple illustration, draws the reader in ('for wiping *your* own breath'), and moves in a slow arc from inert objects through the life they indicate, back to inertia and death in the coating of dust. Mucho suffers from his compulsion to see the cars as part of lives and not simply consumer objects, and yearns for the sort of numbness which, McLuhan argues, *buffers* the individuals from such disturbance. Pynchon takes over McLuhan's actual term to explain the attractions of Mucho's job as disc-jockey where the technical routine, symbolized in his sound-proof glass booth, 'buffers' him against his earlier memories. But this does not satisfy Mucho and by the end of chapter 5 he reveals to Oedipa that he has found a more thorough narcosis through LSD supplied him by Hilarius. Here Pynchon parodies Leary's enthusiasm for the drug's effects; the latter notes in an interview that 'what happens to everyone is the experience of incredible acceleration and intensification of all senses and of all mental processes'.[36] Mucho's hearing has become so acute that he not only perceives the Muzak in a bar but can carry out sound-spectrum analysis in his head, a bizarre and futile capacity which separates him more and more from Oedipa (they 'faced each other through the fluted gold lens of a beer pitcher'). Even Mucho's language parodies Leary's claim of insight:

> 'When those kids sing about "She loves you", yeah well, you know, she does, she's any number of people, all over the world, back through time, different colours, sizes, ages, shapes, distances from death, but she loves. And the "you" is everybody. And herself. Oedipa, the human voice, you know, it's a flipping miracle'.   (99/106–7)

Pynchon shrewdly captures the vague enthusiasm of Leary among others as well as the solemn-minded tendency to read emotional depth into pop-songs. Leary did this extensively in two essays ('the Magical Mystery Trip' and 'She Comes in Colours') subsequently collected in his book *The Politics of Ecstasy*. Mucho begins with obvious incoherence ('yeah well', etc.) and then expands the title of the Beatles lyric until subject and object are all-inclusive. Everybody loves everybody. The crowning irony is Mucho's final enthusiasm for the human voice since his utterance has undermined its efficacy as a means of communication by blurring all distinctions and because his own ego has fragmented virtually out of existence.

McLuhan's statements about the meeting between media shed light on the nature of metaphor in *Lot 49*. He states: 'the hybrid or the meeting of the two media is a moment of truth and revelation from which new form is born. . . . The moment of the meeting of media is a moment of freedom and release from the ordinary trance and numbness imposed by them on our senses.'[37] Interestingly McLuhan applies this notion of the meeting of differences to the hybrid nature of modernistic literature which, he argues, is a source of richness because it energizes our environment in an unusual way. Thus he notes Eliot's use of the lyrical and ironic in 'Prufrock' and Joyce's superimposition of classical parallels on to contemporary Dublin. Oedipa herself experiences key moments of possible insight when sudden unusual analogies present themselves to her. On coming into San Narciso the layout of houses resembles a printed circuit; when she tries to help a derelict she suddenly notices the coincidence between his DT's and the dt's of differential calculus. The narrative explains: 'The act of metaphor then was a thrust at truth and a lie, depending where you were: inside, safe, our outside lost' (89/95). This summary is far less categorical then Fausto Maijstral's condemnation of metaphor as lie in *V.*. Here Pynchon straddles the notions of truth and falsehood by introducing a relativism of perspective. He associates metaphor with religious miracle (again the example is of St. Narcissus) *but also* with psychotic delusion (paranoia) so that the passage insists on the importance of metaphor in a way totally distinct from say verifiability. Slightly earlier in the novel Oedipa meets a Mexican anarchist called Jesus Arrabal who tells her that a miracle is 'another world's intrusion into this one' (83/88). He uses the same awkwardly transcendental language as McLuhan, his definition of miracle almost echoing the other's account of the meeting-point between media. Pynchon himself does not endorse allusions to another world except as describing the mystery of metaphor which emerges in *Lot 49* as a rhetorical peak, a sudden burst of imaginative intensity caused by bringing totally disparate orders of things together. It thus becomes a source of wonderment to Oedipa that DT's could have *any* connection with dt's.

The material which Pynchon brings together in his metaphors usually come from the media, San Narciso's urban 'circuitry' being one clear example, and Pynchon makes comic capital out of the media's capacity to take over an individual. McLuhan declares: 'In this electric age we see ourselves being translated more and more into information' and finds it a constant source of irony that information systems begin as extensions of man but bend solipsistically inwards to translate his environment more and more into versions of himself.[38] In a sense this tendency is a result of McLuhan's constant underestimation of content rather than a provable fact, but his assertion relates directly to Pynchon's continuation of a source of humour from the Whole Sick Crew. The media dominate secondary characters, feeding their obsessions. When Hilarius goes berserk a TV crew arrive almost as quickly as the police, determined to translate his mania into news as soon as possible. Oedipa's lawyer Roseman hates and envies Perry Mason to the extent of drawing up an indictment against him. Metzger is an actor turned lawyer participating in a film 'based loosely' on his career and starring Manny di Presso, a lawyer turned actor who turns out subsequently to have reverted to being a lawyer. The spiral in and out of the media comically prevents any of these characters from having clear borders. Roseman is obsessed with private envies, Mucho's style as DJ is being adjusted to meet what his teenage audience want, and so on.

Since character here is being defined by media, verging on the transformation asserted by McLuhan, we need to turn to the concept of informational entropy which several critics have argued is crucial to this novel. By far the best discussion of this area is an article by Anne Mangel where she examines the importance of Maxwell's Demon and argues that Oedipa's 'clues' yield yet more 'clues' without conclusion, that Oedipa's perception of information increases entropy and that the very transmission of information results in its destruction.[39] In other words it is one of the main ironies of *Lot 49* that the more sensitive Oedipa becomes to information the more chaotic that information becomes. In a whole variety of ways the communication process breaks down entropically towards total disorder. For one thing characters are notoriously redundant as sources of information (Mr. Thoth rambles hopelessly, Mucho's language collapses, and so on); for another sources are either questioned or withdrawn. Or a source could proliferate incredibly. Inverarity becomes the ultimate media personality in only existing *through* the media; Oedipa remembers a telephone call when he mimicked a radio character, she hears of his estate through TV advertisements, and of the Tristero partly through his stamp collection. Information theory also sheds light on Pynchon's fondness for surprise effects since it revolves around predictability. The value of a message is 'bound up with the *unexpected*, the *unforeseeable*, the *original*', so that 'the less likely an event is to happen, the more information does its occurrence represent'.[40] At the same time, however, the more unexpected an event the greater bewilderment it might cause and *Lot 49* exploits the comedy of bewilderment as apparently familiar elements of the Californian scene do startling things. Oedipa's efforts to create order collapse because she cannot even identify the basic rules which would make her information meaningful.

Pynchon draws explicit attention to information theory in one of the most bizarre episodes of the novel. During her visit to Yoyodyne Oedipa hears of an invention called the Nefastis Machine which allegedly can create perpetual motion. It consists of a literal application of James Clerk Maxwell's thought experiment which challenged the second law of thermodynamics. In his study *The Theory of Heat* (1870) Maxwell took the case of a chamber filled with gas and divided into two compartments with a door between them. He then hypothesized that 'if we conceive a being whose faculties are so sharpened that he can follow every molecule in its course, such a being, whose attributes are still as essentially finite as our own, would be able to do what is at present impossible to us' because the being (subsequently called Maxwell's Demon), by separating the slow from the fast molecules, would create a rise in temperature without an expenditure of work. If we substitute items of information for molecules the Demon then becomes a crucial metaphor of the perceptual problems faced by Oedipa, and of the interpretative problems faced by the reader. Anne Mangel has shown that subsequent developments of the Demon-hypothesis by Leo Szilard and others prove that the very act of acquiring information about a system increases that system's entropy.[41]

Apart from this paradox in information theory Maxwell's Demon also represents an ideally efficient sorting process which is obviously not available to Oedipa. Although her faculties too are 'sharpened' the end result is neither efficient nor productive leaving her rather in a state of panicky confusion. In Maxwell's experiment the system is firmly demarcated whereas in the novel systems either seem to proliferate or the very notion of system expands outwards to include more and more aspects of contemporary America. Not only that. The hypothesis of a sorting mechanism occurs inside the system which encloses Oedipa and almost immediately ceases to be a hermeneutic tool but is transformed into a static and enigmatic image – yet another piece of visual information – when Nefastis invites Oedipa to contemplate a photograph of Maxwell (Plate 2). Nefastis himself is anyway an increasingly ludicrous figure who mixes the jargon of spiritualism with scientific terminology and who tries to induce a communication 'at some deep psychic level'. Nefastis (whose name suggests 'impious' or 'wicked') then invites Oedipa to have sex with him while there are news-items on the TV about the Far East, at which point she flees.[42] Ironically Nefastis insists on the very thing which he cannot offer: 'communication is the key!' (72/77). Pynchon simultaneously uses a character to introduce an area of information relevant to the novel's method and at the same time discredits that character as ludicrous. Nefastis proves to be yet another of the obsessives who people Lot 49 and ironically exemplifies the ubiquitous presence of the media in being unable to have sex without technological aid. Even his language in its mixture of the spiritual and secular offers a comic version of a tension within the novel's own style.

4 CALIFORNIA: THE TOPICALITY OF THE NOVEL

Nefastis is only one of the many strange characters Oedipa meets as she travels around California. The self-obsession of Nefastis, Roseman, Hilarius and others (most of whose very names alert us to their ludicrous status) prevents any impression of a corporate life in America from emerging. These characters have withdrawn from the establishment in order to circle endlessly around their pet preoccupations. Any organizations which the disaffected create also fall victim to Pynchon's ironic humour in being politically undefinable (the Peter Pinguid Society is so far to the right that it resembles the extreme left), paradoxical (the Inamorati Anonymous) or ambiguously absurd (is WASTE actually communicating anything?). Pynchon thus hints constantly at an underground without specifying any clear group or programme. Rather the very notion of underground seems to be used almost as a metaphor of the teeming varied life which America's public images of itself neglect. 'Revelations' come to refer to hints of this other America lying behind superficial appearances.

The landscape of *Lot 49* is essentially man-made. All the details of urban sprawl both tease Oedipa's curiosity and block it, until that is she makes her nocturnal tour of San Francisco. This is articulated in terms of penetrating surfaces: 'the city was hers, as, made up and sleeked so with the customary words and images (cosmopolitan, culture, cable cars) it had not been before' (81/96–7). Oedipa demonstrates a humanizing impulse in her desire to see the life these images conceal and to probe behind the Fangoso Lagoons complex, for instance, to see how and why it was created. Her curiosity cuts across Inverarity's implied mercenary treatment of lots of land as mere commodity to be bought and sold. It also relates closely to Pynchon's interest in things. The scrap-heaps of *V.* stand as ominous emblems of man's future. In *Lot 49* Pynchon probes behind objects trying to locate the life as it were embedded in them. Mucho gives up his job as a car salesman because he can sense too clearly all the suffering and poverty they imply. Similarly Oedipa stares in wonderment at the mattress of a derelict, speculating about the cumulative isolation it embodies. The detritus of the Californian environment thus takes on an almost sacramental quality in containing evidence of life within itself.

Unfortunately Pynchon's refusal to allow the physical details of the environment to remain inert as part of an urban wasteland leads him into rhetorical difficulties. Towards the end of the novel Oedipa loses her bearings and seems to be on the verge of despair. Then she stumbles across a stretch of railway track which stimulates a meditation on the disinherited of America. This section has been attacked by Richard Poirier for having an excessive rhetoric and he rationalizes the discrepancy as follows:

> . . . Pynchon desperately needs to magnify the consciousness of his heroine, if he is to validate her encounter with the Tristero system. Only by doing so can he maintain the possibility that the system is distinguishable from the mystery and enigma of America itself. To say that no distinction exists would be to sacrifice the very rationale of his comic reportage: that he is reporting not evidence about America so much as pockets of eccentricity in it . . .[43]

The passage Poirier is describing is too long to quote in its entirety but makes an explicit effort to generalize Oedipa's experiences in San Narciso out into America. Paradoxically but explicably close to her nadir of depression, the tone of apotheosis is hard to miss as the metaphorical weight of the railway lines grows, Oedipa 'knowing as if maps had been flashed for her on the sky how these tracks ran on into others, others, knowing they laced, deepened, authenticated the great American night, so wide and now so suddenly intense for her' (124/135). Even Pynchon seems to have recognized that his rhetoric was excessive, toning down this sentence.[44] Although as a whole it contains questions which link it with the usual tentative hypotheses of interpretation, the passage includes too many images of drifters, squatters and the poor as if linked by the means of communication. Indeed Pynchon refers to the 'secular miracle of communication', a phrase which is not ironic and hence out of key in a novel at pains to demonstrate the *difficulty* of communicating and the distorting effects of media. The passage is also too categorical in tone in that it suggests an actual community whereas the novel as a whole has constantly rendered any reference to the Tristero as problematic. The notion of underground in *Lot 49* is broad enough to include a motley crew of eccentrics, dissaffected drop-outs as well as poor, in other words such a heterogeneous group that the only thing they have in common might be a contacting out of American life. Thus, if Poirier is right that Pynchon wants to validate the Tristero system here, he is damaging the carefully maintained ambiguity which runs throughout the book. The possibility that it doesn't exist must not be allowed to disappear and this carries with it the corrolary that Oedipa's quest and the novel itself is WASTE.

The rhetorical strain in such passages as the one discussed above grows out of Pynchon's impulse to question American culture by leading his protagonist into socially strange areas. One of the key progressions in this novel is that Oedipa begins by travelling insulated in her car along the freeways. She first sees San Francisco from above, and then gradually descends from this middle-class position into a closer and closer contact with the 'infected city'. Whether we see her nocturnal tour of the city as an extension of tourism or a different kind of strip-tease, Oedipa gets access to Mexican and negro neighbourhoods, to drop-outs, derelicts and urban poor, and the symbolic culmination of this penetration comes when she walks under the freeways. In this section Pynchon uses the metaphor of blood-circulation as if Oedipa is investigating a huge organism, a hint of the teeming life in the city which she never knew existed. One of the key moments in the novel occurs at the end of this night in San Francisco when Oedipa comes across an old man sitting in the entrance of a rooming house. Like all the other poor and disfigured mentioned in *Lot 49*, he is more humanized than the physical grotesques of *V.* which are there primarily to be looked at. The old man is attributed with more of an inner life and, acting on this recognition of a fellow human being Oedipa takes him in her arms. It is a masterly scene because Pynchon does not give in to Oedipa's surge of feeling and underlines her inability to help the man. Even when she takes him into the rooming-house she falls victim to middle-class ironies, imagining herself playing a 'scene' with the offending landlord and playing the lady bountiful in giving the man money. In fact her real wonder grows not from the man himself but obliquely from his mattress when she (as Mucho did with the used cars) imagines the life lying behind it.

An important development in the novel then is that Oedipa discovers an alternative America. In 1962 Michael Harrington published his study of American poverty, *The Other America*, which played an important part in stimulating Johnson's 1964 War on Poverty. Harrington addresses the middle class primarily because 'the ordinary tourist never left the main highway, and today he rides interstate turnpikes' and because 'middle-class women coming in from Suburbia may catch the merest glimpse of the other America on the way to an evening at the theater'.[45] Oedipa would exactly fit both categories. She is a suburban housewife and enters North Beach among a group of tourists. It would of course distort the novel to suggest that it was only or even primarily about social concerns. Harrington's definition of another America is social whereas say Timothy Leary's notion of an underground is quasi-political. Pynchon straddles both senses including a heterogeneous collection of eccentrics as well as the socially ignored. The primary fascination of this mixed group seems to be their avoidance of what is to Pynchon one of the besetting sins of American life – its uniformity.

A new edge of social concern characterizes Pynchon's other writings of the mid-1960s. As we have seen his 1964 story 'The Secret Integration' approaches the question of housing and race obliquely through children's fantasies. The alcoholic negro bass-player McAfee desperately needs help like Oedipa's old man but the children can only give him an opportunity to talk. His nightmare and pathetic attempts to make a long-distance telephone call evoke his isolation and make him take on human stature before he is unceremoniously removed by the local police and reduced back to an object, like the unwanted rubbish which supplies the concluding image of the story.

In 1966 Pynchon made his one and only excursion into journalism when he produced an article on the aftermath of the 1965 Watts riot which makes a useful gloss on the values of *Lot 49*. He wrote the piece partly at the invitation of Kirkpatrick Sale who was then editor of the *New York Times Magazine*, and partly, in the words of the current culture editor, 'from his concern for Watts'.[46] Pynchon knew Sale from his Cornell days when he was editor of the *Daily Sun*. His article, 'A Journey Into The Mind of Watts' appeared in the *NYT Magazine* for 12 June, 1966 and was illustrated with photographs showing police cars cruising the area, street scenes, a dominoe parlour, etc.[47] This article has received comparatively little attention in discussions of Pynchon's fiction, rarely getting more than a passing mention. Of the two critics

who have examined it in some detail – Joseph Slade and William
Plater – both agree that it develops important themes in the
fiction, although Slade is rather uncertain about its journalistic
value, describing in on the same page as 'a skillful piece of
journalism' and 'unremarkable'.[48]

The article begins with a straightforward factual account of how
a negro called Leanard Deadwyler was chased by the police and
shot. It is a strategic opening because this event resembles the
arrest of Marquette Frye for drunken driving which triggered off
the 1965 riots.[49] All the way through the piece Pynchon is raising
the possibility of recurrence and so resists any suggestion that the
situation has improved. Secondly the Deadwyler killing introduces
one of the main themes of the article – the enormous gap between
black and white attitudes. White officialdom dismisses it as an
accident, whereas the blacks of Watts cling on to the possibility
that it was murder. The Deadwyler incident is really the only part
of the article which could be described as straight journalism.
From that point onwards Pynchon gives a broad over-view of the
situation in Watts and uses a number of literary strategies towards
this end.

Firstly there is the question of perspective. Intermittent details
in the Deadwyler narrative suggest that Pynchon is locating his
point of view among the blacks; the coroner's verdict of accidental
death comes 'to no one's surprise'.[50] This is confirmed when the
individual confrontations between police and blacks take place:

> . . . how very often the cop does approach you with his
> revolver ready, so that nothing he does with it can then really
> be accidental; . . . how, especially at night, everything can
> suddenly reduce to a matter of reflexes: your life trembling in
> the crook of a cop's finger because it is dark.   (35)

On one level the 'you' applies to any black out on the streets.
There is no point in Pynchon trying to individualize events since
they fit into a stereotyped pattern. But also the 'you' draws the
reader imaginatively into the dramatic predicament of the blacks.
This is certainly the main polemical thrust of the article. Being
written for the *NYT Magazine* Pynchon must have had a primarily
white readership in mind and therefore throughout his piece
exploits perspective to force some kind of awareness of Watts on
to the reader. Here the awareness focuses on the immediate

threat of shooting. Later Pynchon takes us through the visit an average black youth would make to a welfare officer and his search for a job on an average day. The simple device of the pronoun 'you' plays a large part in inviting the reader to participate imaginatively in these experiences, so as to understand black frustration. Although the article begins predictably with the police, Pynchon moves on to the welfare services and 'the white faces of personnel men' with their 'uniform glaze of suspicion' (80). Here he inverts a racist perspective (they all look alike) and puns ironically on their uniformity and the fact that they represent the forces of law and order. By contrast with the police, the white middle-class ('the little man') exerts a more sinister threat to the blacks in the sense that opposition to black self-expression might be masked by smiles or smothered by well-meaning attitudes.

Pynchon is concerned above all in this article with stereotyped attitudes and he only glances briefly at particular political faults before he begins to indicate how both sides are locked into patterns of behaviour. The exchanges between police and blacks form a kind of tense ritual which may or may not lead to a shooting. The welfare workers are burdened with an anachronistic faith in social improvement which is complicated by reflex reactions to nonconformity, violence, etc. In fact the gloomiest and shrewdest insight of Pynchon's article is that both sides react to situations automatically. Behaviour becomes a matter of physical process ('for every action there is an equal and opposite reaction': 82), so deeply ingrained or dictated by the situation that it scarcely seems available to rational scrutiny. Even the welfare workers are presented as naively urging the young blacks to conform to an essentially white image. We have already seen that this is nothing new in Pynchon's writing. In *V.* Esther has cosmetic surgery on her nose in order to conform to an advertising stereotype of beauty. It is presented ironically as a pleasingly sexual act of violence against herself, basically an *individual* act which links Esther to the other self-obsessed members of the Whole Sick Crew. In 'A Journey' Pynchon's attention has broadened socially in that he recognizes the political and communal consequences of such stereotying. At its worst it can cause murder; at the very least it creates an atmosphere of threat.

Pynchon expresses the gap between the blacks and whites as a contrast between reality and illusion. Once again this is a tactic with a political purpose since it de-mystifies Watts – Pynchon is careful to point out that everything there is out in the open – and it introduces two of the most important analogies in the article. As Plater points out, 'A Journey' develops Pynchon's interest in the tour and in colonialism. Partly this involves him in adopting the stance of a guide: 'Pynchon deliberately builds his fictional world from the facts and artefacts of his reader's experience. In part, he fulfills the tour guide's responsibility for familiarity, but he also demonstrates the confluence of illusion and reality in form'.[51] The very title of the article confirms the analogy with a tour. Watts becomes Raceriotland just as Egypt, Italy, etc. become collectively Baedekerland in *V*. The difference here is that Pynchon tries to undermine the tourist's detachment by his use of perspective and by insisting on the constant presence of violence. The average white view of Watts is 'panoramic' (i.e. again touristic) because it is gained from above, from the Harbor Freeway, and Pynchon invites the reader to make a different kind of actual and imaginative journey, down from the freeway into the streets of Watts. In *Lot 49* Oedipa Maas makes exactly this kind of journey down from the California freeways and out of the insulation of her car. The fact she travels by bus and that she now looks under the freeway and not down from it gives her access to the poor and disinherited of San Francisco. Tourism in Pynchon's works regularly shades over into colonialism. This is why he refers to the police as 'white forces' and the welfare offices as 'the outposts of the establishment'. Watts is an area under siege, 'a siege of persuasion' to conform to white images which is not entirely metaphorical because it is supported by arms.

In contrasting one mentality with another, one landscape with another (the two merge obviously, hence the title). Pynchon emphasizes how ordinary, even in a sense how familiar Watts is with its disused railroad tracks and two-storey houses. Against that he uses Watts as a vantage-point from where he can criticize white California, specifically Los Angeles. This place he defamiliarizes as the creation of mass media images:

> It is basically a white Scene, and illusion is everywhere in it, from the giant aerospace firms that flourish or retrench at the whims of Robert McNamara, to the "action" everybody mills along the Strip on weekends looking for, unaware that they, and their search which will end, usually, unfulfilled, are the only action in town.   (78)

Pynchon does not have the space to develop this suggestion that while California is in the grips of a collective self-mystification. That is taken up and developed in *Lot 49* particularly in the sections dealing with Yoyodyne and the drugs scene. The repeated use in 'A Journey' of terms like 'conditional', 'psychosis', 'reflex' and 'unreality' builds up a cumulative sense that the outside white world is the projections of a collectively diseased psyche. By contrast Pynchon insists on the debris of Watts, the bottles which can break and cut a child's foot. As a landscape Watts has all the actuality that Los Angeles lacks and this impression is created novelistically by a constant stress on *things* – on rubbish, houses, railroad tracks and so on.

The objects which culminate the references to rubbish are the Watts towers, built by Simon Rodia. As Joseph Slade point out, they are a metaphor of the wasted lives in the black ghetto.[52] At first Pynchon seems to dismiss the towers as a private dream or fantasy of their creator. They might be a landmark but they are juxtaposed with the nearby railroad tracks where children break more and more bottles: '. . . Simon Rodia is dead, and now the junk just accumulates' (78). When he describes an Easter festival held in memory of Simon Rodia, he dismisses the 'theatrical and symphonic events' in favour of a kind of art of salvage – the objects left behind from the rioting. These Pynchon describes as 'fine, honest rebirths' and he concludes with the following image: 'In one corner was this old, busted, hollow TV set with a rabbit-ears antenna on top; inside, where its picture tube should have been, gazing out with scorched wiring threaded like electronic ivy among its crevices and sockets, was a human skull. The name of the piece was "The Late, Late, Late Show"' (84). This image fits Pynchon's purposes so exactly that one wonders whether it ever existed. But that doesn't really matter because his article works basically through rhetorical strategies rather than new information. The object makes an artistic gesture of defiance against one instrument of power in the white establishment – the television. It both embodies the debris of Watts and at the same time transforms it into an emblem of impending crisis. In his manipulation of the reader's perspective Pynchon extends Rodia's art, attempting to salvage rhetorically the inhabitants of Watts from being written off as social detritus. His treatment of the same process in *Lot 49* is more ambiguous since Oedipa's discovery of new social possibilities both liberates and disorientates her. Her recognition of America's disinherited and her puzzling over the Tristero look forward to the Displaced Persons of the Zone and the equally ambiguous Counterforce in Pynchon's next novel, *Gravity's Rainbow*.

4

Gravity's Rainbow

Gravity's Rainbow (1973) marks a return to the scale of Pynchon's first novel. Both works use a specific period from recent history – 1956 and the last year of the Second World War – as a base for a broad-ranging examination of western culture.[1] *Gravity's Rainbow* assembles a series of narratives, most prominently that of an American GI named Tyrone Slothrop, around the overt subject of the V-2. However, it quickly becomes apparent that this novel is working simultaneously on multiple levels so that the desire to construct the V-2 and subsequently collect data on it involves a Conradian regression into the ancestral unconscious of the novel's main characters. The astonishingly extensive references which underpin these narratives have been recognized by Edward Mendelson who locates *Gravity's Rainbow* within a tradition of encyclopaedic narrative which includes *Don Quixote*, *Moby-Dick* and *Ulysses*. This tradition, he argues characterstically involves a concentration on technology (in this case ballistics), an encyclopedic range of styles and linguistic diversity.[2] Mendelson's category offers a useful warning to the reader not to expect organic unity in this novel, not to be dismayed by its discontinuities and startling shifts in register.

Unlike *V.*, *Gravity's Rainbow* offers no impression of orderliness through titled chapters. In Pynchon's first novel the mock-picaresque chapter-headings – also used by Richard Fariña, the dedicatee of *Gravity's Rainbow*, among other American novelists – comically distance the reader from the absurd sequences which they introduce. By contrast *Gravity's Rainbow* consists of 73 chapters grouped into four sections.[3] The first, 'Beyond the Zero', takes place mainly in England during the last months of 1944, the months of the V-2 bombardment, and raises questions about the nature of death. The second, 'Un Perm' [i.e. 'permission' or leave] au Casino Hermann Goering', is set in the south of France and partly concerns Slothrop's instruction in rocket technology. This section, as M. R. Siegel declares, 'suggests the gambling-like laws of randomness that govern events in an apparently perverse world'.[4] The third and longest section, 'In the Zone' drastically increases the reader's disorientation – hence its epigraph from *The Wizard of Oz* ("Toto, I have a feeling we're not in Kansas any more. . . .") – by multiplying the narrative and thematic strands. On a literal level the Zone represents Germany in that temporary state of flux between Nazi collapse and Allied partition, but as we shall see the Zone is also a place of origins, a mythic as well as geographical area. The concluding section, 'The Counterforce,' synchronizes the disintegration of Slothrop with a progressive dismantling of the novel's own images and themes.

Gravity's Rainbow is constructed on the basis of a worldview that even the most diverse cultural and natural phenomena are interconnected. The repeated metaphors of its own assembly are the lattice and the mosaic. Fictional plots shade into historical and scientific ones, and thereby raise a staggering critical problem. Richard Poirier expresses this problem in the following way: '. . . he [Pynchon] proposes that any effort to sort out these plots must itself depend on an analytical method which, both in its derivations and in its execution, is probably part of some systematic plot against free forms of life'.[5] In other words critical analysis will by its very nature work against the values implicit in Gravity's Rainbow whose rhetoric and associational method are peculiarly resistant to discussion. The critical reader is thus forced to choose between the unacceptable option of silence and the inevitably distorting effects of separating out different aspects of the novel for examination. The latter is the course which most critics have followed to date and which will be followed in this chapter.

1   CHARACTERIZATION: SLOTHROP'S PROGRESS

The question of character has been handled gingerly by Pynchon's critics as if either anachronistic or irrelevant to the concerns of *Gravity's Rainbow*. M. R. Siegel has described the novel's characters as projections of the narrator and C. S. Pyuen has declared that 'each character proceeds to seek meaning according to the particular mode of consciousness he represents'.[6] In fact the process of characterization is rather more complex than either of these propositions suggests. In *V.* Pynchon's characters for the most part act out the necessities of their own comic roles. In *Lot 49* Oedipa, initially a ludicrous stereotype, is gradually liberated and put more at risk by the thrust of events. She thus represents a direction which Pynchon's fiction is taking away from 1960s absurdism towards a rather different mode. It is significant that the section of *V.* which he uses most extensively in *Gravity's Rainbow* – 'Mondaugen's Story' – is also the least comic. Pynchon removes the ironic gap created in his first novel by an impassive narrative stance by drawing the reader into the destinies of his dozen main characters through immediate and concrete description. The love-affair between Roger Mexico, a statistician and Jessica Swanlake is one of the key relationships in the book, representing a possibility that is yearned for by other characters. But Pynchon constantly reminds the reader of their vulnerability, at the end of chapter 9 for instance, where they convert an anxious discussion of pre-war memories into play:

> "And one cried wee, wee, wee all the way –" Jessica breaking down in a giggle as he reaches for the spot along her sweatered flank he knows she can't bear to be tickled in. She hunches, squirming out of the way as he rolls past [. . .] But a rocket has suddenly struck [. . . .] Their hearts pound. Eardrums brushed taut by the overpressure ring in pain. The invisible train rushes away close over the rooftop. . . . They sit still as the painted dogs now, silent, oddly unable to touch.[7]

Speech, gesture and above all contact are suspended by the rocket's thunderclap. Roger and Jessica try to withdraw from the war into a separate intimate space but quite simply the war will not let them. The scene previously full of movement now freezes into immobility. The details of movement convince us that these characters are acting on feelings substantial enough to deny that they are mere puppets. All the major characters in the novel, form relationships out of need. The various makeshift forms of love offer temporary respites from the war but never smother the fear of isolation. Edward Pointsman, a Pavlovian scientist, channels love into his work; hence his only direct sexual experience is with one of his employees. Franz Pökler, a German rocket-technician obsessively loves his daughter as if she will carry him back to childhood; and so on. Love throughout the novel is a term applied to characters' efforts to form contacts with others and sooner or later all fail or are betrayed. Michael Seidel has pointed out that the scenes of love are exempt from satire and seem to be 'vestiges from forgotten novelistic worlds'.[8] The episodes seem old-fashioned because they temporarily give the illusion of autonomous existence to the characters, and temporarily fend off the pressures of the war. In the passage quoted above Roger and Jessica are not simply interrupted by the rocket-blast, they are transformed into two-dimensional shapes. Their very reality changes. For such transformations to carry emotional impact the reader must be convinced of the authentic existence of these characters. It is a weakness of *V.* that with the possible exceptions of Mondaugen and Fausto nothing seems to be at stake, whereas in *Gravity's Rainbow* Pynchon's intermittent use of the realistic mode admits a far greater range of feeling and desire in his characters. The main chapter (40) devoted to Franz Pökler, for instance, shows him sitting in a children's amusement park called Zwölfkinder waiting for his daughter. The specific details of place evoke absence and loss, become that is a concrete expression of his own state: 'Twists of faded crepe paper blow along the ground, scuttling over his old shoes [. . .] Storks are asleep among two- and three-legged horses, rustling gear-work and splintered roof of the carousel, their heads jittering with air-currents [. . .]' (398). As the chapter develops we have to revise our reading of this image away from purely individual reference as we realize that the machinery represented an attempt to bureaucratize children's dreams, to organize them within a cultural system. Pökler thus becomes a double victim, of the failure of an individual *and* a collective dream. The pathos of Pökler's fate does not disappear but shades into a larger historical fate. As we shall see, Pynchon blurs the boundaries of character throughout this novel.

Pynchon's characters regularly act under two related impulses – to love and to know. The repeated ironic use of the quest-motif in his first two novels restifies to the presence of this drive which disperses throughout the major characters of *Gravity's Rainbow* as an urge to rectify their own feelings of marginality. The drive to acquire knowledge represents a resistance to the anonymous pressures of war and that is why characters' self-enactment regularly goes hand in hand with arguments about ways of knowing. In Dos Passos' *U.S.A.* characters argue about the true nature of the First World War (that it is a rigged commercial system, for instance) and similar exchanges take place in *Gravity's Rainbow*. But the discussions characteristically push towards the most abstract topics, towards the very basis of perception. Many characters thus personify different ways of interpreting phenomena, even of interpreting the novel itself, and are arranged in the narrative so that no single possibility gets unconditional authority. Pointsman, for instance, argues with associates over the ethnics of experimentation (with Brigadier Pudding; chapter 13), the nature of analysis (with Mexico), and finally internalizes his doubts into a private voice which attacks his own certainty. Pynchon repeatedly pairs characters of opposing viewpoints (Pökler and his wife Leni, Tchitcherine against Wimpe, etc.) to remind the reader of the intellectual issues which each episode raises. Characters' varying capacities to conceptualize these issues expands a technique Pynchon uses in *V*. of dispersing insight through characters. The repeated use of dialogue and question both clarifies issues and simultaneously keeps the reader in a state of uncertainty particularly as the novel shifts away from modes of rational analysis towards gnosticism, zen, tarot and masonic symbolism.

In view of the intellectually representative role which many characters perform it may seem almost contradictory that Pynchon should make Tyrone Slothrop the novel's closest candidate for protagonist, so *un*intellectual. He differs markedly from his historical counterpart Major Robert Staver, who headed the military/General Electric project to retrieve the V-2, by being so disorganised and passive.[9] In effect Slothrop personifies Pynchon's scepticism about the individual's capacity to perform meaningful action and therefore inevitably contrasts with the clean-cut and predictably heroic role which George Peppard plays in the 1964 film about the V-2, *Operation Crossbow*.[10] *Gravity's Rainbow* constantly stresses the passivity which war-time officialdom induces and locates sources of power in organizations rather than individuals – hence the startling reduction of Hitler's importance.

Slothrop's origins clearly lie with the comic victims of sixties black humour. Like Benny Profane he is easy-going, sceptical and a sexual opportunist and like Joseph Heller's Yossarian he uses a bizarre inventiveness to manoeuvre through situations of danger. In Parts I and II of the novel Slothrop is theoretically gathering data about the V-2, but this search jerks abruptly into self-exploration as he discovers information about his own past. From that point (chapter 30) onwards his already weak sense of purpose disappears and his fate turns into a picaresque series of adventures involving the Zone's black market. More and more at the mercy of chance Slothrop finally fragments out of existence. It is crucial to remember, however, that Slothrop is introduced from the very first as a character under observation, in other words as a phenomenon or freak of nature. Apparently his erections are coinciding with rocket-drops and apparently his map of sexual conquests (of which more later) exactly parallels the distribution of V-2 rockets across London. This grotesque linkage undermines our sense of Slothrop's autonomy long before he realizes it – indeed his narrative enacts the gradual loss of self which haunts most of the novel's characters. Part of Slothrop's role then is to embody in a comically heightened form the fears and misfortunes common to all participants in the war. Initially terrified of the rockets, Slothrop later finds a subtler source of fear when the novel shifts to the Riviera, in sensing a conspiracy around him. One by one those around him disappear and he seeks refuge in a sexual relationship with a Dutch double-agent called Katje Borgesius. The broad irony here is that he is performing an action which he hopes will bring physical and emotional relief, i.e. confirm his autonomy, through the very area of self which we know is strangely programmed. Slothrop gradually realizes that he is falling into a 'seductress-and-patsy' pattern (207). His very lovemaking then turns into an attempt to subdue the functionary in Katje which transforms her into a ghastly simulacrum of a human being; [Slothrop] 'watching her face turned $\frac{3}{4}$ away, not even a profile, but the terrible Face That Is No Face, gone too abstract, unreachable' (222). The nervous edge to this relationship compounds Slothrop's mounting panic which climaxes when he discovers that he has been sold as a child for experimentation.

A novel concerned with intelligence agencies will obviously contain examples of disguise but in the case of Slothrop guises or roles take on such prominence that they smother identity.[11] As he moves around the novel's theatre of operations, Slothrop changes dress again and again from that of a British Officer, to a zoot suit and even a pig costume. At times he resembles Gnossos Pappadopoulis, the protagonist of Richard Fariña's novel *Been Down So Long It Looks Like Up to Me* (1966) who struggles for 'exemption' (i.e. detachment) by borrowing roles from comicbooks (Captain Midnight, Superman etc.). Pynchon comments that 'his life is a day-to-day effort to keep earning and maintaining it' and presents it as a constant exercise in bravado or risktaking.[12] Slothrop's roles and costumes carry rather more sinister implications even though at times they foster an illusion of freedom. The zoot suit suggests an analogy with Ralph Ellison's invisible man and hints that Slothrop is heading for a similar limbo state.[13] The Wagnerian costume which Slothrop dons suggests variously a comic-book role (Rocketman), a Wagnerian role and the mythical 'wishing gear' described by Jacob Grimm in his *Teutonic Mythology*[14] (magic boots, a cloak that confers invisibility, etc.). The still later pig costume explicitly represents a sacrificial role for Slothrop. These guises are complexly determined, the very opposite to liberating, and imply the presence of a ubiquitous stage-director choosing these costumes for him.

It is a traditional confirmation of a realistic character's existence for him or her to appear in different contexts, so that we recognize that character's independence of place. In the case of Slothrop the very opposite happens. As he is introduced into different scenarios we recognize different resemblances which undermine his individuality. An escapade in the Mittelwerke (the underground rocket factory in the Harz Mountains) follows a comic chase-pattern; Slothrop's balloon journey across Northern Germany parallels a similar episode in *The Wizard of Oz*. And Slothrop repeatedly finds himself acting out other characters (e.g. Tchitcherine, a Russian intelligence officer; or Max Schlepzig, a German film-actor). Many critics have noted Slothrop's subsequent 'scattering' but in fact he begins to attenuate as soon as he reaches the Zone. It is impossible to take him as a quester except in a negative sense.[15] Pynchon's parallels between his actions and the Orpheus myth, for example, are repeatedly parodic. Orpheus is a traveller (Slothrop has come from America); he is associated with the lyre or harp (Slothrop with the mouth organ or 'harp'); he is in love with Eurydice who is held in the underworld after her death (Slothrop repeatedly forms sexual attachments to partners who either die or are themselves devoted to death); Orpheus descends into the underworld, Slothrop into a toilet and an underground factory; and Orpheus' death at the hands of the Maenads corresponds to Slothrop's scattering. Thus, although Slothrop evades the activities of the British intelligence agency which wants to analyse his relation to the rocket, and in that sense seems to have moved towards freedom, his actions become more and more determined by previous patterns and archetypes.

Pynchon refers insistently to Slothrop's Puritan ancestry and through the metaphor of a reversed film presents his entry into the Zone as a return to his ancestral past ('Signs will find him there in the Zone, and ancestors will reassert themselves': 281).

The biographical dimension to this regression is nightmarish since Slothrop discovers his father has betrayed him, and Slothrop's performance of Teutonic mythic figures pushes him gradually towards death. Local narrative comment sometimes suggests the opposite as in this allusion to midsummer magic when 'fern seed fell in his shoes. He is the invisible youth, the armored changeling, Providence's little pal' (379). This passage precedes Slothrop's capture of Tchitcherine and his collapse into anaesthesia 'hovering coyly over the pit of Death' (383). Subsequently a horse's head functions as an iconic reminder of this theme (436) and when Slothrop joins the 'Anubis' on the River Oder, named after the Egyptian jackal-god who conducted the souls of the dead to the underworld, his fate seems to have been confirmed.[16] At this point we come to a problem in Slothrop's status. Temporarily he becomes something of a local deity, learning a new sense of wonderment at nature which finds expression in a cosmogonic image: '[. . .] Slothrop sees a very thick rainbow here, a stout rainbow cock driven down out of pubic clouds into Earth, green wet valleyed Earth, and his chest fills and he stands crying, not a thing in his head, just feeling natural . . .' (626). Even though the specific image is reversed through an equally sexual representation of the Hiroshima bomb-blast, any suggestion of the reverential in Slothrop contradicts his comic status and also narrative statements like the following: '[. . .] he is to be counted, after all, among the Zone's lost' (470). If Slothrop is a failure his everyman status links him to all the other victims of the war, but he is too consistently a failure and too comic a character to become affirmative. Thomas Schaub notes a similar strain in his role when he links Slothrop to Osiris and then admits that he cannot bear the weight of this correspondence.[17]

The repeated linking of Slothrop to his ancestors in a strategy which Pynchon follows with other characters in this novel. The past exerts a constant and oppressive pressure throughout *Gravity's Rainbow*, a pressure which Pynchon demonstrates through flashbacks. In chapter 14 Katje Borgesius has arrived in London and the sight of an oven triggers off memories of pornographic rituals she used to perform in Nazi-occupied Holland. Her memory slides into the consciousness of her then master Captain Blicero (also known as Lieutenant Weissmann) and later, this time via the notion of commerce, into the experiences of one of her ancestors on Mauritius who helped to exterminate the dodo. The sequence can only be justified in non-realistic terms. Captain Blicero dominates her whole self and so as it were appropriates her consciousness while the 'flashback' to the 17th century clearly demonstrates Pynchon's conviction that no character exists apart from his ancestral past. This is demonstrated repeatedly through Slothrop who represents the last of his line, possessing only tenuous Puritan reflexes. In chapter 40 Pynchon refers to Jung's notion of the collective unconscious in connection with the fluidity of one character's dreams. The individual consciousness, Jung states, 'is in the highest degree influenced by inherited presuppositions. . . . The collective unconscious comprises in itself the psychic life of our ancestors right back to the earliest beginnings'.[18]

Where Jung demonstrates the relevance of mythic patterns to dream-symbolism Pynchon applies the concept of the collective unconscious to a pathological interpretation of the rise of Nazism. The latter emerges as a collective yearning for the primitive and irrational which leads ultimately to death. Once again Jung is probably an influence. Commenting on the revival of the Wotan-cult in the German youth movement (the *Wandervögel*, which Pynchon mentions scathingly in the novel), he diagnoses 'a gradual rejection of reality and a negation of life as it is. This leads in the end to a cult of ecstasy, culminating in the self-dissolution of consciousness in death. . . .'[19] Pynchon too presents a tribal regression to the primitive as a collective neurosis and builds this into his description of Germany which regularly stresses myths, traditions and local folk-lore. It is a signal to the reader than on entering Section III (i.e. on entering the Zone) we are 'past' St. Boniface, the Christian missionary to the German tribes. We now enter an area full of primitive traces – of nature-rituals and witches' sabbaths (on the Brocken particularly). Previous details have prepared us for this development. Pynchon has already mentioned the ancient symbolism of the swastika (100) and the significance of runes (206) which were taught to SS recruits. He then reinforces the symbolism of place by drawing attention to certain German names. The actress Greta Erdmann tells Slothrop that she adopted her present name as part of a *völkisch* code (395) and Pynchon obligingly decodes the SS name which former Lieutenant Weissmann (i.e. 'white man') as adopted – Blicero. This is related to the symbolism of whiteness in the novel since it is a medieval name for death as bleacher (Bleicher). A nexus of associations are built up around the German stems *bleich-/blick-* (meaning both whiten and shine) which appear in the place-name of the Mittelwerke (*Bleicheröde*, a place of death), the pig-deity who Slothrop impersonated (Plechazunga, i.e. 'lightning' in Old High German) and the Nazi coinage Blitz and Blitzkrieg (i.e. lightning war).[20] The connections between mystical radiance, whiteness and destruction thus seem to be embedded in the etymological matrix of the language itself.

It is axiomatic in *Gravity's Rainbow* that behaviour is determined at pre-conscious levels. In that sense Pynchon's original title for the novel, *Mindless Pleasures*, may not necessarily suggest hedonism so much as the tenuous role which the mind plays in human activity.[21] Greta Erdmann and Blicero are as dimly aware of what they are doing as was Wilhelm Hauer, founder of the German Faith Movement, who used the Eddas and Germanic myths for a 'religious renaissance of the nation out of the hereditary foundations of the German race'.[22] Pynchon mimics this preoccupation with origins in his general use of Jacob Grimm's *Teutonic Mythology* and of the Hansel and Gretel story in particular. Grimm is concerned to show the 'deposit from god-myths' in contemporary customs, folk-tales, etc., and notes that the custom of kneeling before the oven is a relic of fire-worship.[23] This is a posture included in the Hansel and Gretel ritual which Blicero forces Katje to act out, driven by the need for a reassuring pattern to stave off the war's contingency. By chapter 40 Greta has been enlisted into Katje's role, this time to be performed on Lüneberg Heath which Blicero has transformed into a private mythic space, an *Ur-Heimat*. Even Blicero himself, under the pressure of this 'hallucinating of the very old', changes into a werewolf 'on into its animal north, to a persistence on the hard edge of death [. . .] (486). Acting out these roles involves impersonation, as Greta realizes, and ultimate self-destruction.

In Blicero Pynchon dramatizes the cost of mythic enactment, of wilfully subduing the self to mystifying rituals drawn from the primitive depths of culture. In Part I of *Gravity's Rainbow* a different but equally disturbing possibility is raised: possession by spirits. A séance at a London club called Snoxall's gives the quite misleading impression that spiritualism is organized and limited only to the adept few, whereas cases of psychic possession occur throughout this section and even linger into concluding chapters where Tchitcherine is 'haunted'. The very notion of possession could confirm the epigraph to 'Beyond the Zero' ('Nature does not know extinction; all it knows is transformation') and implies that death is a point of transition only. This was, for instance, the message from the spirit of Sir Oliver Lodge who addressed members of the Society for Psychical Research (referred to several times in *Gravity's Rainbow*) in a séance of June 1945, admonishing them not to separate the two worlds: 'There is really one world and we must take down these barriers of illusion.'[24] Instead of offering consolation, however, possession intensifies the fears of the war by resembling madness or other-worldly domination. Jessica Swanlake's niece is haunted by her father and recoils in terror from his visitation (176); Jessica herself experiences levitation and an influx of non-rational images; and the medium Carroll Eventyr yields to his 'voices' and is almost swamped by a flood of information.[25] When the spirit of Walter Rathenau speaks during a German séance we could take the event as a metaphor of one of the novel's most persistent themes – the past's pressure on the present – but this would risk rationalizing the phenomena out of existence. Possession represents an invasion of the self and is repeatedly linked to the activities of wartime agencies; the psychological intelligence unit called PISCES, is only partly comic and becomes progressively less so as we see more of its activities and as the symbolism of white begins to form. The particular threat from possession lies in the self's vulnerability at its innermost point.

The various ways in which Pynchon limits the self's autonomy grow out of the literal fact that war is a collective predicament. The opening two pages establish that fact scenically by presenting an evacuation which becomes more and more nightmarish. Instead of enacting liberation the evacuees descend through deeper and deeper levels of poverty towards a literal dead end. The terminology of 'salvation' and 'judgement', the stress on depth and darkness gradually shift the nature of the journey towards an archetypal pattern of domination. It is a weakness that Pynchon tries to attach this sequence to one character's consciousness ('Pirate' Prentice) because it enacts an essentially collective nightmare. The very fact that the opening scene cannot quite be classified (it is *like* a train-journey, *like* the journey of the souls of the dead, and so on) increases its impact and introduces a series of descents – Slothrop's into the Mittelwerke, for instance – which recur throughout the novel. Just as this dream reverberates

into different areas of the novel so Franz Pökler's dream at the
Peenemunde V-2 base shades into Kekulé's famous dream of the
benzene ring and in turn into another nightmarish journey, this
time by bus. The same threatening monitor is present ('Lord of
the Night'), the same helplessness. Pynchon begins this dream-
sequence as follows: 'Pökler may be only witnessing tonight – or
he may really be part of it. He hasn't been shown which it is.
Look at this' (410). As narrator Pynchon has access to his
character's experiences but refuses to specify a meaning which is
not available to Pökler. Rather he functions as a presenter or as
the voice of a collective humanity towards which the individual
consciousnesses of the novel converge. J. Hillis Miller has argued
that the narrative voices of Victorian novels reflect a faith in a
collective mind: 'To write a novel is to identify oneself with this
general consciousness, or rather to actualize a participation in it
which already exists latently by virtue of a man's birth into the
community.'[26] It is exactly this confidence in a community which
Pynchon's voice does *not* reflect. Communities are either vestigial
or memories in a novel where agonized isolation is the norm and
characters' ultimate merging with the narrative voice in no way
mitigates their actual predicaments. It does not even imply any
consolatory view of humanity for as we shall now see, Pynchon's
vision of human action is bleak indeed.

2   CONDITIONING AND BEHAVIOURISM

After working on patients suffering from war-induced neuroses
Freud posited a death-instinct which acted against and even
overcame the pleasure principle.[27] This notion was further
developed by Norman O. Brown in his study *Life Against Death*
(1959) where he demonstrates the universality of repression.
Brown argues that culture, dominated by the death-instinct,
imposes repression on the individual, but also that repression is
built into the individual from his earliest years. There has been
general agreement among Pynchon's critics that Brown's book
exerted a strong influence over *Gravity's Rainbow* particularly in
presenting history and economics as neurosis, and in establishing
a series of connections between money, faeces and blackness.[28] A
minor character at one point in *Gravity's Rainbow* – it is typical of
Pynchon to raise a major possibility through a minor character –

attempts to convince his associates 'that their feelings about blackness were tied to feelings about shit, and feelings about shit to feelings about putrefaction and death' (276). But his associates (momentary surrogates for the reader) refuse to listen. Nevertheless the connections recur again and again in the novel, and raise the appalling possibilities that western culture is devoted to death and the man is a uniquely cursed species, possibilities which pull against the novel's comedy and virtually transform it into a jeremiad.[29]

Although Pynchon repeatedly mocks dualistic schemes as manichean he exploits black/white contrasts to assemble a complex set of associations around each colour. Blackness is linked variously with nightmare, faeces and the devil; whereas whiteness is related to purity, idealism, the north (ice) and bureaucracy (paper). As usual no contrasts are neat in *Gravity's Rainbow* and both colours converge on death, but the blackness of the anus, for example, carries quite different cannotations of humanity than whiteness which suggests transcendence, an attempt to escape from death. The prominence of blackness is nothing new in American literature. It indicates residual traces of Puritan symbolism throughout the nineteenth century and the problematic significances of blackness and its opposite form a major theme in *Moby-Dick*.[30] Pynchon shows an unusually acute awareness in tracing the kind of colour-symbolism to its cultural and psychic roots, and by so doing clarifies the largely unconscious actions of his character. Greta Erdmann, for instance, acts out her own archetype in the town of Bad Karma (an equally bad pun). Dressed in black she tries to drag a boy ('the offering') into a 'black mud pool' (477) as if to take him back into the primal earth. This sinister and farcical, mythic and theatrical travesty of a pagan ritual expresses itself in a racial revulsion ('little piece of Jewish shit') which connects the pool's mud with faeces. it soon becomes evident in *Gravity's Rainbow* that blackness is a symptom which cannot be read with innocence. That is why *King Kong* becomes linked with Christian mythology as 'the legend of the black scapeape we cast down like Lucifer from the tallest erection in the world' (275). Pynchon's calculated sexual pun transforms the film into an expression of fear of animal sexuality which extends to the racial themes of the novel.[31]

Tchitcherine's obsessive search for his black half-brother Enzian, Blicero's fearful coupling with the latter, and Slothrop's dread of negro buggery all articulate projections of the Jungian shadow. The shadow for Jung embodied the repressed and inherited unconscious of the psyche which takes more solid form the more the conscious self tries to ignore it. In a retrospective article on German fascism Jung diagnosed a collective dissociation of the personality whereby the shadow is avoided internally but projected on to 'everything dark, inferior, and culpable *in others*'.[32] Although Pynchon only names the shadow on the last page of the novel he actually appears under many guises as the Lord of the Night, as a dark and threatening figure hovering on the verges of characters' consciousness. After Tchitcherine has assembled information on Enzian he discovers that it has been transferred to his own dossier, a bureaucratic hint that he is in effect compiling information on a part of himself. By the time that Pynchon explicitly raises the question of the significance of blackness (in chapter 38 Tchitcherine wonders 'is there a single root, deeper than anyone has probed, from which Slothrop's Blackwords only appear to flower separately?' 391), he is simply consolidating the implications of earlier pages. Tchitcherine's struggle to understand Slothrop's statements under sodium amytal recall Pointsman's identical efforts in Section I, and suggest a possible way for the reader to engage with the 'black-phenomenon' of the text itself.

Blackness has a clear sexual dimension in the novel also. Joseph Slade has commented that the sado-masochistic episodes in the novel represent 'attempts by characters to break through the boundaries of the individual self and to re-establish the sense of community that an impoverished spirituality has forestalled'.[33] This could stand as an explanation of *all* the sexual activities in the novel since Pynchon does not distinguish morally between the normal and abnormal, but the characters' sexual activities try to form a slighter contact than Slade suggests – even with one more individual. Virtually the only genuine western community evoked in the novel is a kind of socialist commune which Pökler's wife joins in pre-war Germany, a commune where its members are freed from shame and competitiveness. But this is the exception to the general rule that driving needs distort sexuality towards domination (Pointsman's ambitions for his experimental subjects), manipulation (Katje and Slothrop), regression (Pökler's incest with his daughter) and even magic (Geli and Tchitcherine). Like the protagonist of Mailer's *An American Dream* (1965) Pynchon is fascinated by the diversion of eros towards waste. Rojack draws on a related tradition of Protestant symbolism to allegorize the orifices of his German maid Ruta so that her anus represents the devilish and forbidden. Blicero's buggery of Enzian similarly enacts an engagement with evil which heightens as the boy starts uttering the name of God (100). Chapter 25 gives us an even more startling example of this kind of symbolism. Here Brigadier Pudding, an inmate of the White Visitation, works out his guilt at sending men to their deaths in the Passchendale trenches through a pornographic ritual of humiliation. He passes through a series of cells which embody imagistic variations on his state, (death, shame, humiliation, etc.) and then performs urolagnia and coprophagy with Katje acting the role of witch or Domina Nocturna. Within this general dominance of black the Brigadier performs a submission to death where physical disgust takes on a transcendent significance through a stark visual contrast between black and white: 'A dark turd appears out of the crevice, out of the absolute darkness between her white buttocks' (235). By eating Katje's faeces he is partaking of death, symbolically sharing the fate of the men he loved. Paul Fussell has rightly drawn attention to the mixed tones of this complex scene which is 'disgusting, ennobling, and touching, all at once'.[34] The Brigadier's ritual allows a nexus of psychic associations to surface (between mud, faeces, death and the black men who will punish him) which are otherwise heavily censored, ironically he literally follows the fate of his men since he subsequently dies from an overdose of *e. coli*.

The Brigadier's experience is as grotesque as the fantasy induced by Slothrop's first interrogation under drugs. Here the drug releases taboos on his deepest racial and excremental fears and he fantasizes a journey into a toilet. Farcical literary and mythic parallels are suggested with Alice's descent down the rabbit-hole and Orpheus' descent into the underworld, and disgust is this time evoked in comic terms as the hapless Slothrop battles against waves of sewage in the tunnel. Slothrop's fantasy fits into a whole series of references to toilets and excrement which imply an attenuated Puritan disgust at the body. Slothrop's all-American exclamations ('shit', 'crap', etc.) turn into symptoms of repression which Pynchon later converts into comedy by devoting whole sections of the novel to 'explicating' that area of American slang. Toilets too become comic reminders of humanity from the bowl where Pointsman's foot sticks (chapter 7), through the parodic

German toiletship in chapter 42 which burlesques Nazi efficiency, to knockabout comedy (the bomb in the Transvestites' Toilet – 688–90) and the ludicrous use of the toilet as a source of inspiration ('Listening to the Toilet', 694ff.). The prominence of toilets and the repetition of the bodily functions associated with them insist on man's physical vulnerability and also on the inescapability of his physical existence. Standing behind these emphases are Protestant and Romantic attempts to transcend humanity which find their embodiment in Blicero.

As the representative of a diseased Romanticism Blicero should also be related to the novel's parodic allusions to Wagner. Explicit parallels are drawn between the song-contest from *Tannhäuser* and the Mittelwerke episode which David Cowart has interpreted to mean that Slothrop is redeemed.[35] This is an oddly solemn version of an episode which burlesques Wagner into a drunken brawl and obscene limericks on love for machines. The humour here is reductive, deliberately denying the operatic parallels any dignity, just as Pynchon presents Blicero's dreams of transcendence as exercises in coercion, whether Enzian is acting out a role derived from Rilke, or Katje from Hansel and Gretel, or Gottfried from *Lohengrin*. At the end of that opera his namesake appears transfigured in silver garments just as at the end of *Gravity's Rainbow* Blicero launches him dressed in white to his death, in a specially designed V-2. Pynchon's language now combines arousal, marriage and funeral all in one: 'Deathlace is the boy's bridal costume. His smooth feet, bound side by side, are in white satin slippers with white bows. His red nipples are erect' (750). Blicero 'colonizes' his subjects, drawing them into personal fantasies which mimic the apotheoses of German romanticism. At the end of his long monologue in chapter 70 he expresses a desire common to the novel's characters to 'break out' in terms strikingly similar to a climactic passage from Wagner's essay 'Religion and Art' (1880): 'The soul of mankind . . . soars from the abyss of appearances, and, freed from the terrible Category of Cause and Effect, the restless will feels itself bound by itself alone, by itself set free.'[36] To avoid the reader categorizing Blicero too easily Pynchon depicts him relativistically: to Katje he is a 'dark oven', enigmatic but necessary; to the technician Pökler he is an ageing bureaucrat (running part of the V-2 programme); to Gottfried he is lover and master. In spite of his apparent power Blicero is no less driven than the other characters and has an unimpressive physical appearance, being short and myopic like Himmler. His sections revolve around mental sequences and indicate an inverted religious impulse where dread has replaced faith. Blicero is haunted by presences outside the reach of language ('[. . .] beyond was something heaving, stirring, forever below, forever before his words': 101). Never a strong physical presence, Blicero attenuates outwards as a name, a rumour, a principle of domination. He personifies a certain kind of yearning to escape from the disease of the body which is fed by images of rising, as when Rilke's youth climbs the mountains of primal pain at the end of the *Duino Elegies* (Blicero's favourite book), or of transcendence. The latter could be found in the climaxes of Wagner's operas or in the transformations in Rilke's *Sonnets to Orpheus*; Sonnet 12 of Part II combines transcendence ('O be enraptured with flame') and domination ('that projecting spirit, which masters the earthly').[37] The flight of Blicero's ultimate rocket dramatizes in its bizarre apotheosis three strands of desire: the will to master Nature (or gravity specifically), the yearning to rise above the bounds of human life, and the longing for death. Douglas Fowler has complained that Pynchon does not work out Blicero's destiny for us but in fact his fate is so closely tied to Gottfried's and the final launching that once it has taken place he no longer has a separate existence.[38]

Blicero, the rocket-technician Franz Pökler, and others articulate a collective 'dream of flight'. Growing out of childhood stories, films like Fritz's Lang's *Die Frau im Mond* (1929) which overlapped with the actual rocket industry, and the impulse to conquer gravity, this dream resembles spiritual ascension, which is parodied in Slothrop's balloon-journey, and ironically imitated in the experience of being bombed.[39] The spiritual ambiguity of moving upwards is shown at the end of chapter 59 where a certain Lyle Bland, an American businessman and freemason, discovers the mystical richness of the earth and levitates out of existence. Bland proves to be a spiritual elitist, ignoring the earth's accumulated wastes, and Pynchon turns his experience into parody as soon as he dies through a punning allusion to Hobbes' description of human life: Bland's lawyers are 'Salitieri, Poore, Nash, De Brutus, and Short' (591). In any case the direction of his and other ascensions can become confused. Flight in the novel thus becomes a physical form of sublimation which Pynchon, following Norman O. Brown, presents as a repudiation of reality.[40] Hence his juxtaposition of sado-masochism with idealism, and hence, the reference to the 'Apollonian dream' in the pre-launch section towards the end of *Gravity's Rainbow*. The figure of the parabola and the novel's presentation of landings before launches both set up ironic reverberations for the various forms of idealism on which characters act, implying a metaphorical connection between Pynchon's ironic humour and gravity itself. The rocket thus grows out of a certain death-directed cultural context which for Pynchon lies embedded in German Protestantism. For Norman Mailer similarly the moon-rocket of 1969 (directed by Wernher von Braun) carried a similar symbolism, this time of WASP technology: 'wasps were, in the view of Aquarius [Mailer's persona] the most Faustian, barbaric, draconian, progress-oriented and root-destroying people on earth' partly because of their futile efforts to 'deliver themselves from death'.[41] Both writers treat the rocket as symptom. In *Gravity's Rainbow* the ironies are harsher because the rocket dramatizes the gulf between the yearning elect and the vulnerable preterite at the other end of its trajectory.

Like Swift and Henry Miller, Pynchon uses faeces polemically to undermine idealism of all kinds. Once again Norman O. Brown suggests the connections in his chapters on Protestant imagery which 'reveals the anality behind the sublimation'.[42] In the case of Blicero Pynchon presents his sexual rituals from Katje's point of view (i.e. from the point of view of someone only partially committed to them) and reveals them as primarily physical: '[. . .] Captain Blicero plugged into Gottfried's upended asshole and the Italian at the same time into his pretty mouth' (94). Pynchon does not strike a censorious stance towards Blicero but insists on the physicality of his needs. The emphasis throughout *Gravity's Rainbow* on man's sexual needs, his senses of taste and smell, and on his least dignified bodily functions relocates man within nature rather than poised arrogantly above it. Anality and faeces are both synecdoche and bathos; they tie in with the downward pull of gravity which brings the parabola of flight inevitably back to earth. What Thomas Schaub rightly calls the novel's 'complex determinism' grows partly out of Pynchon's application of Norman O. Brown's proposition that man is caught in a double bind: 'the essence of society is repression of the individual, and the essence of the individual is repression of himself'.[43] As we shall see the novel's comedy often revolves around bursts of disorder where the repressive systems of wartime bureaucracy are temporarily disrupted. But the pressure is internal as well as external and Pynchon's use of ellipses suggest the lack of finality in thought as if censoring processes are taking place within the self. Thought then is represented through vectors, as a pointing towards meaning. When Slothrop is waiting for documents in Zürich he falls asleep; Pynchon explicitly points out the nature of his dreams: '[. . .] step by step he, It, the Repressed, approaches . . . *waitaminute* up out of sleep, face naked, turning to the foreign gravestones, *the what*? *what was it* . . . back again, almost to it, up again . . . (268). The self seems temporarily split into scrutinizing consciousness and a threatening unconscious entity just out of reach. The ellipses here and in other characters' thought-sequences recede towards the lowest depths of the self. Only late in the novel (after repeated descents) is a childhood scenario outlined through a set of sensations suggesting oedipal feelings, fetishism and submission: '[. . .] when you were first learning to crawl, it was her calves and feet you saw the most of – they replaced her breasts as sources of strength, as you learned the smell of her leather shoes [. . .]' (736). Partly by reference to the primal mother, partly through the second-person pronoun, the reader becomes implicated in a general human predisposition towards sado-masochism which makes it impossible to take a moralistic attitude towards characters like the Brigadier and even Blicero. Thus predisposition is one sign of conditioning and at this point we must turn to Pavlov's presence in *Gravity's Rainbow*.

Named after a switching mechanism, Edward Pointsman is introduced into the novel as 'the Pavlovian'.[44] He personifies one possibility of control, namely experimentation, and represents all the limitations of behaviourism. He is the spokesman for a certain kind of analysis (cause and effect) and is associated with different forms of personality measurement.[45] Although through Pointsman Pavlov's presence dominates Section I of the novel it is important to recognize the ways in which Pynchon prevents Pointsman from taking on authoritative status. He is regularly seen with spokesmen for opposing points of view (Mexico, the Brigadier, Gwenhidwy and even his colleague Spectro). Our first absurd view of him stumbling around a bomb-side with his foot stuck in a lavatory bowl pulls against the intellectual weight of his beliefs. Pointsman's attention is drawn to Slothrop because the phenomenon of his erection threatens the scientist's orderly sense of reality. As usual Pynchon draws on actuality in presenting

Slothrop's 'symptoms' as sexual and in comparing him to J. B. Watson's infant Albert (84). The experiments had planned a form of 'reconditioning' using 'as a final resort the sex organs.'[46] Pavlov also used castrates in his work and so it is historically consistent (as well as the most satisfying mistake in the novel) for the fascist racist Major Duane Marvy to be castrated instead of Slothrop. In the event Slothrop eludes rational explanation. Part of his function is to pose as an enigma for the self-styled analysts of Section I. Pointsman is not alone in his puzzlement, only the most single-minded in trying to pursue his investigations to their conclusion. However, even his mentor recognized the way in which conditioned reflexes could outrage our sense of cause-and-effect in the fourth or ultraparadoxical phase which Pavlov describes as follows:

> We cannot therefore judge the degree of extinction only by the magnitude of the reflex or its absence, since there can still be a silent extinction beyond the zero. This statement rests upon the fact that a continued repetition of an extinguished stimulus beyond the zero of the positive reflex deepens the extinction still further.[47]

Pynchon quotes the first of these sentences in the novel and it supplies the title for Section I. Pavlov elsewhere describes this phase as a 'perversion of effects' since a negative stimulus produces a positive result. Similarly Slothrop's physical link with the V-2 disturbs the advocates of cause-and-effect because the rocket was only heard arriving after it exploded. In other words the stimulus (if we accept that terminology at all) either succeeds or coincides with its reflex. Pynchon ingeniously borrows Pavlov's own words to subvert his disciple's common-sense notion of sequence, a tactic which he uses several times in the novel.[48]

Pynchon carefully specifies enough similarities to suggest that Pointsman is a second Pavlov, but he is actually a study in imitation and ultimate failure.[49] It is impossible to consider him the villain of the book because he too falls prey to the prevailing fears of the time. Chapter 17 gives an internal view of Pointsman's nightmares where the deep-level images contradict his surface rationalism. Indeed he clings more and more to the abstract nouns of Pavlov's analysis to stave off his growing superstition that there is a curse attached to the owners of Pavlov's book, his

Lectures on Conditioned Reflexes. 'Beyond the Zero' is saturated with endings and Pointsman imagines the nerve-centres of his cortex being progressively extinguished. By Section II his institution has virtually collapsed as has his rationality. Opposites, previously crucial to his intellectual distinctions, now fall together as he begins to hallucinate an aggressive voice (a kind of anti-Pointsman) which deflates his labours to the level of popular melodrama by quoting from one of the Fu Manchu tales.

Contrasted with Pointsman's manic but futile pursuit of cause and effect stands Roger Mexico the statistician. Statistics offer him a means of negotiating the terrors of the V-2 bombardment by partially demystifying the distribution of rocket strikes. He embodies a capacity to live with uncertainty which marginally reduces his susceptibility to fear without every implying that he is exempt from the general predicament. In other words the contrast between causality and statistics is by no means only a matter of mathematics. It even takes on an erotic dimension. Mexico's capacity to love Jessica – a crucial emotional focus in the novel – represents an impulse which temporarily fulfils itself whereas Pointsman diverts eros into his work and specifically into a lust to dominate his experimental subjects. Pointsman represents an increasingly discredited drive towards control whereas Mexico represents a more open possibility. As Joel D. Black rightly puts it, 'Roger Mexico's secular creed of statistics is a way of breaking out of the closed, deterministic economy of Calvinist exchange.'[50] But no character in *Gravity's Rainbow* can break out and survive intact. The armistice ends Mexico's relationship with Jessica. We should also recognize that he performs an important role in alerting the reader to the related notions of probability and frequency of occurrence. Although the very concept of measurement is brought into question in Part I ('Beyond the Zero' statistically could mean beyond an infinitely rare event), Mexico's way of scrutinizing events proves to be far more useful than Pointsman's linear cause and effect.

In Section II of the novel Pynchon gradually shifts emphasis off the psychological on to commerce and it is appropriate for Pointsman to virtually disappear from the novel at this point. An equivalent shift has taken place in Slothrop's significance as he moves from psychological freak to intellectual prize. Pointsman's presence, however, has helped to alert the reader to a certain lexical set which revolves around the concept of conditioning. The main terms are; 'reflex', 'mosaic' (of the nervous system or cortex), 'maze' (from behaviouristic experiments), and 'labyrinth', the latter three functioning as reflexive metaphors of the novel's own assembly. Pointsman may be forgotten but reflexes never are. Slothrop after all comically reminds the reader of the sexual reflex. The notion of conditioning reinforces the determining nature of psycho-cultural patterns in the characters' behaviour. An anonymous member of the French underworld in Nice tells Slothrop '"we have to play the patterns. There must be a pattern you're in, right now"' (257), and this assertion binds together his own reflexes, the sado-masochistic combinations Blicero uses and, for instance, 'Pirate' Prentice's orgasmic reaction to an erotic drawing in chapter 12. Pynchon presents sexual fantasy in quasi-political terms, work as sexual sublimation and even music as a political phenomena, thus forcing the reader to admit a continuity between apparently quite diverse areas of culture.[51] At the end of chapter 39 Pynchon tries half-seriously to diagnose the stimulative effect of women's stocking-tops and does so by relating then to singular points – on mathematical curves, at the top of cathedral spires and so on. This characteristically lateral explanation leads to further puzzles and questions; '. . . In each case the change from point to no-point carries a luminosity and enigma [. . .] Do all these points imply, like the Rocket's, an annihilation?' (396). It is partly an intellectual *tour de force* to suggest that stocking-tops might be related to a symbolism of death, but completely in keeping with the procedures of the novel which regularly proposes connections between the least obvious materials.

A crucial part of his characters' environment consists of film and Pynchon repeatedly demonstrates that the cinema has a determining effect on behaviour and patterns of fantasy. In the case of 'Pirate' Prentice mentioned above the drawing is both cinematic (in a 'De Mille set': 71) and explicitly located within a context of conditioned reflexes. Characters repeatedly act out cinematic roles so that their behaviour ceases to be individually expressive and resembles a set of routines, of culturally determined patterns. The most complex example of this determinism, one much examined by Pynchon's critics, occurs in chapter 39 where Slothrop regains consciousness from his second sodium amytal interrogation in an abandoned film studio. This location draws on Siegfried Kracauer's thesis that 'what films reflect are not so much explicit credos as psychological dispositions – those deep layers of collective mentality which extend more or less below the dimension of consciousness'.[52] Slothrop surfaces into the theatrical enactment of cinematic roles since he, under his current alias of Max Schlepzig (itself a Nazi 'folk'-name), meets a German actress named Greta Erdmann who invites him to repeat a whipping routine she used to perform with Schlepzig. Layer upon layer of theatre accumulates in this bizarre scene which has real sexual consequences as Pynchon slides into the next chapter opening with Franz Pökler's procreation of his daughter. He can only do this by temporarily transforming his wife into a proxy Greta. This section marks only one of countless examples of characters leading 'paracinematic' lives, i.e. living through cinematic patterns.

Conditioning, whether cultural or genetic, clearly reduces a character's autonomy and adds another example to the many cases of control which fill *Gravity's Rainbow*. The novel directly bears out Tony Tanner's general assertion that 'the possible nightmare of being totally controlled by unseen agencies and powers is never far away in contemporary American fiction'.[53] These threatening forces are usually referred to by the catch-all pronoun 'they' which could include anything from political masters to childhood bogey-men, but always forces opposed to the self. This pronoun contrasts strongly with 'you' which Pynchon uses as an inclusive device to unite reader with character, particularly with character as victim. Pynchon's sympathy and perspectives are regularly employed on behalf of the casualties of war to try to rescue them imaginatively from their reduction to anonymity. A brief but crucial juxtaposition of the Mittelwerke factory with piles of corpses from the nearby concentration camp depicts the cost of the rocket programme as the central (but by no means unique) exploitative system of the novel. The generic term which Pynchon applies to the victims of the war and related systems is the 'preterite'.

3 THE PRETERITE: HEREROS, KAZAKH AND OTHERS

In seventeenth-century Puritan terminology the preterite are those passed over by God in his primal scheme. The *Oxford English Dictionary* gives the following example of its use from 1862: 'The Praeterition and consequent perdition of the majority of mankind does no violence to our sense, either of the Divine justice of sovereignty.'[54] *Gravity's Rainbow* diametrically opposes such spiritual elitism and Pynchon draws no distinction between the various systems – technological, political or religious – which consign the mass of humanity to subservient roles. Chapter 54 opens with a lyrical evocation of the Zone's nationalities thrown into a flux ('a great frontierless streaming') which reverses the division into elect and preterite, and concludes with a block of information on a theological treatise written by one of Slothrop's ancestors which explicitly discusses this division. As Matthew Winston first pointed out, Pynchon is drawing on his own family ancestry here. William Pynchon's *The Meritorious Price Of Our Redemption* (1650) attempted to soften the doctrine of predestination and to emphasize Christ's humanity, as a result of which the Massachusetts General Court ordered it to be publicly burnt.[55] Ultimately driven out of the colony William Slothrop/Pynchon in effect joined the preterite himself. Pynchon discredits the seventeenth-century theocracy as a proto-fascistic system and draws on the language of prayer to invite compassion from the reader for Slothrop as he attenuates out of existence; '[. . .] forgive him his numbness, his glozing neutrality' (510).

Since 'preterite' combines both chronological and moral meanings (the neglected or the past) Pynchon evokes sympathy for them through their traces, through the brassière which Jessica Swanlake finds in a bombed house, through the cartloads of corpses removed from Dora concentration camp and most importantly in a scene where Mexico and Jessica attend an Advent service. Critics have commented on the nostalgia which weighs down this set-piece, a nostalgia for communal forms of worship no longer available.[56] The humanity gathered in the church out of a common need – and it is the signs of this humanity (smells, appearance, etc.) which are emphasized – leads into a lyrical evocation of the piles of toothpaste tubes collected for the war effort:

[. . .] here's thousands of old used toothpaste tubes, heaped often to the ceiling, thousands of somber man-mornings made tolerable, transformed to mint fumes and bleak song that left white spots across the quicksilver mirrors from Harrow to Gravesend, thousands of children who pestled foam up out of soft mortars of mouths, who lost easily a thousand times as many

words among the chalkey bubbles – bed-going complaints, timid
announcements of love [. . .]   (130)

The general tendency of the systems Pynchon examines is to
obliterate humanity, to reduce bomb-blasts to a statistical 'event'
or to reduce people to things, to passive functions. In the Advent
passage Pynchon's rhetoric reverses this process, and even
reverses the flow of time by working backwards from the things
to the life lying behind them through a series of appositional
phrases which literally equate the tubes with the human occasion
of their use. As in Whitmanesque list of items the sequence
becomes expansive, opening out to more and more life ('a
thousand times as many words') so that the passage turns into a
wonderfully moving elegy on the humanity that the war seems
bent on destroying. There is a sad irony in this 'poetry of things'
being celebrated as Advent since Pynchon looks *back* to life in the
past. The main problem for his preterite is how to cling on to
humanity in a situation which mocks spiritual hope virtually out
of existence.

Pynchon refers explicitly to several of the familiar victimized
groups of Nazi Germany (the socialists (joined by Leni Pökler),
homosexuals and Jews), but also devotes his main attention to a
group of Herero exiles and the victims of Stalin's enforced literacy
programme in Central Asia. The Hereros had caught Pynchon's
attention when researching on *V.* and for his third novel he
followed through his interest with more reading (see Appendix)
because he saw analogies between the German treatment of the
Hereros, of the Jews, the American treatment of the Indians, and
of the Vietnamese. Pynchon draws on historical evidence that the
Herero began yielding to a collective death-wish by transposing
his survivors, not only into the Zone but into the very army that
was originally responsible for their massacre.[57] Within only about
fifty years then the Herero have passed from tribal unity through
conversion to Christianity *and* colonization (Pynchon blurs these
two processes together) into a state of cultural limbo, belonging
neither to their past nor to a European future.

It is obviously important for Pynchon to weave his Herero
material into *Gravity's Rainbow* and yet there is an equally obvious
difficulty in the reader's unfamiliarity with the tribe. Accordingly
he lays the ground carefully, preparing the reader for the Hereros'

actual appearance with scattered hints of their existence. When Slothrop first encounters them their leader Enzian plays down their oddity, insisting '"We're DP's like everyone else"' (288). Enzian performs a crucial role here in rescuing the Herero sections from being pure information since he dramatizes the fears of his group. A description of the hairs on his neck, for instance shades into a loose associative sequence heading back into memory: [. . .] iron filings about the south pole of his Adam's apple . . . pole . . . axis . . . axle-tree. . . . Tree. . . . Omumborombanga. . . . Mukuru . . . first ancestor . . . Adam . . . still sweating, hands from the waking day gone graceless and numb, he has a minute to drift and remember this time of day back in Südwest [. . .] (321–2). The drift of Enzian's memory becomes largely notional as it enables Pynchon to insert blocks of information about the Hereros' past. It is appropriate to their predicament for these facts to emerge *as information* because the Herero are virtually cut off from their tribal past. Their geographical exile indicates their cultural dispossession within which they cling on to traces of their earlier life. The fragments of Enzian's memory reflect, for example, the ambiguous importance for the Herero of a leather thong they carry – 'it is a bit of the old symbolism they have found useful' (316). Instead of suggesting a living soul (a knotted thong), they suggest rather death as if they, like other groups in the novel, are going through their last stages before extinction, through a mythic primal return (led to Enzian) and tribal suicide (advocated by his rival Ombindi).[58]

Pynchon researched his Herero materials thoroughly and employs quotation from their language, religious names (as in the memory-sequence quoted above) and allusions to their mythology to stress their exile from their own cultural origins.[59] Even their names (Christian, Enzian, Henryk the hare) ironically reflect their colonized status and they have christened themselves the *Erdschweinhöhlers* (i.e. 'dwellers in the aardvark's hole') in bitter mimicry of the totem animal of the poorest Herero. Living in abandoned mine shafts they enact a multiple derivative role: they resemble the dark dwarves of Teutonic mythology (*Erdmänner*), suggest subversive underground forces in the Zone's psychic geography; they anticipate the historical fate of the V-2 documents which were buried in the abandoned mines of the Harz, and in adopting the V-2 as a substitute totem (they search for rocket 0001) they become an appendage of Blicero's own fantasies.[60]

Indeed the whole agony of the Herero revolves around their uncertainty whether they have survived tribal massacres and disease by luck or by design; are they a saved or a cursed remnant? 'If voices have never been our own, if the Zone-Hereros are meant to live in the bosom of the Angel who tried to destroy us in Südwest . . . then: have we been passed over, or have we been chosen for something even more terrible?' (328). Uncertainty and fear are two of the characteristic signs of suffering humanity in *Gravity's Rainbow* and they confirm that the Hereros are participating in a general predicament.

Pynchon skilfully relates the Herero to the major themes of the novel (dispersal, spiritual absence, cultural breakdown, etc.) and by attributing humanity to them works against the inertial pull of the symbolism of blackness which is to attenuate them into repressed fears within the White psyche. There is thus an intrinsic tendency towards colonialism within this area of symbolism which is perhaps why Pynchon chooses the Herero chapter to make theoretical assertions such as the following: 'Colonies are the outhouses of the European soul . . .' (317). Already in *V.* Pynchon had demonstrated that in a colony the restraints of civilization fall away and the primal fear or hatred of the 'other' can find direct expression. Von Trotha takes the censoring initiative on to himself to give his troops moral permission for slaughter. In *Gravity's Rainbow* the notion of colonialism is extended to include other forms of domination: of nature, in an episode set in Mauritius where one of Katje's ancestors participates in the extermination of the dodoes; of language, in Stalin's literacy programme for Central Asia; and of fantasy, in the fate of a group of Argentinian exiles at the hands of a German film-director.

Gerhardt von Göll a Nazi film-maker and black marketeer believes that a 'cosmic design of darkness and light' licenses him to manoeuvre and manipulate people as if the Zone were a huge film set and he the director. As Charles Clerc points out, 'he sees himself as a ubiquitous god figure' whose repeated speech mannerism 'they're not supposed to' suggests a providential arrogance.[61] Believing that his propaganda film about the Schwarzkommando has made them real (the Herero), he agrees to make a film of the nineteenth-century Argentine epic *Martin Fierro*. He appeals to destiny and history;

'It is my mission [. . .] to sow in the Zone seeds of reality. The

historical moment demands this and I can only be its servant.
My images, somehow, have been chosen for incarnation. What
I can do for the Schwarzkommando I can do for your dream of
pampas and sky . . .'   (388)

This masterly pastiche of fascist rhetoric with its appeal to history
and its contradictory claims to humility and leadership, signals
the takeover of the Argentine exiles' dream of acting out
Hernandez' poem. The whole enterprise is deeply ironic since
Martin Fierro (as witness the opening lines: 'Here I'll sit and
sing/to the beat of my guitar') commemorates the transition of an
oral mode into a written one.[62] Von Göll's planned film formally
distances the Argentinians yet again from the original *payada* or
singing-duel which particularly fascinates the German director.
These exiles are obviously introduced as an analogous group to
the Hereros but the analogy is strained since they exemplify the
domination of central government and the characters are so briefly
and ludicrously sketched that nothing seems at stake in their fate.
They are basically there to cement thematic linkages.

The same cannot be said of the relatively self-contained chapter
34 which revolves around Stalin's compulsory introduction of
literacy among the peoples of Central Asia in the 1920s. This is
not merely an autocratic exercise in central government but
essentially a continuation of Kuropatkin's brutal suppression of
the 1916 uprising in the same area. We have already seen
Pynchon's use of Marshall McLuhan in the attention to media in
Lot 49. Now he adapts the latter's belief in the alphabet as 'an
imperial visual net in which the Western world has captured
every oral culture it has met'.[63] Literacy becomes a political tool, a
means of subjugating oral cultures to a central bureaucracy. The
main teacher in the programme, Galina, is described as if she has
literally become an official implement: '[. . .] she is more like the
shape of an alphabet, the procedure for field-stripping a Moisin'
(339). Similarly Pynchon refers to the Central Asian silences which
the alphabet 'cannot fill, cannot liquidate' (341). 'Liquidate'
combines historical accuracy (the campaign was called the Likbez
or 'liquidation of illiteracy') with political inuendo.[64] Such details
make it possible for the reader to view the literacy programme in
isolation because they keep suggesting analogies. Similarly
Pynchon introduces the idiom of Westerns here (during 1916
'thousands of restless natives bit the dust'), a stylistic coding

which points to yet another analogy with the treatments of the American Indians.

If bureaucracy has its sinister side, it is also the occasion for comedy, particularly in Pynchon's depiction of 1927 Plenary Session of the Committee of the New Turkic Alphabet which took place in Baku. One of the advisers to this committee spoke proudly of the fact that this was a historically unique effort to create a new script and added: 'of course both here and in the West there are many learned philologists who say that this is an impossible task, that this is an absurd experiment'.[65] Pynchon compares the introduction of an alphabet to the hubristic construction of organic molecules, a disruption of 'the mortal streaming of human speech' (355); and then manoeuvres the whole event into farce by grotesquely over-individualizing the members of the committee and stressing inter-departmental rivalry. Tchitcherine, the point-of-view character of this chapter, subverts the session into a series of practical jokes by stealing pencils and sawing through chair legs, and it slides into complete slapstick as the Russians are pursued by furious Arabists who see their script as holy.[66]

The final part of the Central Asian section gives a tableau of the oral culture which will be lost by the introduction of the alphabet, this time specifically among the Kazakhs. The episode contains a singing-duel (another link with the Argentine group) and the song of a Kazakh bard or *aqyn*. It is crucial for Pynchon's purposes for him to evoke the communal immediacy of these performances, symbolized by the holistic circle in which the villagers sit. Thomas Winner, Pynchon's main source for this section, comments:

> Oral art constituted the most important and most highly developed means of cultural expression in Kazakh society. All the varied elements of Kazakh life, the people's mores, beliefs, emotions, and ideals, found expression in their folk literature, and above all in the epos.[67]

Winner's study of Kazakh oral art appeared two years before A. B. Lord's *The Singer of Tales* (1960), McLuhan's source, but is very similar in approach. Like Lord he sees oral art as a manifestation of tribal cohesion, the very thing which the Herero have lost and the very thing which the Nazi revival of primitive myth tried to recapture. Pynchon has only a brief scene to make these points emblematically. That is why he does not only evoke the life of the people through key descriptive details, as Javaid Qazi has pointed out, but also their social order: what instruments they use, the reassurance which emanates from the old singer, and so on.[68] The reader gains access to the singing-duel through Tchitcherine who visits the village to transcribe the songs, a circumstance which prophesies the extinction of the culture and also makes it clear that Pynchon is not simply indulging in nostalgia. The historical inevitability that the culture will disappear is offset by a deliberately colloquial non-literary language to chart the step-by-step reactions of the audience. The references to the equivalent singing-duel in *Martin Fierro* work quite differently. There the oral tradition has been extinct too long for any of the Argentine characters to remember it except as part of a literary work.

Pynchon suggests a resistance to bureaucratic and verbal organization in the land itself which seems to possess a numinous quality through metaphors which shift from light to sound and space. The *aqyn's* song articulates this mystery in its stress on far distances, the legendary depths of time and the 'Kirghiz Light' which probably derives from the seventeen strata of heaven in the Kazakh cosmology which were called the 'realm of light'.[69] Edward Mendelson and Maureen Quilligan have rightly drawn attention to the importance of this episode for the whole novel in demonstrating the desacralization of language and in pinpointing 'the loss of a primitive, holistic experience of the cosmos at the moment of original literacy'.[70] It is an irony of the *aqyn's* song that it incorporates an allusion to the legendary founding of Kazakh music at the very point where that culture is doomed.[71] In spite of Tchitcherine's anarchistic detachment from his own official purposes he, like the reader, becomes a helpless spectator of the process.

4   MAN'S FALLEN STATE: COMMERCE AND ITS ANALOGUES

The preterite were, as we have seen, the disposable human material available to ruling groups. Although Pynchon takes care to complicate the moral values suggested in *Gravity's Rainbow*, there is a clear bias throughout the novel against exploitative systems. The lust to dominate, without which these systems would not exist, is a symptom of man's fallen state for the premise of the novel is that modern man lives in a broken postlapsarian world. In *V.* Pynchon implied a hypothetical state of humanity from which man was declining; here man's origins lie buried in the depths of time. Various emblems – a Gothic sun-wheel, The Kazakh communal circle and the layout of a Herero village (see Figure 1) – point towards an Emersonian sense of nostalgia for a lost wholeness (in 'The Over-Soul' the latter writes: 'we live in succession in division, in parts, in particles').[72] The loss of this wholeness is indicated in allusions to the Christian Fall (in Slothrop's ancestory) and to a primal act of scattering (170) or breaking (148). But there is no going back, for instance, to the Hereros' orderly cosmological balances between male and female, north and south. The mandalas which Jung used for a therapeutic reintegration of the personality turn out to be tainted or ambiguous in this novel. The circular sign of the Herero exiles is adapted from the uniform of their conquerors, resembles the launching-switch positions of the V-2, and later attenuates into graffiti.[73]

The gap left by the loss of religion, implied as an ironic absence in *V.*, leads to a collective yearning for an absolute confirmation of characters' own existence and for a dimension exempt from the flux and uncertainty of this world. The Advent service which Jessica Swanlake and Roger Mexico attend (discussed earlier) represents an attempt to fill the hollow space of the church and enacts a common need without making any spiritual affirmation. Several critics, most noticeably Edward Mendelson and Thomas Schaub, have examined Pynchon's use of Mircea Eliade in this context, particularly the latter's discussion of the myth of the eternal return. Eliade states that: 'Through repetition of the cosmogonic act, concrete time, in which the construction takes place, is projected into mythical time, *in illo tempore* when the foundation of the world occurred'.[74] The possibility of meaningful ritual re-enactment is only available to those who have a faith in their own origins whereas *Gravity's Rainbow* assembles an enormous number of endings. Schaub demonstrates convincingly that the Hereros have become tainted by Protestantism and are therefore caught tragically between linear history and cyclical myth. Their efforts to realize spiritual hope in a Second Firing of rocket 00001 (a re-enactment of Blicero's launch) is therefore 'hybrid, as they themselves are hybrid people'.[75]

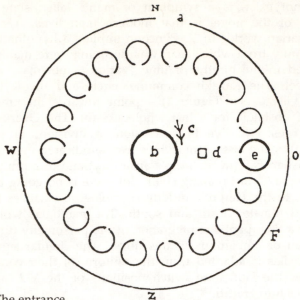

a) The entrance.
b) The calves-pen.
c) *Omumborombonga* Tree or its substitute: The *Omuvapu* bush.
d) *Okuruo:* ashheap where the holy fire burns.
e) Holy hut of the principal wife and of the chief.
f) Thorn hedge.

Figure 1   Diagram of Herero village, from H. G. Luttig's *The Religious System and Social Organization of the Herero*. The southern semi-circle of huts was inhabited by the men, the northern by the women. (cf. *G.R.*, 563).

Eliade helps Pynchon to define an absent Centre which paradoxically by virtue of its absence still attracts characters towards it. The convergence of lines of action on the Zone and of lines of symbolism on the rocket resembles a reversed diaspara and finds articulation in characters' stated desires to return. But the Zone itself only has a temporary existence and fragments into zones moving outwards (519), making the hope of return into an even more elusive possibility. Molly Hite has recently explained the absent Centre as a crucial ordering device in all of Pynchon's fiction, particularly *Gravity's Rainbow*, which demonstrates a 'plenitude of failed revelations'.[76] The novel repeatedly discredits Protestanism for growing out of a loathing of the body, for

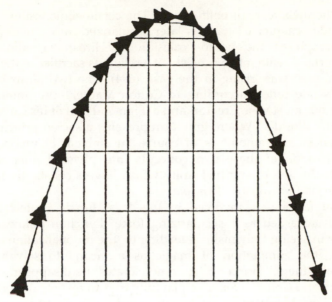

Figure 2   Parabola of the rocket, from Joseph W. Slade's *Thomas Pynchon*. Original ballistics diagrams used the trajectory of cannon balls. Each arbitrary division of the parabola corresponds to a t. i.e. a fragment of time represented spatially. (cf. *G.R.*, 567).

fostering shame and the sense of sin, for being inseparable from commercial activity, and for promoting power-structures through the elect/preterite division. Religion in general appears through inverted images of Death, projections of fear not hope and through ambiguous figures of threat. Angels become harbingers of destruction, seen during the Lübeck bombing raid which triggered off Hitler's programme for the V-1 and V-2 (151), or haunt characters' nightmares of visitation: '[. . .] the Tenth-Elegy angel coming, wingbeats already at the edges of waking, coming to trample spoorless the white marketplace of his own exile . . .' (341). The allusion here is to a line (quoted in German on the same page of the novel) from Rilke's *Duino Elegies* which reads in the translation Pynchon used: 'How an Angel would tread beyond trace their market of comfort.' Rilke explains the Angel in these poems as a being 'who vouches for the recognition of a higher degree of reality in the invisible', who appears terrible to man because he is still tied to the visible.[77] Pynchon tilts the ambiguity towards dread by linking the angel with a whiteness which feeds

Tchitcherine's fears of obliteration. The cosmogonic vision which concludes chapter 63 (626) is later secularized into a newspaper photograph of the bomb-explosion in Hiroshima, and then transformed again into a travesty of a religious sacrifice to the 'pale Virgin' who was 'rising in the east' (694). The two terms of the novel's title reflect according to Cotton Mather, 'the immediate will of our most wise Creator' and a 'Sign and seal of his Covenant with the World'.[78] Where gravity represents a sacred principle of coherence, the rainbow is of course an emblem of union. The secularization of these two concepts into physical phenomena reflects the loss of spiritual unity which hovers constantly in the background of *Gravity's Rainbow*.

What factors are involved in this loss? Firstly Protestantism itself is regarded as a secularizing force. Pynchon follows Max Weber in seeing Calvinism as leading to 'the rationalization of the world, the elimination of magic as a means to salvation'.[79] Ironically then a form of religion accelerates the disappearance of religion and *Gravity's Rainbow* playfully tries to reverse the process by making increasing reference to spirits, dryads and magic in general. In the letter to Thomas Hirsch referred to earlier Pynchon states that German Christianity was the clearest expression of the western analytical tradition (see Appendix). 'Analysis' always carries pejorative connotations in this novel because it implies a proliferation of divisions, a way of dividing in order to control. In the same letter to Hirsch Pynchon cites Leibniz and Gauss as two prime exponents of analysis, the former because he froze motion and segmented it by calculus (Figure 2). In the novel a chain of analogies is set up which includes calculus, German state divisions, German word-formation, and even the step-gables of German houses.[80] Nazi icons like the swastika and runes reflect this fragmentation emblematically. By cross-relating such diverse cultural areas Pynchon even manages to make calculus take on a sinister political significance thanks to its analogical connections with bureaucracy.

Dividing for Pynchon becomes tantamount to bureaucratization and here Max Weber's presence becomes important. He borrows the term 'charisma' from Weber, the latter glossing it to mean 'an extraordinary, supernatural, divine power' which is invested in a hero.[81] The forces of bureaucracy, however, rationalize or routinize charisma into economic or political utility, and thereby, take away its magical power. Pynchon diverts the notion of charisma away from its most obvious application (to the 'führer-principle') on to the V-2 and repeatedly contrasts two broad perspectives on it. The rocket is on the one hand a piece of military hardware, to be perfected and measured; it is on the other hand the closest embodiment of charisma that the novel offers. It is repeatedly discussed in religious terms, linked to the spires of Gothic churches, compared to 'a baby Jesus' (464), and presented as the culmination of 'electro-mysticism' (403–4). It has its devotees in its technicians as well as in the Herero. It also has its shrines (Peenemünde and Nordhausen), its apostolic succession of directors, and appears suddenly out of the sky like a visitation. By describing the rocket as a 'holy text' (520) Pynchon is not indulging in fancy, but rather underlining its cultic symbolism. The V-2 becomes a substitute deity demonstrating its charisma in Weber's sense when it performs randomly, and its routine efficiency when it conforms to its own ballistic equations.

The prime example of exploitation in the novel is the big business cartel, based on bureaucracy, answerable to no national authority, and working on a scale which places it beyond any individual's control. Pynchon's interest is topical and a probable result of the 1960s exposées of the American military–industrial complex. The same year that *Gravity's Rainbow* was published also saw the appearance of William Manchester's book about ITT (*The Sovereign State*) and the ITT-funded coup which toppled Chile's President Allende. Because the novel has traditionally concentrated on individual destinies Pynchon faces an enormous problem in introducing big business into his narrative. One solution is to administer a series of warnings to the reader about the internal momentum of markets (30), the 'real business' of war being 'buying and selling' (105), and about strange lines of power. In the latter case Pynchon sets up a séance where the spirit of Walther Rathenau gives an oracular admonition to his audience (and of course to the reader) that industrial interconnections and even the structure of certain molecules can have political consequences. He concludes: 'You think you know, you cling to your beliefs. But sooner or later you will have to let them go . . .' (167). In this and an earlier séance warnings are met with scepticism but as the reader's sense of possibility changes so detachment becomes more and more difficult to maintain. Forcing an astonishingly extreme meaning on to 'theatre of war', Pynchon proposes early in the novel that the received notion of warfare is an illusion projected in order to distract attention from the commercial dealings which go on behind the scenes.[82] People are reduced to the same level as information – mere items in business transactions. The two key terms which draw attention to the processes involved – 'control' and 'synthesis' – are both raised by Rathenau and embodied in a cynical agent called Wimpe who tries to establish a drugs trade in Russia. In an anonymous 'scientific' tone of voice reminiscent of Burroughs' Dr. Benway he argues that addiction should be brought under control, blended into the market and then fed with synthetic narcotics.[83]

Pynchon takes as his prime example of big business in action the German multinational I. G. Farben which he repeatedly links with arms manufacture. We are never allowed to separate the V-rocket from its commercial matrix (supported by I. G.) nor to view I. G. as a non-political institution. This would be difficult to do historically since it has gone down to fame for its notorious manufacture of Zyklon B and for its Buna-Werke concentration camp/factory on the outskirts of Auschwitz. However, Pynchon scrupulously avoids exploiting such details and concentrates instead on I. G. as a *process*, a steady relentless agglomeration of power through mergers, takeovers and contracts. As Wimpe points out within the novel, I. G. becomes the model of the totalitarian state and Pynchon merely follows history in describing the struggle to take over their intelligence machinery. By referring repeatedly to I. G.'s connections with other companies, the film, chemical and arms industries Pynchon builds up a suspicion in his characters' (and reader's) minds of a super-cartel, what he sign-posts in the text as a 'rocket-cartel' (566) with its tentacles spreading around the globe.[84]

Partly by sheer repetition, partly by the shock of characters' discoveries, Pynchon gives the impression of a politico-economic process taking place which can only be glimpsed and which seems to baffle logic. Slothrop, for instance, suddenly suspects that Shell is straddling the two sides in hostilities, each simultaneously developing weaponry to test on its opponents. By chapter 59, where the American side of these interlocks is being detailed, Pynchon recognizes that these connections must have become rather familiar and incorporates the reader's objections into a mock-dialogue (' – *saw him on*? isn't that a slice of surplus paranoia there, not *quite* justified is it – well, call it [. . .]': 587). Pynchon's teasing refusal to be too categorical reflects the presence of gaps in the reader's knowledge about I. G.'s activities. Since they can only be glimpsed through documents which, as it were, exist outside the boundaries of the text (an impression which Pynchon creates by summarizing the relevant information in a very neutral style), the reader is tantalized by the possibility that more important events are taking place outside the novel then inside it. This impression is partly a result of the partial knowledge of events which is granted to reader and characters alike. In chapter 64 without in any way relinquishing the possibility of a tentacular economic system Pynchon turns conspiracy temporarily into comedy through a pastiche picaresque narrative, 'The Story of Byron the Bulb', based on the eighteenth century 'adventures of a guinea' formula. Byron 'fights' the international light-bulb cartel by surviving all schemes to destroy him.[85] Gradually he discovers the truth about the system, but like Eliot's Tiresias 'he is condemnèd to go on forever, knowing the truth and powerless to change anything' (655). Byron represents in comic form man's passivity before the System he discovers.

Two figures embody the opposing ends of bureaucracy Franz Pökler and Dr. Laszlo Jamf. Pökler joins the rocket programme under the double impetus of a yearning to transcend human life and the failure of his marriage. He exactly fits Wilhelm Reich's thesis in *The Mass Psychology of Fascism* that Hitler drew his support from the sexually repressed masses who willingly collaborated with the forms of authoritarianism. In Pökler's case sexual disappointment leads to a total immersion in his work which later turns into a nightmare:

> [. . .] once or twice, deep in the ephedrine pre-dawns nodding ja, ja, stimmt, ja, for some design you were carrying not in but *on* your head and could feel bobbing, out past your side-vision, bobbing and balanced almost – he would become aware of a drifting away . . . some assumption of Pökler into the calculations, drawings, graphs [. . .] (emphasis Pynchon's).
>
> (405)

The second-person pronoun as usual draws the reader immediately into Pökler's fears until it shifts into the third person as if Pökler has begun to recede from himself, to attenuate into his own technical documents. Pökler's fate is a study in bureaucratic exploitation not technical expertise. Pynchon focuses our attention repeatedly on how Pökler's superior (Blicero/Weissmann) manipulates his emotional needs so as to keep up his productivity. By allowing him a regular visit by his daughter Ilse Blicero builds up a serial sequence which counterfeits Ilse's existence and simultaneously undermines Pökler's certainty that the visitor is his daughter. As Richard Poirier has noted, the effect is like a sequence of cinematic stills which 'frame' Ilse in every sense.[86]

The individual narratives of *Gravity's Rainbow* usually present in detailed form predicaments which extend outwards into the novel as a whole and chapter 40 is no exception. Pökler's loss of self is repeated in Slothrop's discoveries and in many characters' fears of manipulation. In Slothrop's case these fears focus on Laszlo Jamf. In *Lot 49* Pierce Inverarity could be seen as the most important character although he dies before the novel begins. He takes on a sinister force by the frequency and variety of contexts in which his name occurs. Similarly Jamf is hardly seen at all and yet his name constantly reappears in connection with conspiracy and domination. When he is in Switzerland Slothrop goes to Jamf's grave, more precisely to his crypt, and almost has the sense of being visited by his spirit. After his key discovery from his dossier he internalizes Jamf into a nightmarish tyrant. Similarly Pökler transforms his one-time chemistry teacher into a figure of threat who moralizes the discovery of organic chemistry as a second Fall and who then accusingly asks Pökler 'who sent the dream?' (413). It does not matter whether he is specifically referring to Pökler's or Kekulé's but Jamf's appearances in dreams suggest that he can manoeuvre on both sides of the grave.

Partly Pynchon uses simple repetition to surround Jamf's name with mystery, partly he associates him with two kinds of voice. Like the Gaucho in *V*. he models himself on Machiavelli's lion to propose a power politics of chemical bonding: 'move beyond life, toward the inorganic. Here is no fraility, no morality – here is Strength, and the Timeless' (580). Pynchon explicitly links Jamf to pre-war German film characters like the inventor Rothwang (from *Metropolis*) and Dr. Mabuse as possessing a common yearning which ends in death. Briefly it seems that the mad Nazi scientist is not such an improbable figure after all. At his point Jamf has become a caricature fascist. But Jamf's second voice is more important and more sinister. The second time his name appears in the novel is through an AGFA technical brochure advertising a new product. Jamf is closely associated with the anonymous language of business transactions which proves to be more chilling than his manic championing of silicon over carbon. The most convoluted example of such language occurs in the document registering the sale of interests in Slothrop: 'Seller agrees to continue surveillance duties until such time as Schwindel operative can be relieved by purchaser equivalent, acceptability to be determined by seller' (286). Apart from his obvious dehumanization, the entry is in code and such terms as 'surveillance' and 'operative' link the transaction with espionage and imply that the latter is one of particular heightened form of bureaucracy. Jamf here has taken on a compay voice and in tracing out lines of power, Pynchon proceeds to question the traditional Gothic identification of force with an individual such as Montoni or Manfred, whose stature corresponds to their threatening energy. Pynchon implies that this over-humanizes the sources of power in his consistent linking of Jamf with the German business combine I. G. Farben. Both names occur with approximately the same frequency, the latter supplying a context for Jamf who, at best a shadowy figure, repeatedly shades into the company itself.

The outward and visible sign of a culture based on analysis and commerce is the metropolis and Pynchon repeatedly contrasts images of fertile nature with cities in *Gravity's Rainbow*, the latter being repeatedly associated with death or a pseudo-life. London, for example, is described as follows:

> It was one of those great iron afternoons in London the yellow sun being teased apart by a thousand chimneys breathing, fawning upward without shame. This smoke is more than the day's breath, more than dark strength – it is an imperial presence that lives and moves. People were crossing the streets and squares, going everywhere. Busses were grinding off, hundreds of them, down the long concrete viaducts smeared with years' pitiless use and no pleasure, into haze-gray, grease-black, red lead and pale aluminium, between scrap heaps that towered high as blocks of flats, down side-shoving curves into roads clogged with Army convoys. [. . .]   (26)

Pynchon puts a very heavy stress on materials (iron, concrete, etc.) and emotionless movement here as if the whole activity of the city has become mechanical. The grotesque sexuality of the chimneys pulls rhetorically against their inorganic materials. In this description the city has become a generic nexus of power ('imperial') which has no connection with Pynchon's use of actual place-names. It stands as a general emblem of industrialism and – as usually happens with the novel's images – it undergoes a series of transformations which develop its significance. Pynchon's allusions to the city of *Metropolis* imply a fear of a new industrial feudalism; the emphasis on stone and bone in Zürich (268) underlines the city's connections with death; and chapter 67 fills out a futuristic city (the 'Raketen-Stadt') in science-fiction terms. Whereas in *V.* Pynchon used the city street as an image of modern man's estrangement from his own environment, in *Gravity's Rainbow* the city is always shown as the product of political and industrial processes.

In *The Culture of Cities* Lewis Mumford summarizes the phases of urban growth from village community through metropolis to necropolis. In this last phase, he writes, 'war and famine and disease rack both city and countryside. The physical towns become mere shells . . . the streets fall into disrepair and grass grows in the cracks of the pavement. . . . Relapse into the more primitive rural occupations'.[87] Pynchon similarly uses the notion of necropolis to indicate that the cities of western Europe are passing through the last stages of an evolutionary cycle, and to reinforce their symbolic links with commerce (27) and winter death (626). The fate of Berlin is particularly important as it lapses from its fascist order (its 'necropolism of blank alabaster': 372) back into 'organic' shapes. Out of its ruins (Mumford's 'shells') grow trees and grass and its population regresses to a rural nomadic existence huddling round camp-fires. In Section I of the novel we see a metropolis at work; in the Zone the city has been transformed into ruins although there are clear suggestions of industry's capacity to survive the destruction of war (as witnessed in the fate of Krupp).

As the novel moves into the Zone the seasons change from spring into summer and as if to reflect this rebirth of life we repeatedly see Slothrop in rural settings or in close contact with natural creatures – owls, lemmings, pigs, etc. All nature seems to be suffering as a result of the war. Cows are bellowing to be milked; dogs programmed to kill are roaming the countryside; and a troupe of performing chimpanzees get grotesquely drunk on black market vodka. The sheer number of references to seasonal change in the landscape and to animals work polemically against the reduction of nature to a utilitarian commodity and relate to Pynchon's account of technology as a spoliation of nature. J. D. Black has convincingly located Pynchon in a tradition of anti-technological dissent which presents man as the destroyer of a vitalistic earth where even the rocks may have sentience: '. . . he describes a Nature which has been ruthlessly violated, quantified, and technologically transformed by the irreversible, exhaustive processes of History'.[88] The phrase 'Earth's mindbody' (590) suggests the kind of primal unity which has been broken. Technology is partly a specifically masculine impetus: 'Beyond simple steel erection, the Rocket was an entire system *won*, away from the feminine darkness [. . .]' (324: Pynchon's emphasis). Although the Zone is an area of destruction Pynchon's satisfaction at nature's seasonal fertility sharply contrasts his landscape with the 1945 wasteland of John Hawkes' *The Cannibal*. Surreal images such as the following suggest that the ruined town is as dead an organism as the corpses which fill the surrounding countryside: 'The town, without its walls and barricades, though still a camp-site of a thousand years, was as shrivelled in structure and as decomposed as an ox tongue black with ants.'[89] Hawkes grotesquely heightens images of death, decay and pollution whereas Pynchon at times waxes lyrical over nature's reassertion of itself out of the war's destruction. Pynchon's capacity to create lyricism out of such an inhospitable context is as astonishing as his salvaging of comedy from a situation of warfare.

5 THE USES OF COMEDY

The general presence of danger in Section I of the novel, its use of nightmarish effects and repeated stress on mankind's vulnerability to its own creations suggests that *Gravity's Rainbow* belongs to the Gothic mode. The novel seems to present an elegy on doomed humanity, but at the same time Pynchon paradoxically creates comedy out of its situations. Many critics have noticed this dimension to the novel but few have examined it in detail. R. B. Henkle suggests that Pynchon's comedy represents 'the metaphorical reduction of the fearful into the playful. Control of the ominous by converting it imaginatively into a subject for ludicrous parody of all its elements'.[90] Comedy is an extension of the jokes that characters exchange to develop through humour a solidarity against the war. During the pantomime of *Hansel and Gretel* described in chapter 21 (itself a parodic version of Blicero's *Märchen*–routines) Gretel rallies the audience as a V-rocket drops outside with a song that begins: 'Oh, don't let it get you,/it will if they let you [. . .]' (174). The explicit recognition of fear by its conversion into song temporarily mutes that fear. Throughout the novel song, play and comedy in general are the intermittent signs of human resistance to the war. They possess an implicit political dimension in establishing 'we-systems', however briefly, against the exploiting and threatening forces denoted by 'they'.

The first clear example of Pynchon defusing nightmare occurs soon after the opening scene when 'Pirate' Prentice comes up against a giant adenoid in London with a fiendish master plan. Perhaps taking the idea from Adenoid Hynkel in Charlie Chaplin's *The Great Dictator*, Pynchon raises in comic form a possibility that haunts the whole novel: that of domination by an irresistible all-powerful force (Nazis, multinationals, etc.). The scene invites classification in at least two familiar genres (horror movie and musical) which by virtue of their familiarity give the reader temporary relief from the more Gothic effects of nightmare and threat. Similarly the scene in Section II where Slothrop 'rescues' Katje from an octopus seems to be a ludicrous disruption of realistic events, except that this time the humour is more complex. We know that the episode has been staged but Slothrop doesn't so that there is a clear comic gap between the respective awareness of reader and character. We also come to realize that the octopus reifies one of the novel's own metaphors of power-agglomeration ('the octopus IG': 284).[91] In other words both episodes retain the idea of power but divert it into comedy partly because the threatening force can be clearly seen – it is the *un*seen which regularly causes terror in *Gravity's Rainbow*. Critics have pointed out Slothrop's resemblance to a comic-book character (the roles of Plasticman, Superman, etc. feed his fantasies) and a crucial factor underlying responses to cartoons, for instance, is the audience's confidence that the character will survive. When Slothrop, as he thinks, chases someone up a tree on the Riviera, discovers that his branch has been half-sawn through, and then falls to the ground we read the scene (as does Slothrop himself) as a cartoon cliché and laugh because his life does not seem to be at stake. Later in the novel (526) Pynchon explicitly discounts *Schadenfreude*, i.e. the humour growing out of the misfortunes of others, since this would complicate his sympathies for the victims of the war. While it is part of Slothrop's role in the novel to perform prat-falls, to be a *comic* victim, there is at the same time a tense edge to the humour in the octopus or tree-climbing episodes because they revolve around trickery and have been stage-managed by the forces keeping him under surveillance.

Pynchon's comedy plays laterally across the various plots and conspiracies which fill *Gravity's Rainbow,* and delays their working out. Slothrop's search for rocket-data in the Mittlewerke changes into knock-about fun and a chase by the manic racist Major Marvy. The next section of Slothrop's sequence (chapter 33) repeats the chase in an even more light-hearted form, this time by a balloon-flight.[92]

The more Slothrop's purposes attenuate the more easy it is for Pynchon to engross the reader's attention with such local comedy. Briefly we have the illusion of clearly defined 'goodies' fighting 'baddies', even with custard-pies, an impression which cuts across Pynchon's repeated attempts to confuse the reader's sense of sides in the war. The general characteristic of these comic episodes is that their action is naïve and issues have been simplified, thereby granting the reader temporary relief from the general complexities of the novel. It is significant that the two scenes described above frame a particularly dense and serious chapter devoted to the Herero exiles.

Pynchon would not use such extensive comic efforts if he did not find some absurdity in contemporary events. The famous statement on the third line of the novel ('it's all theatre') carries comic connotations as well as suggestions of disguise and Pynchon uses humour anarchistically to highlight or disrupt the war's processes. He parodies bureaucracies of course in acronyms like ACHTUNG and SEZ WHO. He repeatedly burlesques the pomposities of officialdom and directs comedy against institutions and meetings. We have already seen Tchitcherine's disruption of the Soviet alphabet conference. Roger Mexico tries to get revenge on his superiors in PISCES by urinating on their desks and reduces a dinner-party to chaos by playing an obscene foods word-game with Pig Bodine, who Pynchon revives from his first novel. Temporarily these scenes demonstrate an anarchistic exhilaration at breaking down the control of bureaucratic forces. A direct analogy would be with the customs-house scene in the film *Monkey Business* where Harpo Marx seizes one of the rubber stamps and runs amok, stamping anything in sight. Pynchon refers to the Marx Brothers several times in *Gravity's Rainbow* and is clearly sympathetic to their subversive comedy which in his novel he develops into a quasi-political counter-force. The one and only gesture of resistance Slothrop makes is to engage in a 'counter-conspiracy' during his stay on the Riveira, to get Sir Stephen Dodson-Truck so drunk that he will admit he has been sent to observe Slothrop. As his inhibitions drop away Dodson-Truck gives him this confirmation and simultaneously emerges as a victim in his own right, but Pynchon quickly drains off this pathos by turning it into a ribald song – 'The Penis He Thought Was His Own'.[93] Here the comedy is hedged round with broader ironies because although Slothrop scores a temporary victory he has yet to discover his own childhood betrayal. It is anyway an axiom of *Gravity's Rainbow* that power recedes out of sight. When Slothrop discovers links between Shell and both sides of combatants he fantasizes a comic-book raid on Shell-Mex House, only to discover that the central office is empty.

As the adenoid is being introduced in chapter 2 Pynchon briefly evokes a scene from a musical: 'Chorus line of quite nubile young women naughtily attired in Busbies and jack-boots dance around for a bit here' (15). Again and again he suspends the narrative to compose similarly absurd images of performance. 'Loonies on Leave' orchestrates the prevailing madness in Zürich (259); an introductory interlude on space-suits combines operetta, fashion-parade and tour (296–7); and the fraternizing between the armed forces in Cuxhaven develops again into chorus lines (593–4). These intermissions in the action counter the isolating tendencies of Pynchon's stress on plots and paranoia, and draw characters and reader into a collective situation – that of a theatre or cinema during performance. Not only do these images radically alter the tone of the specific situations, they also grant relief from the privacy of reading, locating the reader within an imaginary audience. Even the last words of the novel represent, as Maureen Quilligan has noted, an invitation to communion.[94] By repeatedly theatricalizing his narrative Pynchon is of course playing with his reader's expectations and incorporating them into the text. When he is describing Tchitcherine's father's brief love-affair with a Herero woman the operatic allusion is downright ironic: '[. . .]

even if you'd like a few bars of *Madame Butterfly* about here, she was more probably out hustling or asleep' (351). Here the expectation of pathos is brought to the surface and then blocked, ridiculed by being made explicit. Pynchon demands of his reader a preference for outrageous puns, for comic deflation and a familiarity with certain areas of popular culture (film comedy, comic-books, etc.) to which he refers constantly. The solidarity implied by such references could be related to Pynchon's use of 'dreck' in this novel – i.e. the brand names of commodities, advertising slogans and consumer articles. During a discussion of this general tendency in contemporary fiction Philip Stevick argues that 'naming the object serves to suggest the possibility of a covert indulgence shared by writer and reader.'[95] Stevick cites *Gravity's Rainbow* as the supreme example of fictional 'dreck' and while this method is not intrinsically comic it is certainly related to the direction which Pynchon's comedy takes in establishing a tacit complicity with the reader.

The implicit evocation of an audience is further increased by Slothrop's dialogues with himself and by the narrator's adoption of a comic voice. Slothrop is clearly an anti-hero, bumbling, incompetent and comically lacking in patriotism. At points where he realizes – or rather glimpses – what is going on around him he articulates his thoughts as if speaking aloud. Just after the octopus episode, for instance, he thinks: 'Oh, that was no "found" crab, Ace – no random octopus or girl, uh – uh. Structure and detail come later, but the conniving around him he now feels instantly, in his heart' (188). One problem which Pynchon has with Slothrop revolves around the striking difference in tones between these two sentences. The first is vocal representing Slothrop's speech to himself; the second is to be read and consists of a conventional external narrative description. On the one hand Slothrop emerges as a comic victim, another schlemihl in the mould of Benny Profane; on the other how does Pynchon convince us of the *substance* of his reactions, that he is not *only* comic? This tension emerges again at the crucial point where Slothrop discovers that he has been sold as a child for experimentation. The episode jerks to and fro between melodrama and black humour as Slothrop keeps up an intermittent commentary on his own experiences. His inner voice, which Pynchon fills out with carefully dated slang, proves to be remarkably consistent in contrast with his external speech variations through British English into a whole series of routines. The latter suggest an ironic capacity to stand outside himself, to convert himself into his own audience. Just as Slothrop's various costumes suggest a performance by a quick-change artist, so his comic comments on himself frequently resemble the asides of a vaudeville comedian. After his first interrogation under sodium amytal Slothrop is released in the London streets but notices a change in a comically apologetic way. '. . . don't mean to bitch, folks [. . .]' (114). 'Folks' clearly suggests an audience which Slothrop literally possesses in the sense that he is being watched. But surveillance is aimed at control whereas the reader's observation of Slothrop is not directed towards use at all. The reader's laughter at Slothrop's misfortune is part of his imaginative participation in that character's fate and as often as not in recognizing the comedy involved the reader will take his cue from Slothrop himself. At many points in the novel Slothrop's voice and that of the narrator blur together in idiom. Pynchon is probably indebted to the fiction of Terry Southern and *Portnoy's Complaint* (the latter receives at least one allusion) in devising a very colloquial and heavily emphatic comic voice, such as he uses when explaining the symbolism of a cusp:

> Do you know what the time rate of change *is* at a cusp? *Infinity*, that's what! A-and right across the point, it's minus infinity! How's *that* for a sudden change, eh? [. . .] That's getting hit by lightning, folks. (Pynchon's emphasis)   (664)

Slothrop carries just enough biographical similarities with Pynchon to suggest that he is a partial projection of himself into the fiction so as to balance his intellectualism. By this stage in the novel Slothrop has become a memory, having faded out of the narrative, and Pynchon borrows his nervous stammer and chatty speech-idiom to convert obstruse mathematics almost into comic anecdote.

During one of the more fantastic episodes in Rocket City Pynchon sums up his local effects as a 'nonstop revue' (681) which could also stand for the presence of comedy in the novel as a whole. Comic duos appear and reappear (Mutt and Jeff, Max and Moritz, Speed and Perdoo, etc.); facetious or absurd names like Lloyd Nipple or Säure (i.e. acid) Bummer (a drugs dealer) forcibly distance the reader to observe their actions and words without emotional involvement; stand-up comics go through their routines and comic songs punctuate the text; chorus-lines repeatedly cross the fictitious stage, and so on. There is no end to the sheer variety of theatrical effects which Pynchon manages. It is quite consistent for the novel to end in a theatre, the Orpheus Theatre in Los Angeles, and consistent again for comedy to remind us of political themes. The night-manager of the theatre, Richard M. Zhlubb (i.e. 'shlub' or 'jerk') is a parody of Nixon's paranoia and is known to his friends as 'the Adenoid'. Zhlubb's ludicrous fear of anarchy (in the popularity of the mouth organ) and his collection of audience tapes (a 'stereo rig', as Pynchon puns) revises the image of the theatre towards an exercise of power, in audience manipulation. The process of routinization has converted a western figure of myth into a theatre, and technology has now substituted a pseudo-audience completely under the manager's control.[96]

The ending of the novel thus blends comedy with political anxiety and avoids an overtly affirmative resolution. In general, however, Pynchon's comedy offers escape, temporary relief from the intellectual weight of the novel's materials, without ever breaking the episode's thematic links with those materials. Chapter 15, the Candy Drill, represents a self-contained comic masterpiece which dramatizes Slothrop's American reactions to the most bizarre series of English sweets. It is a section which concentrates in close detail on his reactions to certain taste-stimuli, and weaves a series of comic variations on a by now familiar and ubiquitous theme – reflexes. Pynchon's approach is far from clinical, however, as witnessed by the following lines: 'The meggezone is like being belted in the head with a Swiss Alp. Menthol icicles immediately begin to grow from the roof of Slothrop's mouth. Polar bears seek toenail-holds up the freezing frosty-grape alveolar clusters in his lungs' (118). Pynchon distinguishes his narrative voice here from the 'scientific' observations of Slothrop which have been taking place before this scene by rendering sensation in very concrete images which comically heighten Slothrop's discomfort. Arthur Koestler has described laughter as a luxury reflex because it seems 'unconnected with the struggle for survival' and the reader enjoys the luxury in this episode because Slothrop's sufferings are disconnected from the main urgencies of the novel.[97] The scene fits very well into Section I which is saturated with references to Pavlov and by ingeniously using one kind of reflex (pain) to stimulate another (laughter) Pynchon gives a comic breathing-space away from the solemn absurdities of Pointsman's institution.

Episodes such as these demonstrate a playful inventiveness which relates to one of the novel's most lugubrious themes – repression. Summarizing Johann Huizinga, Norman O. Brown suggests that 'the advance of civilization has repressed the play element in culture'.[98] Pynchon's inventiveness cannot get rid of repression since this is a universal factor in his novel, but at least he can relieve it. By temporarily alienating his reader from his fiction he enables him to laugh at subjects otherwise serious: his deep-lying fear of death, the inauthenticity of his behaviour, and so on. Apart from representing an important possibility of love in the novel, Jessica Swanlake and Roger Mexico also demonstrate a capacity to play; they use film dialogue to each other as if to recognize (as Pynchon points out in a narrative comment) that their relationship conforms to a film stereotype. Pynchon defamiliarizes these stereotyped patterns by playing them off against their context (Slothrop's Western jargon in Berlin) or by mixing words incongruously as in the mock-Western 'Doper's Greed' where the urbane tones of Basil Rathbone clash bizarrely with those of Jewish mother. Play then can destabilize the text of the novel, taking it through a series of increasingly bizarre variations. Chapter 42 would give a clear example of this narrative procedure. It begins with a neutral matter-of-fact description of a German toiletship, a ludicrous embodiment of German bureaucracy's tendency to sub-divide and separate one function from another. Pynchon's description then shades into an even more ludicrous account of toiletship cultism among its proponents which is deflated by a facetious textual aside ('[General, or maybe Admiral, laughter]': 448), and then changed yet again into advice to 'Old warship collectors' (as if military salvage was a hobby). Jealousy between rival G.I.'s is in turn shifted into song, recitative and then back to song. This series of bewildering comic transformations takes place so rapidly it is scarcely possible to articulate them. Pynchon denies the reader a narrative base from which to get his bearings as if the orderliness of the toiletship has provoked an opposingly anarchic inventiveness. It is this inventiveness which Edward Mendelson explains as a carnivalesque mode of writing. Drawing on Mikhail Bakhtin's study of Rabelais, Mendelson suggests that 'Pynchon, like Rabelais, proposes a grotesquerie that governance can never acknowledge, a vital energy that officialdom must always seek to rationalize or destroy.'[99] This helps to explain why, as a result of its continuous association with repressive agencies, the very notion of order becomes discredited as the novel progresses and why Pynchon's textual disruptions become more and more subversive.

6 NARRATIVE FLUX

Pynchon's playfulness alerts us to one of the strangest features of *Gravity's Rainbow* – the fluidity of the text itself. Some of the preceding sections of this chapter could have given a completely misleading impression of stability and orderliness in the novel whereas the experience of reading the word is characterized by the very absence of these qualities. Pynchon's literary strategies such as the extensive use of 'you' or point-of-view characters embed the reader in the text and deny him an over-view. Pointsman, for instance, proves to be as much in a maze as his own rats and the maze supplies a metaphor of the novel's own labyrinthine structure. Pointsman's mentor Pavlov supplies us with an explanation of a mechanism which relates directly to the reader's sense of difficulty in apprehending *Gravity's Rainbow*. He explains reflexes in general as means of preserving an equilibrium with the environment and describes the investigatory reflex as follows: 'It is this reflex which brings about the immediate response in man and animals to the slightest changes in the world around them, so that they immediately orientate their appropriate receptor organ in accordance with the perceptible quality in the agent bringing about the change, making full investigation of it.'[100] In other words the 'what-is-it?' reflex reorientates the perceiver to a changed environment. Pynchon repeats the terminology of behaviourism throughout the novel as if to remind the reader that he too is subject to the same kinds of stimuli. The arrogance of his species blinds Pointsman to his own vulnerability to the unexpected. For the reader also the text becomes a shifting environment within which it becomes more and more difficult for him to orientate himself. The refusal of the Pulitzer jurors to grant Pynchon the prize on the grounds of obscenity and obscurity could be read as demonstrating a hasty disgust-reflex (probably to chapter 25) and a refusal to accept an unfulfilled investigatory reflex.[101]

If the novel's characters converge towards a common humanity and if their behaviour repeatedly shows evidence of being culturally conditioned, then the reader is implicated in a similar predicament, one which Pynchon procedes to exploit by playing games with the reader's expectations. The giant adenoid converts the Gothic expectations of the opening pages into farce and science-fiction, even into a musical, the root idea of conspiracy supplying Pynchon with a continuity on which he can vary the mode of narrative. The constant shifts in genre, the repeated transformations of the text into the non-literary (dream, film, industrial document, etc.) bring the reader's expectations to the surface and force him to revise them. The category of villain, for instance, is implicitly applied to Pointsman and Laszlo Jamf (the evil scientist?) or Blicero (the devil of the Zone?), but the possibility is always undermined so that a company (I. G. Farben) or – even more abstractly – an economic organization (the cartel) comes to focus the fears normally associated with such figures as Fu Manchu.[102] Even narrative continuity is gradually undermined and at some points overtly thwarted as in chapter 37 where our expectations of a collision between a U-boat and an American destroyer are suddenly interrupted as the vessels' courses are wrenched apart in time. The U-boat now becomes an enclosing metaphor of stereotyped mental patterns: '[. . .] what sea is it you have plunged more than once to the bottom of, alerted, full of adrenalin, but caught really, buffaloed under the epistemologies of these threats that paranoid you so down and out, caught in this steel pot [. . .]?' (389). Pynchon demonstrates an astonishing indifference to narrative here as he switches his attention to psychic processes, and in his narrative comments at this point sniggers at the ease with which he has led the reader down a false trail of reactions. These disruptions of the narrative get stronger and stronger as the novel progresses.

If the text is an environment words and images supply the stimuli. We have already noted examples of descents in the novel. The laboratory and the nightmare-journey also offer examples of images which Pynchon obtrusively repeats, always varying their local tone and significance. Similarly he highlights certain words for repeated emphasis such as 'angel' or 'zero'. In the case of the latter the word can connote ultimate endings (the 'Absolute Zero' of the opening scene, or the Zero which the Hereros are hunting) and particularly death or nothingness (Slothrop's crisis of fear over the V-2 takes place at zero longtitude, i.e. Greenwich). The term 'zero' also has a mathematical symbolism again suggesting nothingness. The fact that the Schwarzgerät is numbered 00000 and is fired north into the region of death tends to overshadow more neutral mathematical meanings to the word. Pynchon even contrives to make 'zero' into a verb of its own process: Slothrop realizes that 'there is even more being zeroed in on him from out there than he'd thought [. . .]' (251). It is a brilliant stylistic tour de force that a word which denotes absence should be paradoxically so full of meaning and should support the theme of death so well. Similar 'trigger-words' would be 'cartel' and 'paranoia'. Of the former a correspondent in The New York Times for 1943 wrote: 'the word cartel has become the label for something "bad". As an emotional symbol, it calls for the response of a "secret", "un-American", "contact with foreigners"'.[103] Subtract the chauvinism and this can still stand as an explanation of how Pynchon uses the term to melodramatically highlight the possibility of conspiracy. In the case of paranoia, a much-discussed topic in Pynchon criticism, no one has so far noted how often the word itself appears in Gravity's Rainbow, so much so that the frequency of its occurrence induces the very state to which the word refers.

The recurrence of these words and images teasingly suggests continuities as if repetition were an ordering device, but meanings proliferate outwards. In fact there is a specific kind of repetition in Gravity's Rainbow apparently designed to foster confusion. In chapter 2 Pynchon mentions that the rails have the cross-section of a chess knight (12). In Section II the knight resurfaces as an emblem on a card Slothrop receives from a member of the French underworld (248).[104] Later still we hear about Gerhardt von Göll, alias Der Springer, who 'leaps perpetually [. . .] across the chessboard of the Zone' (376), a phrase which is partly repeated in connection with Franz Pökler (401). Here repetition stylistically implies continuity but then blocks the reader from gaining access to that continuity. A similar process takes place again and again with narrative details. How can Tchitcherine's American horse also be the horse which Greta Erdmann used in a pre-war film (342, 482)? Why does a girl's father disappear from Neukölln which is also the town where a glass-blower takes Byron the Bulb for observation (571, 651)? These recurrences generate an anxiety in the reader by hinting at more connections than can actually be formed.

The impulse to make connections forms part of a predisposition towards paranoia in *Gravity's Rainbow*, a notion which Pynchon uses in a non-pathological sense to mean the conspiratorial organization of events around the self. Paranoia is thus a kind of total ordering and forms the central preoccupation of Section II where it is repeatedly paired with its opposite (contingency). The setting in a casino implies the latter, the events which take place imply the former. Far from being simply 'the last retreat of the Puritan imagination' as Scott Sanders asserts, paranoia proves to be empirically justified in the case of Slothrop and experientially useful to other characters in coping with their fears. As Hendrick Hertzberg and D. C. K. McClelland write, 'paranoia substitutes a rigorous (though false) order for chaos, and at the same time dispels the sense of individual insignificance by making the paranoid the focus of all he sees going on around him – a natural response to the confusion of modern life'.[105] It is an even more natural response to the terrors of war and the melodrama of competing intelligence agencies. Pynchon's series of proverbs for paranoids (perhaps based on Pudd'n-head Wilson's calendar) periodically (and jokingly) remind the reader of a possibility which seems to affront common sense but also opens up a hidden order of history. Moments of discovery are crucial in *Gravity's Rainbow* because they appear to be the epiphanous confirmation of these paranoid fears, whether the moments revolve around apparently trivial details like a strange hair (which Roger Mexico finds in his mouth: 124) or a glimpse of a perfectly working oil refinery (seen by Enzian: 520). Pynchon mockingly sign-posts one such realization (to Tchitcherine) at the end of chapter 56 with a pointing hand in the text, a secularized sign of God which now only points towards unverified possibilities.[106] The repeated references to paranoia sensitize the reader to textual signs and induce in him an urgency comparable to the novel's characters' to strain after certainty. As Thomas Schaub has pointed out, Pynchon's interest in linkage, for reader and character alike, 'becomes a metaphor for the difficulty of knowing from the *inside* whether or not a set of events constitutes a designed plot or is merely coincidental'.[107]

Knowing is an ambition or desire rather than an attainable achievement for the characters of *Gravity's Rainbow* since they are so deeply embedded in the circumstances of their own plot-lines. The reader gradually becomes aware of a lattice of intersections between these plots which does not grant an over-view but does at least remind him of the inadequacy of any one means of explanation. As if to high-light this inadequacy from an early stage in the novel Pynchon repeatedly confronts one explanatory system with its rival; behavioural causation (Pointsman) vs. subject-object patterns reminiscent of Zen (Spectro), and so on. The repeated references to statistics (Poisson and Gaussian distributions), Heisenberg's Uncertainty Principle, Gödel's Theorem and – later still – to different forms of divination build up a commulative subversion of the reader's sense of causality and raise multiple possibilities of arriving at knowledge. At the same time, since there is a continuity between characters' efforts to know and the reader's, Pynchon raises different possible ways of interpreting his own novel, whether from a behavioural stand-point, through Freudian analysis, or through an examination of word-frequencies. All are partial, however. Even when Pynchon alludes to Jung's theory of the collective unconscious (410), he adds a criticism by suggesting a selector-mechanism. And again when calculus, for instance, is used as a metaphor, its applicability is immediately questioned. Dialogue performs the general function of stopping any individual system from being privileged over others. Determination and linear causality are mocked and undermined with the most regularity because the first is closely associated with totalitarianism and the second with the reader's common-sense assumption about explanation.

At one point in Section II Katje voices a sentiment common to most of the novel's characters; '"Beyond them there's so much more, so much none of us know . . ."' (209). The notion of 'beyond' carries crucial implications for the text of the novel. At the end of chapter 31 we leave Slothrop in a laboratory and at the beginning of chapter 33 (the next in his sequence) we see him with Geli Tripping, Tchitcherine's lover. Therefore we infer that during the intervening chapter he has gone back to her. This is of course exactly the sort of inference we might draw when reading a realistic novel, but Pynchon takes this process several steps further. Not only do we see characters intermittently, we also glimpse the activities of the various intelligence agencies which are of course professionally devoted to concealment. Since these agencies wield the power, characters' sense of their own marginality constantly leads them to the conclusion that the crucial events and decisions are being taken elsewhere, somewhere beyond their reach. Pynchon develops our quasi-realistic assumptions of things happening between chapters into a similar suspicion that major processes are taking place off the edges of the text. The repeated catch-all pronoun 'they' points somewhere else, always to agencies beyond the characters' reach. Although Pynchon describes scenes in considerable detail objects take on a surface aspect, like the chairs in the Casino Hermann Goering: 'These are no longer quite outward and visible signs of a game of chance. There is another enterprise here, more real than that, less merciful, and systematically hidden from the likes of Slothrop' (202). There is no ambiguity about the objects themselves but only about their significance. The language of sacramentalism is simply a metaphorical variation on the spatial references to inaccessible meaning.

The notion of 'beyond' denies the novel's text any closure. On the contrary *Gravity's Rainbow* is a work which is constantly referring outside itself. Pynchon quotes actual texts (Pavlov, A. E. Waite, etc.) and fictitious ones. His epigraphs range from actual quotations (to Sections I, II and III) through apparent quotation (71), pseudo-quotation from a fictitious text (83), to facetious quotation from an actual text (357). Like *Ulysses Gravity's Rainbow* also contains allusions to its author's own earlier writings, particularly to 'Mondaugen's Story' from *V.* and to 'The Secret Integration'. To a certain extent these allusions can be explained in quasi-realistic terms as a means of building up a past for Blicero and Slothrop, but when the South-West African materials are being introduced through radio propaganda the broadcaster asks his audience "Remember?" (74). This is an appeal to textual memory which complicates the reader's sense of a clear distinction between the fictional and the real, in this specific case paving the way for the introduction of the Schwarzkommando. Pynchon uses allusion and quotation to blur the boundaries of his text just as he uses historical reference to jolt the reader's sense of possibility. The story of Byron the Bulb begins by establishing an obtrusively fictional narrative (in the picaresque mode, the name of the bulb, etc.) into which Pynchon introduces information about yet another conspiracy 'known as "Phoebus", the international light-bulb cartel, head-quartered in Switzerland' (649). Within a context of apparently fanciful fictional games we suddenly encounter historical fact. The Phoebus S. A. Compagnie Industrielle pour le Développement de l'Eclairage was established in Geneva in 1924 and confirmed in 1935 from where Pynchon takes his ownership figures. It was dominated by General Electric and did possess a virtual world monopoly of light-bulb manufacture.[108] The local context of this information tempts the reader to treat it as fiction but the more or less neutral prose which Pynchon temporarily adopts invites comparison with similar blocks of information on the Herero (chapter 32), the Central Asian Uprising of 1916 (340) and the activities of I. G. Farben. These resemblances in turn include further information of Slothrop's 'sale' and on its economic background related to the American freemason and industrialist Lyle Bland (582). In the latter two cases Pynchon seems to be summarizing actual information on the face of it no less plausible than he summarizes elsewhere except that now historical fact shades imperceptibly into fiction. It is as if Pynchon is challenging the reader to admit a historical possibility which will prevent him from locating the boundary of the novel.

Pynchon is 'democratically receptive to the most common and the most recondite signatures of things'.[109] So wrote Richard Poirier in his review of Gravity's Rainbow, drawing attention to Pynchon's willingness to recognize the various cultural forces which helped to generate the novel. By refusing to close his text, not only in the obviously unresolving ending but throughout the novel, Pynchon places his fiction within its cultural environment. Even within Gravity's Rainbow it makes more sense to talk of multiple texts than any singular one partly because Pynchon has taken 1944–5 as a watershed in the beginning of the cold war which revolves essentially around information rather than combat. His obsessive emphasis on espionage signals a world where representations replace actualities. Hence even the ice patterns on walls become textualized ('the walls read ice': 72) and Slothrop's first interrogation is introduced by a series of stress variations on one repeated phrase: 'Bet you never did the Kenosha Kid' (60–1). Literally everything turns into some kind of text, whether a holy one (the rocket), a film script, a jokingly theatrical 'programme' of nerve-cells (148), or a nightmare search through a dictionary (287). Characters' anxious scrutiny of texts makes reading a central activity within the novel and dramatizes the futile search for the one culminating insight which will make everything clear. As Maureen Quilligan puts it, 'all must be read, interpreted, and perhaps acted upon, for all these signs may be part of the "holy text"'.[110] As the various searches of the novel peter out this possibility seems to recede. The Zone splits into different zones and in Section IV the novel's implicit tendency towards fragmentation is finally realized.

The stylistic signs of the uncertainty which the proliferation of texts creates, are clear to see on almost every page of the novel. Pynchon scrupulously avoids categorical narrative comment, preferring instead to articulate possibilities through questions which draw the reader into the search for meaning. His use of ellipses similarly denies finality and therefore certainty; and he also draws extensively on either/or syntactic patterns, and on deliberately tentative formulations ('perhaps', 'may', etc.). It is quite consistent with this evocation of uncertainty for Pynchon to set up speculative nodes where the continuity of his narrative is suspended so that significances can be enumerated, perhaps on the model of the doubloon episode in *Moby-Dick*. One example of this procedure comes when Slothrop reaches the Mittelwerke and Pynchon speculates about the meaning of the double-ogee tunnel layout (300–2). The speculations cannot be naturalized into any single character's consciousness but are rather related to general themes and areas of the novel's symbolism. Once again Pynchon's narrative comments only extend what his characters do for page 85 lists four possible interpretations of Slothrop's mysterious sexual reflex. Tchitcherine's bemused reaction ('the man is a puzzle': 391) is both typical of other characters' views of Slothrop and hint to the reader that Slothrop poses a comical enigma analogous to other areas of the novel. In spite of the clear textual warning ('but perhaps the colors are only random, uncoded': 19), critics have tended to accept at face value the coincidence between Slothrop's map of sexual conquests and the distribution of rocket-drops over London, but Bernard Duyfhuizen has now shown that this involves the distorting effects of other characters' reading of the map. The issue of Slothrop's map, he argues, points a moral: 'by understanding the unreliability of the map and its readers, we see that the idea of establishing the "pure" text is farcical – another one of Pynchon's pranks on the reader'.[111] It is not simply a matter of jokes at the reader's expense, however. Pynchon refuses to allow his text too categorical an existence because this would imply a more stable reality than his characters glimpse. Instead we get a series of fragments, of partial and distorted views.

Pynchon heightens out sense of insecurity by startlingly changing register, violating our sense of character and questioning the status of the experience under description. When Slothrop arrives at the Mittelwerke his visit shifts from tourism towards pornography, except that the guide offers a visit to a concentration camp instead of filthy postcards. The scene is then shifted yet again towards science-fiction (Rocket-City) but terms such as 'hustles' or 'couturier' disrupt the 'coding' and constantly force the reader to readjust his sense of what is happening. This same kind of process takes place throughout the novel. Pynchon destabilizes the text forcing the reader to revise what has happened previously. Brian McHale (who notes some of the same details as Duyfhuizen) argues that the novel differs from Modernist works in 'deconcretizing' its own narrative and notes that this takes place sometimes with advance warning, sometimes in retrospect and sometimes through local incompatibility.[112] The process he notes is the most extreme manifestation of a general fluidity in the text whereby the status of its elements is constantly shifting. Not only does it become impossible to verify Mrs. Quoad's existence, as McHale notes, but the key documents on the origins of Operation Black Wing (the propaganda scheme to invent the Schwarzkommando) disappear, and characters even deny the existence of Slothrop. An unobtrusive but important series of allusions to the Alice books invites comparison with a world of similar flux where objects constantly change and words slide off their referents. Pynchon's tendency to undermine his own narrative reaches its culmination in the final section of Gravity's Rainbow – 'The Counterforce'.

7   THE COUNTERFORCE

At the end of chapter 52 Katje Borgesius imagines that a counterforce must come into existence as a dialectical probability to oppose the dominant force of the war. The chapter which follows, one of the most mystifying in the novel, investigates this possibility through a surreal location which at first seems hell-like (a place of several levels) and then slides into fairyland fantasy. Roger Mexico supplies the dominant perspective, that of a new arrival bewildered by seeing so many familiar faces in an unfamiliar setting. Terms like 'turn', 'defect' and 'double-agent' suggest a coherent force of political opposition but Pynchon never allows its identity to gell. Note, for instance, his refusal to attribute power:

> Well, if the Counterforce knew better what these categories concealed, they might be in a better position to disarm, de-penis and dismantle the Man. But they don't. Actually they do, but they don't admit it. Sad but true. They are as schizoid, as double-minded in the massive presence of money, as any of the rest of us, and that's the hard fact.   (712)

There is no exemption from a common human predicament and partly for that reason the Counterforce is 'doomed'. But we have already fallen into a trap which Pynchon opens by inviting the reader to over-naturalize this embodiment of resistance to 'Them'. Sometimes the counterforce is capitalized, sometimes not; sometimes it appears to have members, sometimes it emerges as a physical phenomenon, a cross-current in the war. At other points the counterforce shades into the black market, or into the population of the Zone, or into the preterite. Its charismatic hero, John Dillinger, is both romanticized and entangled within layers of fiction since he is shot down outside the Biograph Theatre after seeing a film about a criminal going to his death.[113] In short Pynchon both tempts the reader to attribute an identity to the Counterforce but simultaneously muffles that possibility by elusive, shifting methods of portrayal.

What then is the Counterforce? In the view of what happens to the text of *Gravity's Rainbow* in its concluding section the most useful application of the term within a literary context occurs in J. W. Aldridge's *After the Lost Generation*. Aldridge argues that there are two main processes at work in Dos Passos' *U.S.A.*: there is a gradual corruption and defeat of the characters, and there is also 'the implicit indignation of the harsh, cutting style, which runs persistently counter to the drift of the narrative and comments on it'. Aldridge then adds that 'in the "Camera Eye" and "Biographies" sections the style picks up additional counterforce'.[114] In spite of Aldridge's identification of moral and textual qualities (the non-narrative sections do not simply cut across the others, but halt their drift towards despair) his application of 'counterforce' sheds some light on Pynchon's practice. Critics have generally agreed that Section IV of *Gravity's Rainbow* is the farthest from realism, and as such presents the most extreme cases of alienation-effects like the dog which talks back to its pursuers in a stage-Yiddish accent (44) or Pynchon's wilful interruption of two boats heading for a collision (389). In *U.S.A.* the non-narrative sections of the text are printed separately and given titles which warn the reader what is coming, but in *Gravity's Rainbow* the text is far less orderly and therefore less predictable. It would hardly make sense for a novel devoted to exploring less and less likely interconnections to separate off its different textual strategies. Nevertheless, modifying Aldridge's usage a little, we could propose that the Counterforce suggests the anti-sequential effects of Pynchon's repeated evocations of uncertainty and his drawing of analogies. It suggests the very opposite of orderly linear realistic narrative in other words, and implies that the novel begins to reverse its own assembly. The 'scattering' which Slothrop experiences could be taken as a metaphor for the fate of the text itself.

Section IV is full of the traces of earlier sections of the novel, being haunted by a sense of post-armistice anti-climax as relationships break up and characters begin to attenuate into larger processes. Roger Mexico's sad and comic efforts to get his revenge on the war lead nowhere. Blicero becomes swallowed up into the collective fantasies of the Zone's inhabitants and Tchitcherine learns that he has been 'passed over' by Stalin's bureaucracy. As the characters lose their separate existences an analogous degradation begins to take place in the novel itself. Chapter 62 throws out allusions to previous details and themes (the search for Slothrop, Van der Groov, the discussion of the politics of musical theory, etc.) as if the very text has become preterite, a matter purely of memory. Pynchon now overtly mocks his own fiction, turning his manipulation of characters, as M. R. Siegel interestingly suggests, into a comic radio show between Skippy and Mister Information (644–6).[115] He even turns against his own characters in an extraordinary passage where he declares: 'I am betraying them all . . . the worst of it is that I know what your editors want, *exactly* what they want. I am a traitor. I carry it with me. Your virus' (739). The combined vocabulary of politics and disease suggests that the transaction between writer and reader has become treacherous and contaminated. Pynchon's insert denies the text any finality and gives us the impression of reading galley-proofs, the impression of the very text being betrayed.

At the beginning of 'The Counterforce' Pynchon gives a warning not to expect sequence: 'no serial time over there: events are all there in the same eternal moment and so certain messages don't always "make sense" back here: they lack historical structure, they sound fanciful, or insane' (624). We have already seen how the fluidity of the text constantly undermines the reader's expectations that the narratives will make sense and how the gaps between the chapters (and even *within* the chapters) thwart any clear continuity. The predicament of the reader worsens. Now he is not so much in difficulties as at the mercy of Pynchon's direct mockery. Chapter 66 begins ironically 'you will want cause and effect' and launches into a ludicrous account of how Thanatz (Greta Erdmann's husband) was saved from the sea by a Polish undertaker who is fascinated by Franklin's theory of lightning. Pynchon's sardonic opening sentence together with the fact that the reader has almost certainly forgotten Thanatz (he fell over-board some 200 pages earlier) set up an ironic context for a brief meditation on discontinuity which Pynchon dismisses as soon as it is formed. The 'explanation' then consists of a facetious performance which ridicules the reader's desire for continuity. Similarly when Pynchon lists a series of place-names he suggests that they form a roll of honour for the dead, but the reader accepts the suggestion at his peril. Pynchon triumphantly interrupts the text:

> Well, you're *wrong*, champ – these happen to be towns all located on the borders of *Time Zones*, is all. Ha, ha! Caught *you* with your hand in your pants! Go on, show us *all* what you were doing or leave the area, we don't need your kind around. There's nothing so loathsome as a sentimental surrealist.
>
> (695–6)

The 'sentimental surrealist' is of course a comic construct which burlesques conventional response as a kind of emotional onanism. The notion of an audience is retained ('us') but now as a means of comic exposure just as Pynchon's insertion of pseudo-references into the text mock the reader's desire for verifiability, for some external sense of the real.

As characters and narrative lines blur in Section IV Pynchon isolates different themes and images into separate episodes. 'In the Zone' has already demonstrated an episodic tendency in repeatedly interrupting Slothrop's sequence with comparatively self-contained chapters on the Herero, Central Asia, Franz Pökler, etc. Now, however, Pynchon dismantles the narrative, summarizing and separating out items for individual scrutiny. He gives a resumé of directional symbolism (chapter 69), of the rocket's significance (726–7) and a recapitulation of themes in chapter 73 (the city, sado-masochistic fantasy, the existence of Jamf, etc.). As the variety of styles broaden to include picaresque ('The Story of Byron the Bulb') and science-fiction the discontinuity between individual sections increases. The most startling examples of discontinuity occur in chapters 69 and 73 where items are further separated by headings. The effect is slightly similar to the 'Aeolus' section of *Ulysses* where Joyce mimics the fragmenting effect of a newspaper layout. In Pynchon's novel no single analogy is applicable, but this method clearly poses certain critical questions. Are the items arbitrarily chosen? Are they relevant and how do they affect the pace of the ending?

Let us examine the sub-sections from chapter 73 to see what sort of a sequence, if any, they make. There are fifteen whose titles run as follows:

1. The Occupation of Mingeborough (744)
2. Back in Der Platz. (745–6)
3. Weissmann's Tarot (746–9)
4. The Last Green and Magenta (749)
5. The Horse (749)
6. Isaac (749–50)
7. Pre-Launch (750–1)
8. Hardware (751)
9. Chase Music (751–3)
10. Countdown (753–4)
11. Strung Into the Apollonian Dream . . . (754)
12. Orpheus Puts Down Harp (754–7)
13. The Clearing (757–8)
14. Ascent (758–60)
15. Descent (760)

The first section draws partly on Pynchon's story 'The Secret

Integration' to sketch out an American scenario related to Slothrop's childhood. The second jumps abruptly to the two characters who were arguing about musical theory and weaves a hallucinatory fantasy around the kazoo (an instrument associated with the Counterforce) which they are now using to consume drugs. Weissmann's Tarot gives a summary of his significance and attenuates him into his own archetype (just as Slothrop recedes into the Fool). The next two brief fragments relate to endings and introduce the theme of sacrifice while 'Isaac' contrasts two mystic ways (the positive/masculine as against the passive/feminine) which parallels the contrast between Weissmann and his victim Gottfried. Sections 7 and 8 begin outlining the interior of the sacrificial rocket until 'Chase Music' interrupts the sequence and repudiates a last-minute reprieve. 'Countdown' returns to the serial sequence, relating it to film and to the kabbala (as if the launch was a travesty of God's primal firing of energy into the universe). Section 11 develops the symbolism of whiteness and cements the connection between apotheosis (ascent) and death. Section 12 further delays the serial sequence by presenting a parody of Nixon and introducing the image of the theatre. 'The Clearing' takes us through the launch ritual which opens the film *Operation Crossbow*. The ascent is constantly interrupted by 'CATCH' as if to suggest a film sticking and in the final section Pynchon naturalizes the breaks in the text by returning to the image of an auditorium. The novel stops with images of suspended motion, a closeup or a still.

Most of the sections relate directly to each other, with titles which suggest static scenes for the most part, many consisting of nouns or noun phrases. Pynchon has already arrested movement by drawing comparisons between scenes and the frames of a comic-book, a daguerrotype or a card. The Tarot becomes relevant here as a kind of proxy text, not because it predicts the future, but because it freezes Weissmann into a static position which then has to be read. Pynchon draws extensively on A. E. Waite's *Pictorial Guide to the Tarot* (1911) for his details and yet is careful to emphasize the ambiguity of the cards. The Tarot layout becomes a temporary metonymic substitute for the text itself, inviting but eluding interpretation. Waite himself admits different meanings to the cards but Pynchon goes a significant step further in stressing their enigmatic quality. The Tower, for instance, is a 'puzzling card', teasing the reader but also drawing him into complicity with the narrator ('we know by now that it is also the Rocket': 747).

Since the sub-sections do make up a partial sequence the repeated allusions to film in the novel invite us to compare the ending with cinematic cross-cutting. Richard Pearce, in the course of a discussion of the tempo of modern fiction, has recently examined the accelerating effect which cutting to and fro between two different scenes can have on film and novel alike.[116] This effect depends on the cuts becoming briefer and briefer but Pynchon does not maintain a steadily increasing momentum, nor does he cut between two clear lines of action. Rather he varies the length of the sections to *decelerate* the ending and bring it in line with his explicit repudiation of climaxes in 'Chase Music'. The novel further confuses our sense of an ending by juxtaposing a beginning (ascent) with an ending (descent) that never takes place.

Like *The Crying of Lot 49*, *Gravity's Rainbow* ends on a note of threatening imminence. It refuses to close its text, simply stopping at the end of a section which has done everything possible to question its earlier procedures. Partly this involves shifting the reader's attention from the historical time of the novel (1944–45) through anachronistic references to the Rolling Stones, Nixon and even Pynchon's friends, to the present of narration. More is involved here than an exploitation of our sense of historical retrospect. The novel shifts from a semi-realistic mode into increasingly fantastic sections which draw attention to their own fictiveness. As if Pynchon were acting on the implications of his earlier implications that print is tainted by political oppression he turns against his own fiction. There is also the risk in the encyclopaedic mode that the sheer wealth of materials used will flood the text. The deconstruction which takes place in 'The Counterforce' both denies the text any formal stability and draws the maximum attention to the technologies and media out of which the novel grows.

5

Pynchon in Context

Apart from his published fiction since 1967 Pynchon has been writing promotional statements for various novelists some of whom were his personal friends.[1] The works which he has endorsed have the value of shedding more light on the themes and concerns of his own fiction even when their methods diverge quite widely from his own. By expressing interest and approval for these books Pynchon in effect is creating a context for himself, locating his own novels in relation to those of his contemporaries. His earliest support went to Richard Fariña's *Been Down So Long It Looks Like Up To Me*, a novel whose comic methods closely resemble Pynchon's own. We have already seen how both Fariña and Pynchon picked up on the Beats and popular culture. A similar path has also been pursued by the comic novelist Tom Robbins whose works suggest a direct influence from Pynchon as well as a common background.

Robbins' first novel, *Another Roadside Attraction* (1971) expresses a reaction against what he calls 'economic totalitarianism', the reduction of all life to economically measurable quantities. The narrative divides into two main strands. The first centres on John Paul Ziller (an elusive combination of artist, magician and con-man) and his wife Amanda, the sexual focus of the novel, who both establish a wild-life preserve in what was a roadside diner. The second strand forms a sacrilegious comedy in which one Plucky Purcell steals the mummified body of Christ from the Vatican cellars. In reality the two narratives cannot be separated because while Amanda embodies reverence for Nature Plucky penetrates the institutions of Christianity. In his burlesque of an adventure story Robbins directs his irony against Christianity as a political force; Plucky, for instance, infiltrates an order of armed monks working for the CIA in south-east Asia. Even the myth of the Fall becomes rewritten as a triumph of censors and 'the Management'. Like Pynchon Robbins turns towards Zen in revulsion against a discredited Christianity which has become a means of control and repression. Amanda's celebration through enjoyment of sexuality and fertility acts against the entropic downward drift of this Christianity.

Robbins' second novel, *Even Cowgirls Get the Blues* (1976), like his other works takes its bearings from the 1960s, this time from the Beats. Its protagonist Sissy Hankshaw (like Robbins and for that matter Pynchon) grows up in the Eisenhower years afflicted with elephantiasis of the thumbs. This abnormality – which we are later guided to see as a difference – is an unavoidable physical sign of Sissy's inability to fit into her parents' lifestyle; and, true to their decade, they treat it as a social embarrassment. So Sissy takes the time-honoured way out by going on the road. Robbins naturally is aware enough to realize that without any explanation he would just be producing a pastiche of earlier American fiction here, so he explicitly locates Sissy's action in the context of a national literary tradition and of recent pop culture: 'From Whitman to Steinbeck to Kerouac, and beyond to the restless broods of the seventies, the American road has represented choice, escape, opportunity, a way to somewhere else.'[2] Escaping from her parents, Sissy meets and gets to know the Countess, a homosexual cosmetics tycoon and on her travels ends up at his Dakota ranch, a kind of health farm run by the cowgirls of the novel's title. One of these cowgirls, a feminist called Jelleybean, takes over the ranch in a kind of coup but is shot down during the dénouement when law-enforcement officers surround the ranch. Robbins lightly and humorously touches on a whole series of issues here. The West – specifically Dakota – is contrasted with the claustrophobia of New York. The latter (the home of the Countess represents big business, confinement, repression. The ranch represents space and freedom. Jelleybean's 'revolution' revises the sexism of traditional Western images. The arguments which she and Sissy have with the Countess question the assumption behind female cosmetics; they promote acceptance whereas the Countess is driven by disgust and revulsion. And so on.

The ludicrous plays an important role here in testing the reader's sense of humour. Now Robbins is far more successful because his narrative is both comic and politically alert (one of the cowgirls is a 'revisionist'; Richmond, Virginia at midday 'felt like the inside of a napalmed watermelon'). Basically Robbins is an intense moralist and the besetting weakness in his fiction has been a tendency to the garrulous, to offer opinions about everything masked by a rather laboured humour. In *Even Cowgirls* he controls this tendency partly by (again like Pynchon) setting up characters who represent particular attitudes and then letting these attitudes clash through dialogue. This neatly anticipates some of the criticisms which might be levelled against Robbins himself (of romanticizing the primitive, for instance) and also gives a dialectical progression to the novel. The dialogues are both funny and thought-provoking. At one point in *Another Roadside Attraction* Robbins switches the person of the narrative and immediately anticipates the reader's reaction by denying objectivity because he is so engrossed in the narrative ('I am irreversibly enmeshed in the events').[3] The narrator glosses over his shifts from idiom to idiom by disarmingly adopting a mock-eighteenth-century role as 'host', creating a fictive sociability between himself and the reader. In *Even Cowgirls* he projects himself directly into the fiction as a Dr. Robbins, a psychiatrist who ultimately rejects the repressive scholasticism of his superior Dr. Goldman. By creating this character Robbins mocks his own didacticism – Sissy, like Bellow's Herzog, is constantly confronted with 'instructors' – and also repeats and endorses Sissy's original gesture of rejection in setting out on the road.

In working against repression Robbins embraces the ludicrous (Sissy's thumbs, the non-realistic character-names, etc.) and risks the obscene. At one point Sissy is being instructed by a hermit called Chink through anal intercourse, symbolically purging herself of a Christianity which has blocked her psyche. But even more importantly Robbins has now built his resistance to authority into the very act of narrating. Here we need to remember the politics of Pynchon's own humour. His famous punning on 'gravity', the comic exploitation of simultaneous different meanings, his shifts in time and register, and his final dismantling of the text prevent it from gelling into a fixed system. Similarly Robbins uses alienation effects such as the 'cowgirl interludes' which punctuate the narrative or the constant interruptions in order to resist the authority of authorial comment. Indeed at one point he admits 'the author frankly doesn't know'. He repeatedly reminds the reader that his fictions are provisional sometimes apologizing for his antics with a tongue-in-cheek solemnity reminiscent of Fielding ('if he has confused you, the author apologizes. He swears to keep events in proper historical sequence from now on'); or, like Pynchon in *Gravity's Rainbow*, he will adopt the role of a theatrical entertainer.[4] Towards the end of the novel when Sissy has taken up residence with the Chink the narrative becomes rather weighed down by his enigmatic philosophizing. Accordingly Robbins inserts a facetious chapter (111a) which lays down some generalizations about poetry and then immediately wipes them out, transforming his own chapter into a ludicrous military area:

> Poetry is nothing more than an intensification or illumination of common objects and everyday events until they shine with their singular nature . . . [Definitions are limiting. Limitations are deadening. To limit oneself is a kind of suicide. To limit another is a kind of murder. To limit poetry is a Hiroshima of the human spirit. DANGER: RADIATION. Unauthorized personnel not allowed on the premises of Chapter 111a].[5]

The free-ranging discussions in the novel have already demonstrated that there is no such thing as a no-go area in this context.

Resistance to authority through humour, argument and disengagement is a constant theme throughout Robbins' fiction. He sums up the rationale for his fictional stance in chapter 65 of *Even Cowgirls*. In the past the burden of the artist was to create order. 'In times such as ours, however, when there is too much order, too much mangement, too much programming and control, it becomes the duty of superior man and women to fling their favourite monkey wrenches into the machinery.'[6] In other words Robbins' narrative antics have a calculated function in causing disruptions, whether to the reader's expectations or his beliefs. Significantly Robbins figures this disruption in a spontaneous gesture of sabotage to machinery, and in his later novel, *Still Life With Woodpecker* (1980), he enacts this resistance through a striking and unusual means. The novel consists of a romance between an American princess and an anarchist bomber called the Woodpecker. At the height of their romance the Woodpecker is caught and imprisoned. Robbins now takes one of the most familiar consumer-objects in America, a Camel cigarette packet, and transforms it first into a historical object and second into a means of communication between the two lovers. Just as it 'contains' the novel (whose covers mimic this design), so the packet contains also the romantic imaginings of the lovers. This tactic directly exemplifies a general point Pynchon has made recently about fiction: 'To insist on the miraculous is to deny to the machine at least some of its claims on us.'[7] Robbins similarly articulates narrative purpose through a gesture against the machine and in *Still Life* brings an inert object to life by imaginatively salvaging it from the cycle of consumerism.

Robbins' resistance to the machine of American life involves a reaffirmation of nature which he has made personally by living in the countryside of Washington State for the past few years.[8] The local varieties of mushroom become a focal object in his first novel, representing a natural plenty which the characters discover afresh. In *Even Cowgirls* nature is more threatened. The fate of the cowgirl ranch is a synecdoche for the fate of the landscape in general and the great whooping cranes perform exactly the same function as the dodoes in *Gravity's Rainbow* (though without the Protestant context) in that they are one natural species threatened with extinction by another more arrogant species – man. In *Gravity's Rainbow* man is presented as the spoiler of nature, looting the bowels of the earth for fuels and minerals which can be converted into means of political domination. As Slothrop penetrates deeper and deeper into the Zone he encounters more and more traces of Teutonic nature-rituals which, although only available in the present as memory or masquerade (like his pig-costume), represent the signs of a culture where man was related to Nature in a magical oneness. Throughout the novel Pynchon establishes a polarity between differentiation and integration. Differentiation, championed by Calvinism, modern analysis and more recently, by Nazi bureaucracy, represents virtually every negative direction man takes in the novel whether towards an ostensible knowledge or in realizing political aims. Holism represented by the closed circle seems to have been irretrievably lost by Pynchon can make at least a token resistance to this process by constantly hinting at inner-relations between the most diverse narrative materials. This nostalgia for a lost unity also informs the fiction of Tom Robbins and Mary Beal. At one point in *Another Roadside Attraction* Tarzan lectures Christ on exactly this subject of the primitive world-view: 'The point is, J. C., we had a unified outlook on life' and in *Still Life With Woodpecker* Robbins puts details together for no other point than to raise the 'possibility that everything is connected'.[9] The style of expression is characteristically facetious but the possibility is a serious one, not to rationalize a return to the primitive, but rather to puncture man's arrogance of species and to startle him into a new attitude which, as Robert Nadeau has shown, is actually consistent with the latest theories of physics.[10]

Since Pynchon seeks to relocate man within Nature it is consistent for him to express admiration for the writings of the naturalist Peter Matthiessen, whose 1975 novel *Far Tortuga* he describes as a 'deep declaration of love for the planet'.[11] This is only true in a very oblique sense because the novel promotes an extremely harsh view of Nature. In an earlier work like *At Play in The Fields of the Lord* (1965) Matthiessen is clearly didactic. He sets two groups of characters – naïve Christian missionaries and cynical smugglers or men of fortune – in a remote Latin American state and exploits the comic interplay between them. At the heart of the novel is the question how they will react to the Niaruna Indians. The missionaries try to convert them, the smugglers are ordered to bomb them. But Lewis Moon, one of the latter who is himself of Amerindian blood, joins the Niaruna. This action is didactic in trying to promote a less hostile attitude towards the 'primitive' in the reader. *Far Tortuga* in contrast narrates a turtle-fishing expedition in the Caribbean by a ramshackle schooner called the *Lillias Eden*. Part of the novel's action is to establish the tension between the members of the crew which Matthiessen manages skilfully through variations in Caribbean dialect. Through their speech, J. P. Grove argues, 'one becomes more aware of the work's primary conflict between the pastoral world of the old turtle fishing days and the modern wasteland'.[12] While there is this conflict, however, the novel's action moves remorselessly towards death. This even more important theme virtually transforms the voyage into a metaphor of man's life-span. From the very beginning the signs of death strike the reader. A gravestone ominously anticipates the shipwreck to come, and living creatures prey off others.[13] The crew of the *Eden* are no exception to this because they themselves live off fish and later turtle-meat. The stories they exchange revolve around murder and death by obi (a kind of voodoo). Death is witnessed, imagined and dreamt by them before they actually encounter it. Without any hint of consolation Matthiessen grimly places the crew and other human characters within a physical continuum of life and death which none of them can escape. Thus physical characteristics are emphasized (one man Brown has the 'feral air of a *bandito*').

The *Eden* meets a boat where an old man (the captain's father, it turns out) is seated clutching a conch as if expecting an imminent death. Immediately afterwards they land on a shore littered with rubbish and stinking of human excrement, where two figures copulate while another crouches in a foetus-like position. This sequence emblematically places man in three elemental positions – death (the old man dies later), copulation and birth, the latter two degraded by their context. Predation from pirates forces the captain of the *Eden* to try to escape across a reef at night and directly causes the wreck, from which only one man survives.

The single most striking aspect of *Far Tortuga* is Matthiessen's brilliant exploitation of the white space on the page. In a subsequent interview he explained:

> I was moved by the stark quality of that voyage, everything worn bare by wind and sea. . . . So from the start I was feeling my way toward a space: I wanted the descriptions to be very clear and flat, to find such poetry as they might attain in their very directness and simplicity.[14]

He attains this starkness by cutting out identificatory tags from the dialogue and by strictly limiting description to movement and appearance. In mimetic terms the white gaps which surround his characters' words correspond to the wind (which sweeps the words away) and the space which surround the *Eden*. The characters are thus dwarfed, rendered all the more vulnerable to the sea is like a huge maw waiting to swallow up vessel and men. The climax of the novel, the sinking of the *Eden*, is described in the following lines which take up an entire page:

> A shriek of twisting timber.
>
> The gear in the galley crashes, and bound turtles slide overboard.
>
> Shuddering, the Eden rights herself, and in a din of flopping canvas, screeching blocks, drifts downwind from the reefs.
>
> Black wind and rush of water. Figures running.[15]

Although Matthiessen prided himself on only using one simile in the novel this passage is implicitly metaphorical. In the context of ubiquitous violence it is as if a creature is dying ('shriek', 'shuddering', etc.), but without sacrificing naturalism. The spatial arrangement of the lines retards the action which is expressed through astonishingly fine attention to sound and movement. The boat is taken into the sea as the shifting matrix of life in this novel, preparing (by the play on synonyms 'rush' and 'running') to overwhelm the human figures. In *Far Tortuga* humans are locked into sequences of Nature and Matthiessen evokes the sheer scale and inevitability of these processes. Man's place in a unified nature offers no consolation at all. M. F. Beal's treatment of the same idea is, however, more positive.

Towards the end of Section 3 of *Gravity's Rainbow* (612) Pynchon inserts an apparently gratuitous Argentine legend about a young mother following her lover into the wilderness and dying but somehow continuing to suckle her child for a week. The miracle is related to a belief held by one of the Argentine exiles that rocks have consciousness just like flora and fauna. At this point Pynchon throws out a reference to his friend Mary Beal with whom he used to discuss the limits of sentience.[16] If there is such a thing as mineral consciousness then the earth's crust becomes a living mantle and man becomes a part (a small part) of a living continuum instead of being defined against an inert environment. This is the sort of discovery Lyle Bland makes earlier in the novel, and it is also a belief which informs Mary Beal's own short stories. In 'Gold' (1972) the narrator has left the city to join a mountain commune. His memories of Ruth suggest a use of Wordsworth here and sure enough one of the main themes of the story is the search for 'some linkage, some congruence of mountains/humans whose meaning would fall open like a Chinese puzzle at the right touch'.[17] No decisive moment of insight comes; the narrator is left, even after prolonged fasting, with trying to formulate a precise meaning. The gold which the mountain produces is actually part of a psycho-physical process, the members of the commune also producing gold crystals after periods of spiritual discipline. Gold thus stops being a simple metal and becomes invested with spiritual quality. Similarly in 'Space Time' (1975) which describes a pregnant woman living near a burnt-out house in the country an old man, the last surviving member of the family, is described through the following kinds of analogies: 'His cheeks were packed with silver bristles bulging like the sides of a fish'; 'His cheeks were flecked with light like a rock crowded with crystals.'[18] These similes locate him within his own rural environment. Character and setting become inseparable.

These stories relocate man within the natural order. Connectedness is here a biological point, but it can also have momentous political implications. Many critics have discussed Pynchon's treatment of conspiracy and there are clear historical reasons why his novels should suggest with increasing emphasis that the forces of conspiracy are located within America. In one of the sections of *Gravity's Rainbow* devoted to Greta Erdmann's past (presumably one noted by Tom Robbins) we are told that she played a cowgirl in a film called *Weisse Sandwüste Von Neumexico* (482). White Sands was the location where the US first tested out a captured V-2 in 1946 as a result of a contract between the military and General Electric. This none too obvious allusion is of course anachronistic and anachronisms occur with increasing frequency towards the end of the novel. Many (to Ishmael Reed, to 1966 and 1971, etc.) are blatant disruptions of one historical period (1944–45) with references to contemporary America. In other words by violating our sense of period Pynchon constantly nudges the reader towards bringing the events within the novel's historical fiction to bear on the present of its narration, on America during the Nixon years. When planning the novel he clearly saw German actions in south-west Africa as analogous with American actions in Vietnam (see Appendix), implying that the South-West African materials, in spite of their apparent remoteness, bear an implicit topicality. In the 1968 letter where he outlines his thinking on the fate of non-literary peoples at the hands of western industrialized states, he makes no bones about his indignation and it is reported that he temporarily withheld his income tax as a gesture of protest against the Vietnam War. If the V-rocket is the outward and visible sign of technopolitical power in *Gravity's Rainbow* there is a crucial historical symbolism in the fact that at the end of the novel a V-2 apparently flies from Germany to America, thus reflecting a power-shift which took place once the war was over. The lack of closure to the novel thus invites the reader to see a continuity between 1945 and contemporary America.

Pynchon has recently identified the American military-industrial complex as being a modern development of the factory system. It is entirely in keeping with the imagery and references of *Gravity's Rainbow* that he should single out 'the Manhattan Project, the German long-range rocket program and the death camps' for special mention.[19] By the 1980s these developments have merged into what Pynchon calls a 'permanent power establishment' made up of business executives and representatives of the military. Three months after the publication of *Gravity's Rainbow* Pynchon's friend Kirkpatrick Sale came to a very similar conclusion. In a long and well-documented article he sets out to examine the increasing Southern presence in the Washington establishment but broadens his scope to locate a 'second government', a 'very important nexus of power behind the acknowledged civics-text book institutions'. Admitting that he is only dealing with glimpses, he nevertheless hypothesizes that 'there are important operations going on beyond the reach of ordinary citizens or of party politics'.[20] The nexus Sale identifies includes the CIA and organized crime, and makes an important contemporary gloss on Pynchon's novel. *Gravity's Rainbow* deals at length with hidden political orders and attempts to track down some of the sources of their exploitative energy. Sale pinpoints exactly the same kind of political activity which he sees as characteristic of Nixon and his cronies. Given this diagnosis of the establishment it is not surprising that Sale should have written a history of one of the 1960s protest movements – the Students for a Democratic Society.[21] The SDS (the kind of organization Oedipa Maas encounters on her visit to the Berkeley campus) went through four phases as it progressively took shape, practising first reformism and then widespread confrontations, ending in isolated revolutionary pockets. For Sale (and for Pynchon in his introduction to *Slow Learner*) the turning-point in this movement was its failure to form a students–workers alliance in 1967–68. Not only did Pynchon promote Sale's book but he is thanked in the acknowledgements for his help. These interpretations of what is tantamount to conspiracy in the government establish the best context for approaching the fiction of Mary Beal and Marge Piercy.

Mary Beal's first novel *Amazon One* (1975) takes its bearings from the student activism of the sixties. The novel begins with a series of 'documents' (an FBI wanted notice, a driving licence, an excerpt from an inquest, etc.) and then establishes a narrative which tries to give the reality lying behind melodramatic media-phrases like 'pinko plot to murder innocent'.[22] The novel centres on a group of young activists based in California who have decided to bomb key establishment buildings. Near the beginning of the narrative some explosive detonates prematurely, killing some of the group and sending the rest into hiding. *Amazon One* is a narrative of how inevitably these fugitives will be captured and at the same time a study in the fears they experience. Beal sets out to put flesh on the names which appear in the opening documents, to show the mixtures of motive which brought the group together in the first place. One member is writing a novel about them, a surrogate for Beal which enables her to dispose of the notion of an exposé. Apart from the explosion events in the novel are held at a low key, to keep the narrative as far as possible from sensationalism. At the same time the method used sets up ironies against the political purpose of the group. The main character Marina Karsh declares bravely in an interview that 'the political revolution is advance notion of the Millenial Revolution'.[23] But there is no sign anywhere in the novel of even wide-spread support for the group, never mind of impending revolution. The group is betrayed by one of its members (later tracked down and shot) and is riven by petty rivalries. Beal's method of jumping from one perspective to another further undermines our sense of any group purpose. On the contrary characters are harried by nightmares of attack and enclosure (ironically contrasting with their chosen role as aggressors). Instead of working forwards towards the realization of a political aim the action in the novel's present dramatizes the erosion of the group, and constantly tugs the reader back into the past into characters' memories of their parents and earlier relationships. So although *Amazon One* has telling points to make about police brutality and the repression of American law-enforcement agencies, it is profoundly pessimistic about the possibility of change or even of making symbolic gestures against this system. In spite of the panic and fears experienced by the main characters it is not until her second novel that Beal manages to evoke the atmosphere of suspense through a sheer concentration on all the details of incidental speech and appearances. *Amazon One* uses the Weathermen as a prototype for its central group; her next novel deals more obliquely with domestic intelligence networks.

The Rockefeller Commission in the mid-1970s elicited notorious admissions of CIA investigation of left-wing organizations such as the SDS and of the covert administration of drugs to unwitting subjects, all in the name of counter-intelligence. These investigations evidently acted as a trigger to Mary Beal's second novel *Angel Dance* (1977) which narrates the efforts of Kat, a Chicana detective, to locate a former friend, a feminist journalist called Angel Stone. Angel has been making a film about the use of drugs at a marine base and hence is a fugitive from the FBI and the CIA. Beal combines the tradition of the American private eye novel with some influences from Pynchon. Her spare style of narration is not a form of understatement but reflects Kat's close scrutiny of all appearances for signs or clues of Angel's whereabouts. In Chandler's novels the forces of corruption usually have human faces whether they are febrile millionaires or brutal city cops, but Kat has to contend with far more tenuous and technically more sophisticated adversaries who have unlimited resources at their disposal. The result is to induce suspicions about everything, especially about so-called accidental deaths. Like Oedipa Maas she enumerates possibilities including her own paranoia. Ruminating on the death of Angel's husband, she thinks: 'Maybe up and down some invisible hierarchy everybody owed one to Tarleton. . . . Or maybe not. . . . Suppose it was accidental, then it could be dangerous to act like there had been foul play.' And then she wryly adds: 'In the books the private eye always got to look at the body, it was a big help.'[24] Unlike Philip Marlowe she has to struggle with hypotheses based on vestigial evidence, hypotheses which seem to lead her towards political murder, uncontrolled phone-tapping – in short to the apparatus of a totalitarian state. It is a friendly throw-away reference to Pynchon's treatment of conspiracy that a minor character should be called I.G. Farbus. Beal is as skilful as Pynchon at evoking an atmosphere of anxiety and threat, but without the latter's injections of comic relief. Kat's rape half-way through the novel is an experience equivalent to the hounding of Angel. Both are symptoms of a national (gender-determined) mania for control. In Angel's case the issue, the preservation of secrecy, is more explicitly political.

For Mary Beal and Marge Piercy alike the Cold War manifests itself within the USA not through American foreign policy. The enemy is the American establishment itself against which both writers' characters struggle. Piercy's *Dance the Eagle to Sleep* (1971) begins with four narrative strands centring on figures who define themselves in opposition to the patterns of American life, and dramatizes their convergence into a revolutionary group. Corey, the most important of these characters, is part-Indian and takes upon himself the burden of his ancestors' betrayal, trying to redress their dispossession through the establishment of an activist organization called the Indians. Partly a return to the tribal, the Indians perform certain rituals, central among them being the dance. The novel's title suggests the overcoming of a national symbol (a symbol specifically of American power) by a physical act although the meaning of dance remains ambiguous throughout the novel. It can be communal or individual; it can be spontaneous; it can involve sexual display, or it could act as therapy. Even the fact that a dancer cannot necessarily articulate its significance (one thinks: 'it was an image of something in her blood') does not prevent the dance from being liberating.[25] Like Robbins and Pynchon, Piercy describes conventional American life in terms of conditioning deliberately exploiting connotations of political manipulation. Each of the four characters who begin *Dance the Eagle to Sleep* search for a freedom beyond this conditioning – through rock music, Indian mythology or intellectual dissent. Like Dos Passos Piercy expresses their hostility to the establishment as hostility to a machine and when a member of the group betrays the rest she is immediately transformed into a robot, a 'plastic doll with rubbery skin and a smell of plastics about it'.[26] In depicting the clashes between these militants and the forces of law and order Piercy emphasizes their paraphernalia (the clubs, gas canisters, etc.) and vehicles. They represent regimented repression whereas the dissidents stand for an easy spontaneity in self-expression. Piercy is too shrewd to describe their hopes and their New Jersey commune without anticipating a hostile reader's criticisms. The latter are put in the mouth of Billy, the intellectual genius of the movement, who harangues them for indulging in a bogus primitivism. The point is not that Billy is right exactly, but that expressions of revolutionary purpose are vulnerable because words themselves have become suspect after their abuse in the characters' schools and in the media. One of the most telling ironies of the novel is that the movement's defeat begins with assimilation by the media. The group is classified and the Indian dress becomes a clothing fashion.

The plot of this novel forms a summary of student unrest during the 1960s from individual dissatisfaction through the relief of pop concerts, the formation of a commune and then of a hardline political core. The broad outline of events parallels that of Kirkpatrick's Sales' *SDS*, and the details of police raids and confrontations in the New York streets no doubt draw on Marge Piercy's own firsthand experiences in these years. The last sections of the novel diverge from historical fact to imagine the consequences of a confrontation so severe than Manhattan is bombed: 'All day Saturday the city shook with the bombardment and planes came in screaming on their metal bellies, dropping load after load.'[27] By this stage, although it still uses the narrative past tense, the novel has become predictive of a total breakdown in civil order. Piercy follows the tactic of Jack London's *The Iron Heel* to move unobtrusively from realistic description to apocalyptic confrontation as an autocratic regime asserts, or in Piercy's case reasserts itself. Billy's group attacks the key buildings in lower Manhattan (the banks, courts, etc.) but they are defeated by the national guard, as are the other groups and, as if she sensed the negative political direction the novel was taking, Piercy tries to inject a positive note at the end in one of the dissidents giving birth. Her most famous novel *Vida* (1979) is even more sombre politically. Like *Amazon One* it is a narrative of erosion. The last survivors of a 1960s activist organization are gradually hunted down. They are the victims of a shift in American politics towards conservatism as well as of the police forces and the very form of the novel reads more conservatively than *Dance the Eagles to Sleep* which uses metaphor, theoretical commentary and political fantasy. In spite of its dramatization of how revolutionary activity can escalate to the point where it threatens civil order this narrative and for that matter *Vida* and Mary Beal's two novels are ultimately sceptical about the possibility of revolutionary change. The hope of the militants in these works is for a liberating breakdown in law and order but the novels stress too much internal disagreement and betrayal, and depict the police and intelligence agencies as too powerful for these ambitions to be realized. Disillusionment with America can take another direction altogether. In the next group of novels personal breakdown and failure is described as part of a national malaise, a general collapse of national values.

David Shetzline's *De Ford* (1968) presents a protagonist in the last stages of failure. De Ford, a carpenter/craftsman, has travelled around the West to prove the size of the country to himself but space has contracted in the novel's present down to the streets of the Bowery. Once again a contrast is set up between America's main metropolis and the open land but it is not an even contrast. De Ford's memories of country life where issues have simplified down to the practice of his craft, or of travel which has turned into impersonation (he carries his father's IWW card with him everywhere), recede before the sordid necessities of avoiding a local debt-collector. The novel is static and contracted, exploiting the narrowness of the streets, the claustrophobic interiors of rooming-houses or exteriors of building lots to convey a powerful sense of endings. De Ford is driven by fears of disintegration (he constantly dreams of being attacked) and preserves a vestigial identity with other cronies who have rejected their own class or the whole country, like Leggatt a disenchanted painter who complains: 'I'd swallowed all the head-cheese of American education: the myths, the heroes, the facts . . .'.[28] Until that is, he fought in the Korean War.

Politics for the most part is kept in the background of Schetzline's novel, unlike John Speicher's *Didman* (1971) where the eponymous protagonist is a publishing executive who has lived through the Depression and fought in World War II, Korea and Vietnam. Although the novel works in a realistic mode, Didman personifies America's recent history and also embodies (to the point of self-parody) the contradictions of American liberalism which neutralize each other. Even his life is split between professional prosperity and personal failure, between his luxury apartment and flat in a Puerto Rican tenement block. Didman's motivating force is a political and social guilt which constantly leads him to make futile gestures of atonement. He confronts his racial opposite in marrying a Puerto Rican woman and finally decides to commit the very act of pointless terrorism which he had mocked in others by shooting up the New York Stock Exchange. But the police have been informed and he is shot down, futile to the last. Like Porpentine in 'Under the Rose', Didman is at odds with his context. Throughout the novel he seems incongruous, especially in the Puerto Rican settings. Detached from his own social group and unable to identify with a new one, he is paralyzed by an inability to act. His decision to go to the Stock Exchange is not a positive act but rather a calculated gesture of suicide.

In his earlier novel *Looking For Baby Paradise* (1967) Speicher hints at a similar futility through oblique ironies. Narrated by Charlie Kremmel, a youth worker in Washington Heights, the novel demonstrates the precarious balancing act performed by Kremmel between the law on the one hand and the ethics of the local community on the other. It can only be managed through an element of theatre. Kremmel's 'costume' consists of a long coat, battered hat, dark glasses and cane; these earn him his nickname of The Blind Man. In a way he is wilfully blind, only maintaining his position by deliberately not following out the implications of the poverty he sees for the New York establishment and the country as a whole, and deliberately closing his eyes to the crime going on around him. Kremmel recounts his experiences in an ironic self-mocking style full of local slang which confirms his awareness of the neighbourhood but also his separation from it (he works mainly with Puerto Ricans). One of these youths, the Baby Paradise of the novel's title, goes into hiding under suspicion of murder and after a crisis of allegiance Kremmel helps the police to find him. He rationalizes this decision as working for Paradise's ultimate good but the boy is later killed in a prison riot. Speicher brilliantly captures the day-by-day drama of the social worker's struggle to maintain his own status and sets it against the background inevitability of ultimate failure. The youth centre is doomed and Kremmel can only make a series of symbolic gestures against this fate. Paradise's death is both a metaphor of this failure and the literal trigger to the Harlem riot which concludes the novel. Even here Kremmel has miscalculated. An effort to lead his youths in an orderly participation in the demonstrations backfires and several of his friends are shot down. At the very end of the novel Kremmel, now a member of a quasi-military commune, has realized the elusiveness of his search for any kind of 'paradise'.

Laurel Goldman's *Sounding the Territory* (1982) shifts the emphasis from the politics of breakdown to its pathology. Her novel is the first-person narrative of one Jay Davidson who declares:

> The truth is I am not crazy. I hover on the brink, drawing up tiny grey lists in my head, pros and cons, regurgitating this or that failed time. Did I? Why didn't I? Should I? Would I? It keeps one precariously on the straight and narrow. I sway at the edge but do not fall. But I yearn to plunge into the darkness, whatever it is. Babble and scream, hallucinate till I am wrung out and so clean that my bones would be bleached.[29]

The admission of near or partial mania has become virtually routine in American fiction since the 1960s and Jay's precarious images recall the famous balancing act of Mailer's Stephen Rojack in *An American Dream*. Rojack wilfully confronts his own dread through near-fatal acts of bravado by walking around the balcony-edge of a New York high-rise apartment. Jay Davidson has no room for bravado. Balancing is not a physical action but a metaphor of how delicately he maintains his sanity in the first part of the novel. Even in the passage quoted he manages a mixture of self-mockery, lucidity and frenzy – a combination of 'laughter and vertigo', as Pynchon puts it. He has taken the alias (and the cowboy boots) of Jesse James during his spell in a psychiatric clinic but without ever projecting the clinic as a totalitarian institution. There are partial literary echoes in this novel of Kesey, Salinger (Jay like Holden Caulfield improvises on-the-spot stories to manoeuvre through difficult situations) and Sylvia Plath. In the first section of the novel blocks of narrative are jumbled up chronologically, reflecting Jay's own mental disorder. Memories of psychosomatic crises gradually surface in a quasi-therapeutic sequence so that by the end of part I he has been discharged from the clinic. His newly gained health is signalled by the novel's shift to a neutral, orderly narrative. Jay's psychoses seem to have been caused by family pressure to follow out conventional career-patterns. Once out of the clinic he drifts into a relationship with two girls in New York but decides to light out for the territory when domesticity becomes too stifling. His way out is not to go hitch-hiking like Sissy Hankshaw but to yield passively to a Greyhound journey towards the West. The journey, however, is ironically suspended at the end of the novel when the bus crashes through a roadside Marlboro hoarding.

The preceding novels deal with breakdown in individual terms through modifications of realism, but the disintegration of forms has also been the central preoccupation of Rudolph Wurlitzer's experimental novels. In an interview conducted soon after the publication of his first novel (*Nog*, published in Britain as *The Octopus*, 1969) he makes the following statement about the cultural contrasts within America: 'Forms have disintegrated here [i.e. in the east] so you're involved in disintegration. But out there in the west forms just *aren't there*. In that sense it's a weird frontier . . . it's easier not to have conditioning.'[30] What makes Wurlitzer's fiction so impressive and original is his capacity to follow out the implications of this notion of breakdown for the very forms of his fiction and this experimentation has drawn praise from Robert Creeley, Donald Barthelme and Michael Herr as well as Pynchon. In his first novel the protagonist derives from the Beats, following out his search for an ideal disengagement by travelling around the West with two chance acquaintances. Even here the acts of narrating and of travelling are dovetailed so closely that it is virtually impossible to identify any time-gap of recollection. The narrating literally is the action. *Flats* (1970) moves even farther from conventional narration. Where Wurlitzer saw his first novel as 'anti-psychological', he now was interested in 'going outside of psychology all together'.[31] *Flats* is a post-apocalyptic work which explores displacement in the most literal sense. Its references to the past imply a disaster (a war?); thus the first narrator remarks 'I know I stumbled through rubble, blown-up boulders or smashed statues'.[32] The landscape is littered with such broken cultural traces, the garbage and detritus of a world which has ceased to exist. Disaster is also the central subject of *Quake* (1972) where a massive earthquake shakes Los Angeles and symbolically destroys the coherence of urban society which breaks down into anarchy and cultural regression. In both cases Wurlitzer gives the most literal articulation to the disintegration of forms he discusses in his interview. Not only the landscape but the characters and sequence of *Flats* prove to be broken.

There is nowhere to take bearings from. As D. T. Bolling points out, 'the national myths, the media output, the indoctrination and other societal controls have ceased functioning for the emptied, shadowy survivors in *Flats*' and the reader is faced to participate in the potentially futile search for structures followed out by the characters.[33] The first dislocation is the 'characters' who consist of American cities, sketched so as to contain identifiable geographical or social features. The first example of this process identifies himself both as a place and as a literary character ('Call me Memphis') but in this minimalist novel 'characters' turn out to be little more than personified names. Their movement about the terrain thus enacts the detachment of names from their referents. The landscape has returned to its primal inchoate state as sheer expanse but simultaneously contracted down to a small area littered with debris and polluted perhaps by industrial waste. The influence of Beckett is strikingly evident in the characters' physical debility, inertia and in their fragmentary and inconclusive dialogues.

From the first anonymous narrative voice come the stylistically identical voices of the other characters. In fact character could be explained in this novel as the temporary adoption of a role which is quickly abandoned in favour of a new one. Wurlitzer denies realistic illusion by shifting between the first and third persons and then making an explicit comment on those shifts: 'The third person handles the changes, keeps me from getting popped. I don't want to knock the third person. I like to travel there. It avoids stagnations and the theatrics of pointing to myself'.[34] Such reminders of the fictive nature of events pull *Flats* towards self-reference but characters' place-names by definition refer to external entities, so that there is a constant internal–external tension throughout the novel. Not only that but Wurlitzer's use of contradiction and repetitive sentence-patterns undermines our sense of narrative progression. In the following passage utterance starts as minimal and then turns in on itself, obliterating its own meanings as it goes along:

The ground is cold. I can say that. I can say that in unison with myself. I can say that with a host of places: Toledo, Denver, Tucumcari, El Paso. I say that with no one. I had thought it would take longer. The darkness felt so located. I won't repeat myself. I have repeated myself. The litany isn't in the words. There is no telling. I have told nothing. I can recognize separations as they arrive. There is too much to say. I could bring it all around. My words are still the same. They are still the same. I don't want to manage the repetitions. I know about that. I don't know about that. I don't want to create a conclusion. That has already happened.[35]

The paradox in this sort of language is that it creates meaning (albeit *negative* meaning) even while it denies itself. 'There is no telling' simultaneously rules out coherent narration and coherent knowing. By the end of the paragraph the words have almost become reified objects or events in their own right. Does 'that' in the last sentence, for instance, point to an earlier event in time, to 'conclusion' (where sign and referent have blurred together) or to itself? The impossibility of finally answering such questions is a measure of the uncertainty which Wurlitzer generates in the reader, and it is that uncertainty which prevents narrative closure at the end of *Flats*.

Wurlitzer does not explain what has befallen his landscape since explanation is part of the sense-making processes which his novel works against. And yet the repeated references to a machine humming and to a blue light flashing implicate technology in what has happened. The littered landscape of *Flats* recalls the dump of 'Low-lands' and the junk-heaps of *V.* which are moralized in *Gravity's Rainbow* by juxtaposing the spare parts from the Mittelwerke with the piled corpses from the Dora concentration camp. In the fiction discussed above technology is regularly associated with political control, abuse of the media or cultural entropy. The authors variously resist these associations through subversive humour (Robbins), through narratives of surveillance (Beal and Piercy), or through the obliteration of the human figure (at the end of *Flats* light 'covers' the last speaker). In a recent essay Pynchon has put the issue of technology into a broad historical perspective. His essay 'Is It O.K. to Be a Luddite?' (1984) argues that the Luddite movement and Gothic fiction were only two aspects of a general resistance to the machine which stretches back at least to the sixteenth century: 'Each in its way expresses the same profound unwillingness to give up elements of faith, however "irrational", to an emerging technopolitical order that might or might not know what it was doing.' This tradition of resistance, he continues, has manifested itself latterly in the Beat movement (which, as we have seen, gave an important reference-point to most of the fiction discussed in this chapter) and in Science Fiction. Pynchon even risks a SHROUD-like prophecy: that the 'next great challenge' will come 'when the curves of research and development in artificial intelligence, molecular biology and robotics all converge'.[36] Only time will tell if Pynchon is right.

Appendix: Pynchon's Reading for *Gravity's Rainbow*

During research for a graduate paper on the Bondelzwarts Thomas F. Hirsch read *V.* and wrote to Pynchon about his use of South-West African materials in chapter 9. On 8 January 1969 Pynchon replied to Hirsch. The text of his reply, which is reproduced with Pynchon's permission, reads as follows:

Dear Mr. Hirsch,

As you say, I got much of the information for chapter 9 of *V.* from a government report. I didn't know there was an administrator's report *and* a commission of enquiry's report.[1] I'm afraid I went at the whole thing in a kind of haphazard fashion – was actually looking for a report on Malta and happened to find the Bondelzwarts one right next to it in the same, what the NY Public Library calls, "pamphlet volume".[2] But since then I've been hooked on it. Trying at the moment, in fact, to work into the novel I'm writing now more of the Südwest material. For some reason I can't leave it alone, and I'm glad you and possibly others have been picking up on it. When I wrote *V.* I was thinking of the 1904 campaign as a sort of dress rehearsal for what later happened to the Jews in the '30's and '40's.[3] Which is hardly profound; it must occur to anybody who gets into it even as superficially as I did. But since reading McLuhan especially, and stuff here and there on comparative religion, I feel now the thing goes much deeper.[4] Oddly enough I found most of the material I should have researched for *V.* long after I'd written the book, things I assume you've already been into: the official General Staff history of the campaigns, a species of souvenir program called *Deutsche Reiter im Südwest*, a personal memoir by Klaus Somebody who looks like a nine year old kid with a mustache and talks a lot about his Mother called, I think, *Im Kämpfe Gegen Die Herero*.[5] I wish I could be more specific on those, but I didn't take down any notes, only looked at pictures (my German

240

being nearly nonexistent) and you've probably read them anyhow. I did find a couple things [sic] you might be able to use, especially if you're interested in African motivations: one is a monograph by a Luttig, H. G., *The Religious System and Social Organization of the Herero*, Kemink en Zoon, Over den dom, Utrecht, no date though someone has written in pencil, in brackets on the title page "1933?"[6] The other is a pamphlet by a Steenkamp, W. P., *Is the South-West African Herero Committing Race Suicide*? Unie-Volkspers Bpk, Cape Town, again no date, though internal evidence suggests around 1935.[7] The problem as I guess you appreciate, with getting the African side of it, is that the Hereros were preliterate and everything available from them is (a) anecdotal and (b) filtered through the literate (McLuhan), Western, Christian biases of European reporters, usually missionaries. But I feel personally that the number done on the Herero head by the Germans is the same number done on the American Indian head by our own colonists and what is now being done on the Buddhist head in Vietnam by the Christianity minority in Saigon and their advisors: the imposition of a culture valuing analysis and differentiation on a culture that valued unity and integration.[8] It is impossible, I think, to consider the pre-colonial Herero apart from his religion, which in turn governed his social organization. Their villages were circular, set up like the ancient yang/yin diagram, women living on the north half, men on the south, the whole thing oriented like a mandala on the points of the compass, each direction having a special meaning. Their god embodied male and female, creation and destruction, life and death. The missionaries came in and set up dichotomies, busted up that unity, created categories, and historically nobody has been better at this than the Germans. Both in mathematics and in politics, as witness the whole Kleinstaaterei hangup dating from before the peace of Westphalia.[9] Contrast the shape of a Herero village with the Cartesian grid system layout in Windhök or Swakopmund, read Lewis Mumford or talk to somebody in the city planning department here.[10] The physical shape of a city is an infallible due to where the people who built it are at. It has to do with our deepest responses to change, death, being human. I doubt it was only firepower and aggressiveness that beat the Herero during that "complex and terrible" time. I think the Hereros had as much to do with it as von Trotha did. For perhaps the same reasons the Incas, with everything going for them, let a crippled and hopelessly outnumbered one-time hog drover from Estremadura hand them their ass.[11] This is why I find Steenkamp's pamphlet so fascinating, though I don't know how valid his arguments are. He attempts to explain the declining birth-rate among the Hereros with numbers like overpopulation and Vitamin E deficiency, and to discount the notion, apparently widely-held at the time, that the Hereros were deliberately trying to exterminate themselves. But I find that perfectly plausible, maybe not as a conscious conspiracy, but in terms of how a perhaps not completely Westernized people might respond. They had no concept of property in the European sense before the missionaries came, they felt themselves integrated into everything, like mystics in deep trances or people up on acid; their cattle had souls, the same souls as their own and possible part of a universal soul, though you'd better check that out. But they had no hangups sacrificing cattle, it was part of a universal scheme, and so it's doubtful if they'd have any hangups sacrificing themselves either, given a unified concept of creation, which shows up in religions all around the world, Christianity being a glaring exception. And German Christianity being perhaps the most perfect expression of the whole Western/analytic/"linear"/alienated shtick. It is no accident that Leibniz was co-inventor of calculus, trying to cope with change by stopping it dead, chopping it up into infinitesimals, going in to look at it, the cannonball frozen in midflight, little piece by little piece – no accident that Gauss, who contributed most heavily to Modern Analysis, spent his time moonlighting as a diplomatic trouble-shooter travelling from little state to little state, trying to cool off hassles among the hundred princes of the period.[12] This may all sound irrelevant, but it's not. I don't like to use the word but I think what went on back in Südwest is archtypical of every clash between the west and non-west, clashes that are still going on right now in South East Asia. [. . .][13]

Hopefully this will all show up, before long, in another novel. I don't know if any of it helps, but I hope so – obviously I haven't got it all completely clear in my own head yet. Writing to you has begun to clarify it a little, so I'm glad you wrote to me. If you want to talk about it more, feel free to do so. Good luck on your thesis, though I suspect it's not such a "little undertaking". I hope someday you, or somebody, does a full scale book on the subject.[14] Far from being a minor side-show in African history, I think it could be vitally important to people's understanding of what's going on in the world these days.

Yours truly,
Thomas Pynchon

P.S. – For *V.* I also used a British propaganda pamphlet printed around 1917, whose name I've long forgotten. Good for an anti-German review of 1903–7 events, as well as some pretty frightening atrocity pictures. It was in the Seattle Public Library, if that helps any.[15]

T. P.

Notes

INTRODUCTION

1. Oakley Hall, *Warlock* (University of Nebraska Press, 1980) pp. 13–14.
2. 'A Gift of Books', *Holiday*, 38.vi (Dec. 1965) p. 164.
3. Marshall McLuhan, *The Mechanical Bride* (London: Routledge & Kegan Paul, 1967) p. vi.
4. *The Mechanical Bride*, p. 94.
5. *V.* (Philadelphia: J. B. Lippincott, 1963; London: Picador, 1975) p. 411. The pagination of these editions is identical and will be used throughout.
6. *The Mechanical Bride*, p. 98.
7. Irving Howe, 'Mass society and post-modern fiction' in Marcus Klein (ed.), *The American Novel Since World War II* (New York: Fawcett, 1970) p. 130.
8. *The Collected Works of Nathaniel West* (Harmondsworth, Middx: Penguin, 1975) pp. 46–7.
9. *Slow Learner* (Boston: Little, Brown, 1984; London: Jonathan Cape, 1985) p. 9.
10. In a letter to the author of 10 Oct., 1984.
11. John Clellon Holmes, *Nothing More to Declare* (London: André Deutsch, 1968) p. 217.
12. Lawrence Lipton, *The Holy Barbarians* (New York: Grove Press, 1962) p. 48.
13. *Slow Learner*, p. 14.
14. The most reliable account of Pynchon's known biographical details is Mathew Winston's 'The Quest for Pynchon' in George Levine and David Leverenz (eds), *Mindful Pleasures. Essays on Thomas Pynchon* (Boston: Little, Brown, 1976).
15. J. C. Batchelor, 'Thomas Pynchon is Not Thomas Pynchon, or, This is the End of the Plot Which Has No Name', *Soho Weekly News* (22 Apr. 1976) pp. 15–17, 21, 35. This facetious article elicited a suitably ironic reply from Pynchon who advised Batchelor to 'keep trying'.
16. Details of the award and the text of Pynchon's letter can be found in 'Presentation to Thomas Pynchon of the Howells Medal for Fiction of the Academy by William Styron', *Proceedings of the American Academy of Arts and Letters*, 2nd series 26 (1976) pp. 43–6.
17. *Slow Learner*, p. 8.
18. *The Holy Barbarians*, p. 214. Both Lipton and Pynchon refer specifically to the 1955 paperback edition.
19. Helen Waddell, *The Wandering Scholars* (Harmondsworth, Middx: Penguin, 1954) p. 186.
20. J. C. Batchelor, 'The Ghost of Richard Fariña', *Soho Weekly News* (28 Apr. 1977) p. 20.

21. Richard Fariña, *Been Down So Long It Looks Like Up To Me* (Harmondsworth: Penguin, 1983) p. 128.
22. *Been Down So Long*, pp. 12–13.
23. *Been Do So Long*, p. viii. I have discussed the novel in more detail in 'Richard Fariña's Protest Novel', *Journal of American Culture*, 5.ii (Summer 1982) pp. 104–14.
24. R. C. Goolrick, 'Pieces of Pynchon', *New Times* 11 (16 Oct. 1978) pp. 65, 67; Lewis Nichols, 'In and Out of Books', *New York Times Book Review* (28 Apr. 1963) p. 8.
25. Jules Siegel, 'Who is Thomas Pynchon. . . . and why did he take off with my wife?', *Playboy*, 24, iii (Mar. 1977) p. 170.
26. Bill Roeder, 'After the Rainbow', *Newsweek*, 92 (7 Aug. 1978) p. 7. The information came from Pynchon's then agent Candida Donadio.

1   THE SHORT STORIES

1. Winston, p. 258.
2. Baxter Hathaway, 'Hathaway Recalls Cornell Writers of the '50s', *The Cornell Daily Sun* (5 May, 1978) p. 38.
3. First located by Mathew Winston, ('The Quest for Pynchon', p. 259).
4. Siegel, 'Who is Thomas Pynchon', p. 122.
5. *Slow Learner*, p. 27. All page references to Pynchon's stories except in section 2 are to this collection and are subsequently incorporated into the text.
6. *Been Down So Long*, p. viii.
7. Winston, p. 259.
8. Levine reads an article in a local paper with a similar headline. Internal details (the mention of Biloxi airforce base, oil company boats, etc.) suggest that Pynchon probably used the *American Press* article for details in this story.
9. This source is noted by Thomas Schaub in his survey-article 'Where Have We Been, Where Are We Headed?: a Retrospective Review of Pynchon Criticism', *Pynchon Notes* 7 (Oct. 1981) p. 13. Hemingway quotes the poem beginning 'Blow, blow, ye western wind' in ch. 28 of *A Farewell to Arms*.
10. Joseph W. Slade, '"Entropy" and Other Calamities', in *Pynchon: a Collection of Critical Essays*, edited by Edward Mendelson (Englewood Cliffs, N.J.: Prentice-Hall, 1978) p. 69.
11. Slade, p. 70.
12. 'Mortality and Mercy in Vienna', *Epoch* 9 (Spring 1959) p. 195. This is the only story which Pynchon has not collected in *Slow Learner* and page references in this section are therefore to the *Epoch* printing.
13. Allon White, 'Ironic equivalence: a Reading of Thomas Pynchon's "Mortality and Mercy in Vienna"', *Critical Quarterly*, 23.iii (Autumn 1981) p. 58.
14. The line from Eliot is of course a quotation itself from Baudelaire which makes a referent recede even farther away.

15. White p. 60; Sir J. G. Frazer, *The Golden Bough* (London: Macmillan, 1924) pp. 460–2. Frazer also mentions (p. 73) the significance of frogs as custodians of rain, which adds a possible extra dimension to the ludicrous frogs chorus which accompanies Levine's love-making in 'The Small Rain'.
16. Slade, p. 71.
17. Eliot's 'The Hollow Men' would be directly relevant here, not only because of its epigraph from Conrad. Its attention to emptyness and endings, and the speaker's sense of theatre ('Let me also wear/Such deliberate disguises') find answering echoes in 'Mortality and Mercy'.
18. Cf. Slade, p. 72.
19. White, p. 62.
20. 'Low-lands', first appeared in *New World Writing*, no. 16 (1960).
21. Sigmund Freud, *Introductory Lectures on Psycho-Analysis* (London: Allen & Unwin, 1940) p. 135.
22. According to the biographical note in *New World Writing* (p. 85) Pynchon had 'done a stint in the U.S. Navy'. It is another autobiographical similarity that the Pynchon family home is in East Norwich in the northern part of Long Island.
23. Jules Siegel writes that when Pynchon was in the navy he wrote to Siegel describing himself as a 'jolly jack tar' ('Who is Thomas Pynchon . . .', p. 169).
24. '"Entropy" and Other Calamites', p. 74.
25. Richard F. Patteson, 'Architecture and Junk in Pynchon's Short Fiction', *Illinois Quarterly*, vol. 42, pt. 2 (1979) p. 39.
26. This scene is partly indebted to the cab-shelter section of 'Eumaeus' in Joyce's *Ulysses*.
27. John O. Stark, *Pynchon's Fictions: Thomas Pynchon and the Literature of Information* (Athens, OH: Ohio University press, 1980) p. 165.
28. Cf. *The Waste Land*, ll. 37–41.
29. Cf. *The Tempest*, Act I.ii, ll. 399–405.
30. '"Entropy" and Other Calamites', p. 75.
31. Slade, loc. cit.
32. Schaub 'Where Have We Been, Where Are We Headed?' pp. 12–13.
33. Tony Tanner, *City of Words: A Study of American Fiction in the Mid-Twentieth Century* (London: Jonathan Cape, 1971) p. 153.
34. *Webster's Third New International Dictionary*, 2 vols. (Springfield, Mass.: G. & C. Merriam Co., 1971) vol. I, p. 759b. Pynchon has denied (*Slow Learner*, p. 12) that he had anything but a rudimentary understanding of entropy when he wrote the story.
35. *City of Words*, p. 154.
36. 'Entropy' first appeared in the *Kenyon Review*, vol. 22 (Spring 1960).
37. Henry Miller, *Tropic of Cancer* (London: Calder, 1963) p. 1.
38. It is typical of Pynchon's scrupulous attention to fact that there *was* freak weather in early Feb. 1957, including widespread snowfalls and flooding (*Newsweek* (11 Feb. 1957) p. 14).
39. This is discussed in Robert Redfield and Peter L. Hays, 'Fugue as Structure in Pynchon's "Entropy"', *Pacific Coast Philology*, vol. 12 (1977) p. 55.

40. Samuel Beckett, *Endgame* (London: Faber, 1964) p. 13.
41. Henry Adams, *The Education of Henry Adams*, Modern Library Edition (New York: Random House, 1931) p. 377.
42. *The Education*, p. 389.
43. *The Education*, p. 414.
44. *The Education*, p. 451.
45. *The Degradation of the Democratic Dogma* (New York: Peter Smith, 1949) p. 236.
46. *The Degradation*, p. 308.
47. Norbert Wiener, *The Human Use of Human Beings* (Boston: Houghton Mifflin, 1950) p. 22. Wiener's book is virtually a compendium of Pynchon's fictional themes, including cybernetics which is discussed by Saul and Mulligan.
48. As usual Pynchon's details about the instruments are precise and are summarized from Stravinsky's own memoirs; v. Igor Stravinsky, *An Autobiography* (New York: W. W. Norton, 1962) p. 72.
49. E. W. White, *Stravinksy: a Critical Survey* (London: John Lehmann, 1947) pp. 81, 79, 78.
50. Peter Bischoff, 'Thomas Pynchon, "Entropy"' in P. L. Freese ed., *Die Amerikanische Short Story der Gegenwart* (Berlin: Schmidt, 1976) p. 228.
51. William M. Plater, *The Grim Phoenix: Reconstructing Thomas Pynchon* (Bloomington: Indiana University Press, 1978) p. 139.
52. *City of Words* p. 153.
53. Rudolf Arnheim, *Entropy and Art: an Essay on Disorder and Order* (Berkeley: University of California Press, 1974) pp. 11–12.
54. *The Human Use*, p. 23.
55. John Simons, 'Third Story Man: Biblical Irony in Thomas Pynchon's "Entropy"', *Studies in Short Fiction*, vol. 14 (1977) p. 92.
56. Arnheim has criticized the application of entropy to information theory as being full of internal contradictions (*Entropy and Art* pp. 19–20). Pynchon seems to be using the simple notion of inefficiency in this story.
57. Simons, p. 89.
58. Leonard Feather, *The Encyclopedia of Jazz* (London: Quartet Books, 1978) pp. 344b–345a.
59. Technical details are from Willi Apel, *The Harvard Dictionary of Music* (London: Heinemann, 1944) p. 285.
60. Redfield and Hays, p. 51. Throughout my examination of the story's fugal structure I am indebted to their article.
61. *The Human Use*, p. 25.
62. Joseph Slade, for instance, excludes the story from his survey of Pynchon's short fiction on precisely these grounds.
63. 'Under the Rose', first appeared in *The Noble Savage*, 3 (1961).
64. 'Introduction', *Prize Stories 1962: the O. Henry Awards* (New York: Doubleday, 1962) p. 11.
65. David Cowart, *Thomas Pynchon: the Art of Allusion* (Carbondale: Southern Illinois University Press, 1980) p. 70.
66. John Buchan, *Greenmantle*, 6th ed. (London: Hodder & Stoughton,

1917) p. 186. The protagonist of Pynchon's second story, 'Mortality and Mercy in Vienna', is compared to a John Buchan hero at one point. Pynchon has acknowledged the influence of Buchan in this context (*Slow Learner*, p. 18).

67. Alan Sandison, *The Wheel of Empire* (London: Macmillan, 1967) p. 139.

68. The Marquis of Zetland, *Lord Cromer* (London: Hodder & Stoughton, 1932) p. 128.

69. Karl Richard Lepsius (1810–84) was working in Egypt in the 1840s. Pynchon probably took his name from the 1898 Baedeker to Egypt which mentions him several times.

70. Lord Cromer, 'The German Historians', *The Spectator* (28 Aug. 1915) p. 275.

71. Plater, pp, 70, 101.

72. Karl Baedeker, *Egypt: Handbook for Travellers*, 4th ed (Leipzig: Baedeker, 1898) pp. 21–2. Most these phrases were cut out during the revisions for *V.* Pynchon may also have drawn on E. M. Forster's history and guide to Alexandria. By his own account found a copy of Baedeker in the Cornell Co-op (*Slow Learner*, p. 17). Internal evidence shows that he used the fourth edition.

73. This connection is examined by Joseph Slade in his *Thomas Pynchon* (New York: Warner Books, 1974) pp. 55–9.

74. Mark Twain, *The Adventures of Huckleberry Finn* (Harmondsworth, Middx: Penguin Books, 1966) p. 57.

75. 'The Secret Integration' was first published in the *Sunday Evening Post*, vol. 237, no. 45 (19 Dec. 1964).

76. Mark Twain, *The Adventures of Tom Sawyer* (London and Glasgow: Blackie, 1974) pp. 122–3.

77. *Huckleberry Finn*, p. 88.

78. Benjamin Muse, *The American Negro Revolution* (New York: Citadel Press, 1970) p. 260.

2 *V.*

1. *Best Sellers* 23 (1 Apr. 1963) p. 12; F. J. Hoffman, 'The Questing Comedian: Thomas Pynchon's *V.*.' *Critique*, 6.iii (Winter, 1963–64) p. 176; Christopher Ricks, 'Voluminous', *New Statesman*, 66 (11 Oct. 1963) p. 492; *London Magazine*, n.s. 3. ix. (Dec. 1963) p. 87.

2. *V.* (London: Jonathan Cape, 1963 and Picador (Pan Books), 1975, p. 18, New York: Bantam Books, 1964, p. 9). The Cape and Picador editions have identical pagination. Subsequent page references incorporated into text.

3. Richard Poirier, 'Cook's Tour', *New York Review of Books*, 1.ii. (1963) p. 32.

4. Leo Rosten, *The Joys of Yiddish* (Harmondsworth, Middx: Penguin Books, 1971) p. 352.

5. Hence Jeremy Larner's distinction between *V.* and Jewish–American

fiction in 'The New Schlemihl', *Partisan Review*, 30.ii (Summer 1963) pp. 274–5.

6. According to Jules Siegel Pynchon himself took summer jobs doing road repairs ('Who is Thomas Pynchon', p. 122).

7. E.g. in the painting 'The Melancholy and Mystery of a Street'. This work is referred to in *V.* together with Di Chirico's novel *Hebdomeros*. Pynchon is almost certainly drawing on these works in chapter 14 where a lay figure becomes an erotic substitute. Di Chirico similarly uses a *manichino* (lay-figure) in his paintings from 1913 onwards.

8. Terry Caesar, 'A Note on Pynchon's Naming', *Pynchon Notes*, 5 (Feb. 1981) pp. 5–10. K. B. Harder also gives useful comment on this area of the novel in her 'Names in Thomas Pynchon's *V.*', *Literary Onomastics Studies*, 5 (1978) pp. 64–80.

9. Ludwig Wittgenstein, *Philosophical Investigations* (1953) S.2. The presence of these allusions should alert the reader not to attach inordinate weight to references to the *Tractatus* elsewhere in the novel.

10. *The Image: a Guide to Pseudo-Events in America* (New York: Harper Colophon Books, 1964; first published 1961) p. 204.

11. Cf. *City of Words*, p. 158.

12. Wladyslaw Sluckin's *Minds and Machines* (1954) gives very useful comments on Pynchon's cybernetic themes (the resemblance between neural loops and negative feedback, communication theory, etc.) Even the fly-leaf to the novel comments visually on the theme of mechanization by printing V's into a V-shape. The very title of the novel is a repeatable mechanical sign.

13. Compare Kenneth A. Thigpen's 'Folklore in Contemporary American Literature: Thomas Pynchon's *V.* and the Alligators-in-the-Sewers Legend', *Southern Folklore Quarterly*, 43 (1979) pp. 93–105.

14. 'Embattled Underground', *New York Times Book Review* (1 May 1966) p. 42.

15. Stanley Edgar Hyman, 'The Goddess and the Schlemihl', in Richard Kostelanetz, (ed.), *On Contemporary Literature*, 2nd ed (New York: Avon Books, 1969) p. 509.

16. John Clellon Holmes, *Go* (New York: Appel, 1977) p. 161.

17. *The Performing Self* (London: Chatto & Windus, 1971) p. 24.

18. 'The Questing Comedian', p. 177.

19. Denis de Rougemont, *Man's Western Quest* (London: Allen & Unwin, 1957) p. 197.

20. Freud cites this habit as a retrogressive form of conscience as if the subject were receiving parental criticism (*Collected Papers*, vol. iv [London: Hogarth Press, 1957] pp. 52–3).

21. M. R. Siegel, 'Pynchon's Anti-Quests', *Pynchon Notes*, 3 (June 1980) p. 7.

22. E.g. Joseph W. Slade, *Thomas Pynchon* (New York: Warner Bros, 1974).

23. *The Education of Henry Adams*, p. 389.

24. Hausdorff, p. 263. Adams sees himself as an 'American in search of a father' (*The Education*, p. 229).

25. D. R. Mesher discusses this influence in his 'Pynchon and Nabokov's V', *Pynchon Notes* 8 (Feb. 1982) pp. 43–6. Nabokov's general impact on Pynchon's work is examined in Susan Strehle, 'Actualism: Pynchon's Debt to Nabokov', *Contemporary Literature*, 24 (1983) pp. 30–50.

26. Vladimir Nabokov, *The Real Life of Sebastian Knight* (London: Weidenfeld & Nicolson, 1960) p. 128.

27. *The Performing Self*, p. 40.

28. Robert Graves, *The White Goddess* (London: Faber & Faber, 1961) p. 9.

29. *The White Goddess*, pp. 488, 61, 372.

30. Paul Fahy, 'Thomas Pynchon's *V.* and Mythology', *Critique*, 18.iii (1977) p. 9.

31. David Cowart has put forward evidence for this hypothesis (*The Art of Allusion*, pp. 73–4).

32. Plater, pp. 70, 72.

33. *The Image*, p. 105.

34. David Cowart notes parodic parallels with the Alice books here (*The Art of Allusion*, p. 112).

35. Alain Robbe-Grillet, *L'Année dernière à Marienbad* (Paris: Editions j'ai lu, 1974) p. 25.

36. *City of Words*, p. 157.

37. Walter Pater, *The Renaissance* (London: Macmillan, 1910) p. 55.

38. *The Art of Allusion*, p. 14.

39. Niccolo Machiavelli, *The Prince* (Harmondsworth, Middx: Penguin Books, 1975) pp. 99, 100.

40. *The White Goddess*, p. 395.

41. Melvyn New, 'Profane and Stencilled Texts', *Georgia Review* 33 (1979) p. 404.

42. *Report of the Commission Appointed to Enquire into the Rebellion of the Bondelzwarts*, U.G.16. (Cape Town: Cape Times, 1923) p. 24 [v. Appendix].

43. *Report on the Natives of South-West Africa and their Treatment by Germany* Cmd 9146 (London: HMSO, 1918). Pynchon takes his population figures, details of the forced labour, some names and anecdotes such as the murder of the old woman digging onions (*V.*, 264/246) from this source. The blue book also uses Gustav Frenssen's contemporary novel *Peter Moor's Journey to South-West Africa* (English translation, 1970). [v. Appendix].

44. The Nazi hopes of regaining Germany's colonies are discussed in Derwent Whittlesey, *The German Strategy of World Conquest* (London: F. E. Robinson, 1942) pp. 158–9.

45. Plater, ch. 1 ('All That Is the Case').

46. Hanjo Berressem points out Pynchon's debt to 'The Mask of the Red Death' in Godolphin Goodolphin . . . [etc.]: a Question of Integration', *Pynchon Notes*, 10 (Oct. 1982) pp. 3–4. It is likely that Pynchon took the figure of the hot-house as a place of psychic enclosure both representing and encouraging ennui from the poetry of Maeterlinck. Cf. particularly the poems 'Serre Chaude' (which appears in chapter 14 of *V.*), 'Cloches de Verre', and 'Ame de Serre'.

47. Fahy, p. 13.
48. Plater, p. 227.
49. *Pour un nouveau roman* (Paris: Gallimard, 1964, p. 60).
50. Giorgio di Chirico, *Hebdomeros* (London: Peter Owen, 1968) p. 122.
51. There are allusions to 'the still point of the turning world' (205/189), to 'The Hollow Men' (308/288, 325/304), to the pub scene in 'A Game of Chess' (385/361), to 'Ash Wednesday' (308/288), and to the hyacinth girl (312/292). The list could be considerably extended.
52. Fahy, p. 14.
53. *Collected Papers*, vol. IV, p. 31.
54. Mary Allen, *The Necessary Blankness: Women in Major American Fiction of the Sixties* (Urbana: University of Illinois Press, 1976), pp. 44–5.
55. *The Art of Allusion*, pp. 74–7; Stravinsky, *Autobiography*, p. 31; R. F. Nijinsky, *Nijinsky* (Harmondsworth, Middx: Penguin Books, 1960) p. 158. Stravinsky used a puppet in *Petroushka* (*Autobiography* p. 31).
56. *The Golden Bough* p. 536.
57. *Reports of the Commission appointed to inquire into the events of the 7th and 8th June 1919 and into the circumstances which led up to those events – 18th and 19th September, 1919* [Valletta]: Government Printing Office, 1919. Pynchon discovered this report in a 'pamphlet volume' in New York Public Library [v. Appendix].
58. *City of Words*, p. 172.
59. D'Annunzio figures rather ambiguously in the novel as a figure associated with totalitarianism and as an anachronistic embodiment of virtù.
60. Max F. Schulz, *Black Humor Fiction of the Sixties* (Athens, OH: Ohio University Press, 1973) p. 80.
61. Richard Patteson, 'What Stencil Knew: Structure and Certitude in Pynchon's *V.*' in Richard Pearce (ed.), *Critical Essays on Thomas Pynchon* (Boston: G. K. Hall, 1981) p. 27.
62. Denis de Rougemont, *Passion and Society*, rev. ed (London: Faber & Faber, 1961) p. 15 (published in USA under the title *Love in the Western World*); L. V. Groves, 'Love and the Western World in Pynchon's *V.*', *South Atlantic Review*, 47.i (Jan. 1982) p. 63.
63. *Passion and Society*, p. 19; *Man's Western Guest*, p. 64.
64. Edward Mendelson, 'The Sacred, the Profane, and *The Crying of Lot 49*', *Pynchon: a Collection of Critical Essays*, p. 117.
65. *Thomas Pynchon* (London: Methuen, 1982) pp. 50, 52.
66. *City of Words*, p. 157.
67. 'Love and the Western World', p. 65.
68. *City of Words*, p. 159.
69. On pp. 388/363 and 462/434–5; 53/42 and 279/260 respectively.

3   THE CRYING OF LOT 49

1. Joseph Slade suggests (*Thomas Pynchon*, p. 125) that the differences resulted from the charge of formlessness being levelled against *V.*

2. *The Human Use of Human Beings*, p. 123; cf. Plater, *The Grim Phoenix*, p. 87. Cathy Davidson examines the parallels between Oedipa's search and the quest pattern in her 'Oedipa as Androgyne in Thomas Pynchon's *The Crying of Lot 49*', *Contemporary Literature* 18.i (Winter 1977) pp. 38–50.

3. Maureen Quilligan points out the pun in Oedipa executing a will since she seems will-less (*The Language of Allegory* (Ithaca, NY: Cornell University Press, 1949) pp. 42–3).

4. Joseph Slade discusses the allusions to pregnancy in his *Thomas Pynchon*, p. 151.

5. The play's relation to the novel has been examined by David Cowart (*The Art of Allusion*, pp. 102–6) and John Stark (*Pynchon's Fictions*, pp. 79–80).

6. *The Duchess of Malfi*, i.i l. 190.

7. *The Revenger's Tragedy*, i.i ll. 5–7.

8. Robert Ornstein, *The Moral Vision of Jacobean Tragedy* (Madison: University of Wisconsin Press, 1960) p. 44.

9. *The Crying of Lot 49* (London: Picador Books, 1979, p. 53; New York: Bantam Books, 1967, p. 55). Page-references subsequently incorporated into text with Picador edition first, the Bantam edition second. There are significant textual differences between the Picador edition and the first British and American editions.

10. *The Human Use of Human Beings*, p. 123.

11. Mendelson 'The Sacred, the Profane', p. 137.

12. Thomas Schaub, *Pynchon: the Voice of Ambiguity* (Urbana: University of Illinois Press, 1981) pp. 21–42.

13. 'The Sacred, the Profane', p. 132.

14. *The Art of Allusion*, pp. 104–5.

15. Jean-Baptiste Moëns, *Timbres de l'office Tour et Taxis depuis leur origine jusqu'à leur suppression (1847–67)* (Brussels: Le Timbre Poste, 1880).

16. Manfred Puetz, 'Thomas Pynchon's *The Crying of Lot 49*: the World as a Tristero System', *Mosaic*, 7.iv (Summer 1974) pp. 131–2; *The Voice of Ambiguity*, p. 115.

17. Frank Kermode, 'Decoding the Trystero' in Mendelson, *Pynchon*, p. 164.

18. Tanner, *Thomas Pynchon*, p. 56 and Slade, *Thomas Pynchon*, p. 126.

19. *The Voice of Ambiguity*, p. 105.

20. Cf. Tanner, *Thomas Pynchon*, p. 62.

21. Molly Hite, *Ideas of Order in the Novels of Thomas Pynchon* (Columbus: Ohio State University Press, 1983) p. 71.

22. 'The Sacred, the Profane', p. 120. David Cowart suggests that music in this novel refers to another heightened dimension of awareness (*The Art of Allusion*, p. 81) and Annette Kolodny and D. J. Peters argue that Oedipa achieves an 'altered consciousness of space and time' ('Pynchon's *The Crying of Lot 49*: the Novel as Subversive Experience', *Modern Fiction Studies*, 19.i (Spring 1973) p. 83). Schaub first expressed his objections to Mendelson's standpoint in his 'Open Letter in Response to Edward Mendelson's "The Sacred, the Profane,

and *The Crying of Lot 49*"', *Boundary* 2 5.i (1976) pp. 93–101, and then developed his argument in ch. 2 of *The Voice of Ambiguity*.

23. *Esquire*, 44:6 (Dec. 1965) pp. 164–5. The text of this excerpt varies considerably from that of the novel.

24. Harold Innis, *Empire and Communications* (Oxford: Clarendon Press, 1951) p. 14.

25. The various references to death in the novel have been discussed by Marie-Claude Profit in her 'The Rhetoric of Death in *The Crying of Lot 49*', *Pynchon Notes*, 10 (Oct. 1982) pp. 18–36.

26. D. K. Kirkby has explained this significance to Oedipa's first name in 'Two Modern Versions of the Quest', *Southern Humanities Review*, 5.iv (Autumn 1971) p. 388. Considerable speculation has been expended over her surname although Maas is a perfectly plausible Dutch–American name.

27. M. R. Siegel, *Pynchon: Creative Paranoia in 'Gravity's Rainbow'* (Port Washington, NY: Kennikat Press, 1978).

28. Richard Hofstadter, *The Paranoid Style in American Politics and Other Essays* (London: Jonathan Cape, 1966) p. 4.

29. Pynchon's possible use of Jung is discussed by Cathy Davidson ('Oedipa as Androgyne') and Thomas Schaub (*The Voice of Ambiguity* p. 35).

30. *The Art of Allusion*, pp. 24–30. Tony Tanner also comments on the importance of this painting in his *City of Words*, p. 175.

31. *The Voice of Ambiguity*, p. 38.

32. H. M. McLuhan, *Understanding Media* (London: Sphere Books, 1967) p. 16.

33. 'A Journey into the Mind of Watts', *New York Times Magazine* (12 June 1966) p. 78.

34. *Understanding Media*, pp. 32, 90.

35. *Understanding Media*, p. 56; *The Voice of Ambiguity*, pp. 25–6.

36. Timothy Leary, *The Politics of Ecstasy* (London: Paladin Books, 1970) p. 104.

37. *Understanding Media*, pp. 65–6.

38. *Understanding Media* p. 68. Wallace Stevens argues that Narcissism is a basic principle of observation: 'When we read Ecclesiastes the effect of the symbols is pleasurable because as symbols they are resemblances and as resemblances they are pleasurable and they are pleasurable because it is a principle of our nature that they should be, the principle being not something derived from Narcissism since Narcissism itself is merely an evidence of the operation of the principle that we expect to find pleasure in resemblances' (*The Necessary Angel* [New York: Vintage Books, 1965] p. 80).

39. Anne Mangel, 'Maxwell's Demon, Entropy, Information: *The Crying of Lot 49*' in *Mindful Pleasures* pp. 87–100. Other discussions of entropy in the novel are: P. L. Abernethy, 'Entropy in Pynchon's *The Crying of Lot 49*', *Critique*, 14.ii (1972) pp. 18–33; J. P. Leland, 'Pynchon's Linguistic Demon: *The Crying of Lot 49*', *Critique*, 16.ii (1974) pp. 45–53; Zoltan Abadi-Nagy, 'The Entropic Rhythm of Thomas Pynchon's

Comedy in *The Crying of Lot 49*', *Hungarian Studies in English*, 11 (1977) pp. 117–30; and Mendelson, 'The Sacred, the Profane', pp. 127–8.

40. Abraham Moles, *Information Theory and Esthetic Perception* (University of Illinois Press, 1966) p. 19; Arnheim, *Entropy and Art*, p. 15.

41. J. Clark Maxwell, *Theory of Heat*, 2nd edn (London: Longmans, Green, 1872), p. 308. Mangel, p. 91. A useful article on this subject from a journal Pynchon is known to have read is Walter Ehrenberg's 'Maxwell's Demon', *Scientific American*, 217 (Nov. 1967) pp. 103–10.

42. R. M. Davis comments on the religious significance to Nefastis' name in his 'Parody, Paranoia and the Dead End of Language in *The Crying of Lot 49*', *Genre*, 5 (1972) p. 368.

43. 'Embattled Underground', *New York Times Book Review* (1 May 1966) p. 43.

44. I have discussed some of these alterations in 'Pynchon's Textual Revisions to *The Crying of Lot 49*', *Pynchon Notes*, 12 (1983) pp. 39–45.

45. Michael Harrington, *The Other America* (Baltimore: Penguin Books, 1963) pp. 11, 12.

46. Letter from Gerald Walker (27 August 1981).

47. 'A Journey into the Mind of Watts', *New York Times Magazine* (12 June 1966) pp. 34–5, 78, 80–2, 84. The article was illustrated by a freelance photographer called Bill Bridges.

48. Slade, *Thomas Pynchon*, p. 45.

49. Benjamin Muse, *The American Negro Revolution* (New York: Citadel Press, 1970), p. 206.

50. 'A Journey', p. 34.

51. *The Grim Phoenix*, p. 104.

52. Slade, *Thomas Pynchon*, p. 45.

4 GRAVITY'S RAINBOW

1. Khachig Tölölyan has usefully examined the chronology of the novel in his 'War as Background in *Gravity's Rainbow*', in Charles Clerc (ed.), *Approaches to 'Gravity's Rainbow'* (Columbus: Ohio State University Press, 1983) pp. 33–40.

2. Edward Mendelson, 'Encyclopedic Narrative: From Dante to Pynchon', *MLN* 91 (Dec. 1976) pp. 1267–75.

3. Picaresque chapter headings can be found in Richard Fariña's *Been Down So Long It Looks Like Up To Me* (1966), John Barth's *The Sot-Weed Factor* (1960), and Philip Roth's *The Great American Novel* (1973). The 'chapters' of *Gravity's Rainbow* are unnumbered and untitled but will for the sake of convenience be referred to by number.

4. M. R. Siegel, *Creative Paranoia*, p. 108.

5. Richard Poirier, 'The Importance of Thomas Pynchon', in Levine and Leverenz (eds.), *Mindful Pleasures* p. 23.

6. *Creative Paranoia*, p. 40; C. S. Pyuen, 'The Transmarginal Leap; Meaning and Process in *Gravity's Rainbow*,' *Mosaic*, 15. ii (1982) p. 39.

7. *Gravity's Rainbow*, p. 59. The pagination of the Viking Press (New York, 1973), Jonathan Cape (London, 1973) and Picador (London: Pan Books, 1975) is identical and therefore used here. Subsequent page references are incorporated into the text. Ellipses other than Pynchon's will be marked by square brackets.

8. Michael Seidel, 'The Satirical Plots of *Gravity's Rainbow*' in Mendelson (ed.), *Pynchon*, pp. 210–11.

9. For details on Staver v. James McGovern, *Crossbow & Overcast* (London: Hutchinson, 1965) ch. 8; and Tölölyan, 'War as Background', pp. 49–50.

10. The climax of this film grossly distorts history as the Nordhausen underground rocket factory is destroyed by bombing. In fact Nordhausen was more or less impregnable and was left intact at the end of the war.

11. In this context William Plater notes the relevance of Simmel's stranger-theory (*The Grim Phoenix*, p. 102).

12. 'Introduction', *Been Down So Long*, p. viii.

13. Thomas Schaub (*The Voice of Ambiguity*, p. 138) notes the allusions to Ellison. M. R. Siegel points out related allusions to Malcolm X and Conrad Aiken's 'The Kid' as being ironies which Slothrop cannot possibly recognize (*Creative Paranoia*, pp. 46–59).

14. Jacob Grimm, *Teutonic Mythology* translated by James Steven Stallybrass (London: W. Swann Sonnenschein & Allen, 1880–88; vol II (1883)) pp. 870–1.

15. Cf. Siegel, 'Pynchon's Anti-Quests', pp. 8–9.

16. The fern seed is an allusion to the magical properties of plants (*Teutonic Mythology*, vol. III [1883] p. 1210). The horse's skull is a sign of death (*Teutonic Mythology*, vol. III [1883] p. 850). J. M. Krafft gives a useful discussion of Puritanism in his '"And How Far-Fallen": Puritan Themes in *Gravity's Rainbow*', *Critique*, 18.iii (1977) pp. 55–73.

17. *The Voice of Ambiguity*, p. 71. Joseph Slade addresses the same problem (Slothrop as failed redeemer) in his 'Religion, Psychology, Sex and Love in *Gravity's Rainbow*' (in Clerc, (ed.), *Approaches*, pp. 178–9).

18. C. J. Jung, *The Structure and Dynamics of the Psyche* (London: Routledge & Kegan Paul, 1960) p. 112.

19. C. J. Jung, 'Wotan' [1936], *Civilization in Transition* (London: Routledge & Kegan Paul, 1964), p. 181. The general presence of Jung in the novel has been examined by M. V. Adams ('The Benzene Uroboros: Plastic and Catastrophe in *Gravity's Rainbow*' in James Hillman, (ed.), *Spring 1981* (Dallas: Spring Publications, 1981) pp. 149–61); Schaub, *The Voice of Ambiguity*, pp. 49–57; and Siegel, *Creative Paranoia*, pp. 62–4.

20. Steven Weisenburger has shown that much of Pynchon's play on German etymologies derives directly from Grimm: 'Notes for *Gravity's Rainbow*', *Pynchon Notes*, 12 (June 1983) p. 5.

21. The phrase occurs at least twice in *Gravity's Rainbow* (pp. 270, 681).

22. *Civilization in Transition*, p. 190.

23. *Teutonic Mythology*, pp. 11, 629.

24. *Journal of the Society for Psychical Research*, 23 (June 1945) p. 146.
25. Eventyr (i.e. 'once upon a time') is the title of an orchestral piece by Delius based on a Norwegian fairy-tale by Asbjørsen.
26. J. Hillis Miller, *The Form of Victorian Fiction* (Notre Dame: University of Notre Dame Press, 1968) p. 67.
27. William Plater (*The Grim Phoenix* p. 247) suggests that Pynchon took the name of Weissmann from a biologist discussed in *Beyond the Pleasure Principle*.
28. L. C. Wolfley, 'Repression's Rainbow: the Presence of Norman O. Brown in Pynchon's Big Novel' in Pearce, *Critical Essays*, pp. 99–123.
29. Marcus Smith and Khachig Tölöyan have discussed this aspect of the novel in their 'The New Jeremiad: *Gravity's Rainbow*' in Pearce, *Critical Essays*, pp. 169–86.
30. The classic discussion of this American theme is Harry Levin's *The Power of Blackness* (1958).
31. Cf. David Cowart, *The Art of Allusion*, pp. 40–8.
32. 'After the Catastrophe' [1945], *Civilization in Transition*, p. 203. A relevant discussion of Jung's concept of the shadow can be found in Jolande Jacobi's *The Psychology of C. J. Jung* (London: Routledge & Kegan Paul, 1962) pp. 106–10.
33. 'Religion, Psychology . . .', *Approaches*, p. 189. Slade also discusses the novel's perversions in his *Thomas Pynchon*, pp. 232–3.
34. Paul Fussell, *The Great War and Modern Memory* (London and New York: Oxford University Press, 1975) p. 333.
35. 'Pynchon's use of the Tannhäuser-Legend in *Gravity's Rainbow*', *Notes on Contemporary Literature*, 9.iii (1979) pp. 2–3.
36. Quoted in Alice Leighton Cleather and Basil Crump, *The Ring of the Nibelung* (London: Methuen, 1903) pp. 130–1.
37. The various allusions to Rilke in the novel are identified and explained by J. O. Stark (*Pynchon's Fictions*, pp. 149–52).
38. Douglas Fowler, *A Reader's Guide to "Gravity's Rainbow"* (Ann Arbor: Ardis, 1980) p. 15.
39. Fritz Lang's role in the novel has been explained by S. E. Grace ('Fritz Lang and the "Paracinematic Lives" of *Gravity's Rainbow*', *Modern Fiction Studies*, 29.iv (Winter 1983) pp. 655–70). An account of 'rising' from a rocket-blast (cf. *Gravity's Rainbow*, p. 49) is given in the *Journal of the Society for Psychical Research* 33 (1945) p. 179.
40. Cf. Norman O. Brown: 'Sublimation . . . presupposes and perpetuates the loss of life and cannot be the mode in which life itself is lived' (*Life Against Death* [New York: Random House, 1959] p. 171).
41. Norman Mailer, *A Fire on the Moon* (London: Weidenfeld & Nicolson, 1970) p. 9.
42. *Life Against Death*, p. 225.
43. *The Voice of Ambiguity*, p. 101; *Life Against Death*, p. 3.
44. J. W. Earl suggest that the Pointsman is taken from Clerk Maxwell and is a 'metaphor . . . for the free will itself' ('Freedom and Knowledge in the Zone', *Approaches*, p. 232).
45. Cf. I. P. Pavlov: 'The true mechanical explanation always remains the ideal of natural sciences . . . no effect without cause' (*Lectures on*

Conditioned Reflexes, vol. III [London: Lawrence & Wishart, 1941] p. 149). Thomas Schaub gives an excellent account of Pavlov's presence in the novel (*The Voice of Ambiguity*, pp. 90–4). The various forms of personality measurement referred to include MMPI, Bernreuter Inventory and F-scale (pp. 81, 90). All these methods exist within behavioural psychology, and all are presented as partial and inadequate in *Gravity's Rainbow*.

46. J. B. Watson and Rosalie Rayner, 'Conditioned Emotional Reactions', *Journal of Experimental Psychology*, 3.i. (1920) p. 12. Watson and Rayner took issue with Freudians' assertion of the primacy of the sex-impulse arguing that 'fear is as primal a factor as love in influencing personality' (p. 14).

47. *Conditioned Reflexes* (Oxford University Press, 1927) p. 57.

48. A. J. Friedman discusses some examples of reversed sequence in his 'Science and Technology' (*Approaches*, pp. 84–5).

49. Douglas Fowler rehearses the similarities between Pointsman and Pavlov in *A Reader's Guide*, p. 141.

50. J. D. Black, 'Pynchon's Eve of De-struction', *Pynchon Notes* 14 (Feb. 1984) p. 29.

51. Musical theory is discussed in overtly political terms at two points in the novel (pp. 440–1, 621–2). Cf. Cowart, *The Art of Allusion*, pp. 84–6.

52. Siegfried Kracauer, *From Caligari to Hitler* (Princeton University Press, 1947) p. 6. Film has been discussed extensively by Pynchon's critics, in particular by the following: Charles Clerc, 'Film in *Gravity's Rainbow*', *Approaches*, pp. 103–51; D. F. Larson, 'The Camera Eye: "Cinematic" Narrative in *U.S.A.* and *Gravity's Rainbow*' in Peter Ruppert (ed.), *Ideas of Order in Literature and Film* (Tallahassee: University Presses of Florida, 1980), pp. 94–106; Bertram Lippman, 'the Reader of Movies: Thomas Pynchon's *Gravity's Rainbow*', *University of Denver Quarterly*, 12.i (1977) pp. 1–46; Antonio Marquez, 'The Cinematic Imagination in Thomas Pynchon's *Gravity's Rainbow*', *Rocky Mountain Review*, 33.iv (Autumn 1979) pp. 166–79: Scott Simmon, 'Beyond the Theatre of War: *Gravity's Rainbow* as Film', *Literature/Film Quarterly*, 6 (1978) pp. 347–63; David Cowart, 'Cinematic Anguries of the Third Reich in *Gravity's Rainbow*', *Literature/Film Quarterly* 6 (1978) pp. 364–70.

53. *City of Words*, p. 16.

54. *O.E.D.* 'preterition', IV. The quotation is from *Evangelical Christianity*.

55. 'The Quest for Pynchon', *Mindful Pleasures*, pp. 253–5.

56. E.g. Tanner, *Thomas Pynchon*, pp. 87–8.

57. As usual there is a proportion of fact underlying Pynchon's fiction. He drew here on a pamphlet by W. P. Steenkamp entitled *Is the South-West African Herero Committing Race Suicide?* Steenkamp tried to account for their increasing death-rate by vitamin deficiency but Pynchon wasn't so sure (v. appendix).

58. Heinrich Vedder, 'The Herero' in *The Native Tribes of South West Africa* (Cape Town: Cape Times, 1928) p. 176. Thomas Schaub discusses the futile attempts at a mythic return in *The Voice of Ambiguity*, pp. 86–7.

59. I have explained the Herero terms in 'Pynchon's Herero', *Pynchon Notes*, 10 (Oct. 1982) pp. 37–44. Even the very language was subject to colonization. Vedder recounts how Dr. Hugo Hahn, a Lutheran missionary responsible for publishing the first books in Herero, manufactured 1000 new words to express abstractions (*South West Africa in Early Times* [1938] [London: Cass, 1966] pp. 241–2).

60. *Crossbow and Overcast*, ch. 1.

61. 'Film in *Gravity's Rainbow*', p. 121.

62. José Hernandez, *The Gaucho Martin Fierro*, (trans. by F. G. Carrino *et al*. (Albany: State University of New York Press, 1974) p. 11. Pynchon quotes the opening lines of the poem in Spanish (pp. 386–7).

63. *Counter-blast* (London: Rapp Whiting, 1970) p. 80.

64. T. G. Winner, *The Oral Art and Literature of the Kazakhs of Russian Central Asia* (Durham, NC: Duke University Press, 1958) p. 142. Winner's writings were first identified as Pynchon's sources by Edward Mendelson ('Gravity's Encyclopedia', *Mindful Pleasures*, p. 170).

65. T. G. Winner, 'Problems of Alphabetic Reform among the Turkic Peoples of Soviet Central Asia, 1920–1941', *Slavonic and East European Review*, 31 (1952) p. 139.

66. There was strong opposition to a Turkic alphabet on exactly these grounds ('Problems of Alphabetic Reform', pp. 135–6).

67. *The Oral Art*, pp. 84–5.

68. Javaid Qazi, 'Pynchon in Central Asia: the Use of Sources and Resources', *Rocky Mountain Review*, 34.iv (Autumn 1980) pp. 229–42.

69. *The Oral Art*, p. 9. Qazi suggests a different source from a local cinema called 'Light' (p. 239).

70. Maureen Quilligan, *The Language of Allegory* (Ithaca: Cornell University Press, 1979) p. 207.

71. *The Oral Art*, p. 47.

72. Ralph Waldo Emerson, *Essays: First Series*, The Riverside Edition. (London: Waverley Book Co., [1883]) p. 253.

73. Mandalas in the novel are discussed by J. M. Muste ('The Mandala in *Gravity's Rainbow*', *Boundary* 2, 9.ii (1981) pp. 163–79).

74. Mircea Eliade, *The Myth of the Eternal Return* (London: Routledge & Kegan Paul, 1955) p. 20.

75. *The Voice of Ambiguity*, p. 87.

76. Molly Hite, *Ideas of Order in the Novels of Thomas Pynchon* (Columbus: Ohio State University Pres, 1983) p. 31.

77. Rainer Maria Rilke, *Duino Elegies*, trans. by J. B. Leishman and Stephen Spender (New York: W. W. Norton, 1967) pp. 79, 87.

78. Cotton Mather, *The Christian Philosopher* [1712] (Gainesville: Scholars' Facsimiles, 1968) p. 82; 'The Saviour with his Rainbow' [1714], *Days of Humiliation* (Gainesville: Scholars' Facsimiles, 1970) p. 221.

79. Max Weber, *The Protestant Ethic and the Spirit of Capitalism* (London: Allen & Unwin, 1978) p. 117. Pynchon's use of Weber has been examined by William Plater (*The Grim Phoenix*, p. 210), M. R. Siegel (*Creative Paranoia* pp. 96–8), Joseph Slade (*Thomas Pynchon*, p. 180) and Thomas Schaub (*The Voice of Ambiguity*, pp. 57–8).

80. V. Appendix. Discussions of Pynchon's use of mathematics can be found in L. W. Ozier's 'Antipointsman/Antimexico: Some Mathematical Imagery in *Gravity's Rainbow*', *Critique*, 16.ii (1974) pp. 73–90; and 'The Calculus of Transformation: More Mathematical Imagery in *Gravity's Rainbow*', *Twentieth Century Literature*, 2.iii (May 1975), pp. 193–210. Norman O. Brown discusses isolation as a technique for protecting the ego from its own instincts which 'Consists in fragmenting experience into separate parts; time intervals are interpolated, and the result is a safe obsession with routine . . .' (*Life Against Death*, p. 276).

81. *On Charisma and Institution Building* (University of Chicago Press, 1968) p. 39. Cf. V. D. Balitas, 'Charismatic Figures in *Gravity's Rainbow*', *Pynchon Notes* 9 (June 1982) pp. 38–53.

82. In this case Pynchon is writing within an American tradition of anti-war protest which would include Dos Passos and Ezra Pound (cf. the latter's *Selected Prose 1909–1965* [New York: New Directions, 1973] p. 222).

83. Dr. Benway appears in *The Naked Lunch* (1959) as a Pavlovian administrator of the Freeland Republic, where ostensible therapy masks total exploitation. Pynchon also shares something of Mailer's hatred of plastics because the construction of large molecules feeds the arrogance of exploiting systems.

84. Albert Speer notes in his memoirs that Hitler had agreed in 1944 to build an economic cartel for the SS which by then controlled the V-2 programme (*Inside the Third Reich* [London: Weidenfeld & Nicholson, 1970], pp. 372–3). Pynchon's sources for details on I. G. Farben are Joseph Borkin and Charles A. Welsh, *Germany's Master Plan* (1943) and Richard Sasuly *IG Farben* (1947) (cf. Tölölyan, 'War as Background', pp. 53–8).

85. Here again Pynchon is drawing on fact since a light-bulb cartel called 'Phoebus' was active in the inter-war period. V. below, section (f).

86. 'Rocket Power' in Mendelson *Pynchon*, p. 175.

87. Lewis Mumford, *The Culture of Cities* (London: Secker & Warburg, 1944) pp. 291–2. The phases are: eopolis (village), polis (association of villages), metropolis, megalopolis (city's decline begins), tyrannopolis, and nekropolis. In the novel *Metropolis* Thea von Harbou repeatedly uses animal images to represent the city's machine-life.

88. J. D. Black, 'Probing a Post-Romantic Palaeontology: Thomas Pynchon's *Gravity's Rainbow*,' *Boundary 2*, 8.ii (Winter 1980) p. 233.

89. John Hawkes, *The Cannibal* (London: Sphere Books, 1970) p. 23.

90. R. B. Henkle, 'The Morning and the Evening Funnies: Comedy in *Gravity's Rainbow*' in Clerc, *Approaches*, p. 274.

91. The metaphor was used repeatedly in anti-nazi propaganda, e.g. H. F. Artucio, *The Nazi Octopus in South America* (1943).

92. Perhaps this episode was suggested by the abortive balloon-flight in ch. 17 of *The Wizard of Oz* which was to have taken Dorothy back to Kansas.

93. The song is a lyrical improvisation on a line from Norman O. Brown

('the penis we are is not our own'), *Love's Body* (NY: Vintage Books, 1966) p. 57.

94. *The Language of Allegory*, p. 290.

95. Philip Stevick, 'Prolegomena to the Study of Fictional *Dreck*' in S. B. Cohen (ed.), *Comic Relief* (Urbana: University of Illinois Press, 1978) p. 275.

96. There may be veiled allusions here to the media 'packaging' of Nixon for the 1968 presidential election and to the tapes which he ordered to be kept in the White House from 1971 onwards.

97. Arthur Koestler, *Insight and Outlook* (New York: Macmillan, 1949) p. 3.

98. *Life Against Death*, p. 36.

99. 'Gravity's Encyclopedia', p. 173.

100. *Conditioned Reflexes*, p. 12.

101. Peter Kihss, 'Pulitzer Jurors Dismayed on Pynchon', *New York Times* (8 May 1974) p. 38.

102. It is one of the ironies surrounding Pointsman, the supposedly rational scientist, that he should replace Pavlov's *Lectures on Conditioned Reflexes* with Sax Rohmer's novels as an authoritative text to guide his actions.

103. Quoted in Ervin Hexner, *International Cartels* (London: Pitman, 1946) p. 7.

104. The chess knight is used as a personal sign on his MSS by Nabokov's Sebastian Knight.

105. Scott Sanders, 'Pynchon's Paranoid History', *Mindful Pleasures*, p. 140. Hendrick Hertzberg and D. C. K. McClelland, 'Paranoia', *Harper's Magazine* 248 (June 1974) p. 52. Paranoia has been much discussed by Pynchon's critics, notably the following: M. R. Siegel, *Creative Paranoa*: Michael Friedbichler, 'Towards a Redeemed Imagination: the Role of Paranoia in the Novels of Thomas Pynchon', in Sonja Bahn *et al.* (eds.), *Forms of the American Imagination* (Institut fur Sprachwissenschaft der Universität Innsbruck, 1979) pp. 147–56; Louis Mackey, 'Paranoia, Pynchon, and Preterition', *Sub-Stance*, 30 (1981) pp. 16–30.

106. The finger of God is a traditional sign of his power (cf. Exodus 8:19) but Pynchon uses it in connection with election (e.g. p. 27).

107. *The Voice of Ambiguity*, p. 105.

108. *International Cartels*, pp. 358–9.

109. 'Rocket Power', p. 177.

110. *The Language of Allegory*, p. 217.

111. Bernard Duyfhuizen, 'Starry-Eyed Semiotics: Learning to Read Slothrop's Map and *Gravity's Rainbow*', *Pynchon Notes* 6 (June 1981) p. 27.

112. Brian McHale, 'Modernist Reading, Post-Modernist Text: Pynchon's *Gravity's Rainbow*', *Poetics Today*, I.i-ii (Autumn 1979) pp. 85–110.

113. Cf. Fowler, *A Reader's Guide*, p. 207.

114. J. W. Aldridge, *After the Lost Generation* (New York: Noonday Press, 1966) p. 72.

115. *Creative Paranoia*, p. 41.

116. Richard Pearce, *The Novel in Motion* (Columbus: Ohio State University Press 1983) pp. 8–9.

5 PYNCHON IN CONTEXT

1. The works which have received comment from Pynchon are the following; M. F. Beal, *Amazon One* (1975); Richard Fariña, *Been Down So Long It Looks Like Up to Me* (1966); Phyllis Gebauer, *The Pagan Blessing* (1979); Laurel Goldman, *Sounding the Territory* (1982); Peter Matthiessen, *Far Tortuga* (1976); Marge Piercy, *Dance the Eagle to Sleep* (1971); Tom Robbins, *Even Cowgirls Get the Blues* (1977); Hughes Rudd, *My Escape from the C.I.A. (and into C.B.S.)* (1976); Kirkpatrick Sale, *S.D.S.* (1974); David Shetzline, *DeFord* (1968); John Speicher, *Looking For Baby Paradise* (1970); Rudolph Wurlitzer, *Flats* (1970).
2. Tom Robbins, *Even Cowgirls Get the Blues* (London: Corgi, 1977) p. 52.
3. *Even Cowgirls*, p. 224.
4. *Even Cowgirls*, p. 124.
5. *Even Cowgirls*, pp. 379–80.
6. *Even Cowgirls*, p. 229.
7. 'Is It O.K. to Be a Luddite?', *New York Times Book Review* (10 Oct. 1984) p. 41.
8. A useful companion essay to Robbins' fiction is his 'Why I Live Where I Live' (*Esquire* (Oct. 1980) pp. 82–4).
9. *Another Roadside Attraction* (New York: Ballantyne, 1972) p. 303; *Still Life With Woodpecker* (London: Corgi, 1981) p. 91.
10. Robert Nadeau, *Readings from the New Book Of Nature* (Amherst, Mass.: University of Massachusetts Press, 1981) ch. 7 and 8.
11. Matthiessen, a co-founder of the *Paris Review*, had already four novels to his credit when *Far Tortuga* appeared as well as numerous naturalist studies.
12. J. P. Grove, 'Pastoralism and Anti-Pastoralism in Peter Matthiessen's *Far Tortuga*', *Critique*, 21 (1979) p. 16.
13. Cf. Bert Bender, '*Far Tortuga* and American Sea Fiction Since *Moby-Dick*', *American Literature*, 56 (1984) p. 237.
14. Peter Matthiessen, 'The Craft of Fiction in *Far Tortuga*', *Paris Review*, 60 (Winter 1974) pp. 79–80.
15. *Far Tortuga* (New York: Random House, 1975) p. 369.
16. In a letter of 27 Feb. 1980 Mary Beal explained that they discussed the age of rocks among other things (hence the reference in *Gravity's Rainbow* to frames per century) and referred me particularly to the physical entry under 'sentience' in the *OED*.
17. M. F. Beal, 'Gold' in Martha Foley (ed.), *The Best American Short Stories of 1972*, (Boston: Houghton, Mifflin, 1972) p. 8.
18. 'Space Time', *Paris Review*, 16 (Spring 1975) pp. 16, 18.
19. 'Is It O.K. to Be a Luddite?', p. 41.

20. Kirkpatrick Sale, 'The World Behind Watergate', *New York Review of Books*, 20. vii (3 May 1973) p. 14.
21. *S.D.S.* (New York: Random House, 1973).
22. M. F. Beal, *Amazon One* (Boston: Little, Brown, 1975) p. 53.
23. *Amazon One*, p. 251.
24. *Angel Dance* (New York: Daughters Pub. Co., 1977) p. 44.
25. Marge Piercy, *Dance the Eagle to Sleep* (New York: Fawcett Crest, 1971) p. 63.
26. *Dance the Eagle to Sleep*, p. 212.
27. *Dance the Eagle to Sleep*, p. 186.
28. David Shetzline, *DeFord* (New York: Random House, 1968) p. 67. Shetzline is mentioned in *Gravity's Rainbow* and *DeFord*, like Pynchon's novel, is dedicated to Richard Fariña.
29. Laurel Goldman, *Sounding the Territory* (London: Faber, 1982) p. 4.
30. 'Interview with Rudolph Wurlitzer', *The Rutgers Anthologist* 41.i (1970) p. 37.
31. 'Interview' p. 36.
32. Rudolph Wurlitzer, *Flats* (London: Victor Gollancz, 1970) p. 7.
33. D. T. Bolling, 'Rudolph Wurlitzer's *Nog* and *Flats*', *Critique* 14.iii (1973) p. 12.
34. *Flats*, p. 22.
35. *Flats*, p. 159.
36. 'Is It O.K. to Be a Luddite?', p. 41.

APPENDIX

1. The document which Hirsch drew to Pynchon's attention was the *Report of the Administration on the Bondelswarts Rising 1922* (U.G. 30) (Cape Town, 1922).
2. The *Report of the Commission Appointed to Enquire into the Rebellion of the Bondelzwarts* (U.G. 16) (Cape Town, 1923) is bound together with *Reports of the Commission Appointed to inquire into the events of 7th and 8th June 1919 and into the circumstances which led up to those events – 18th and 19th September, 1919* (Valletta, 1919) in New York Public Library. Pynchon used both reports in *V.* (in ch. 9 and the Epilogue respectively).
3. Cf. *V.* p. 245/227.
4. Pynchon certainly knew Marshall McLuhan's *Understanding Media* (1964), was probably familiar with his earlier study *The Mechanical Bride* (1951) and also with McLuhan's later more politically-oriented writings. There is clear evidence that he used Mircea Eliade's *The Myth of the Eternal Return* (English Translation, 1955) in *Gravity's Rainbow*.
5. This subsequence reading was done in the UCLA Research Library. The texts referred to here are: (a) Grosser Generalstab. Kriegsgeschichtliche Abteilung. *Die Kaempfe der deutschen Truppen in Südwestafrika*, 2 vols (Berlin: E. S. Mittler, 1906–7); (b) Freiherr Friedrich von Dincklage-Campe, *Deutsche Reiter im Südwest* (Berlin:

Bong, 1908); (c) Erich von Salzmann, *Im Kämpfe gegen die Herero* (Berlin: Globus Verlag, 1912).

6. Luttig (published 1933/4) supplied Pynchon with information about the layout of the Herero village, etc. (V. *Gravity's Rainbow* p. 321.)
7. The Herero birth decline is discussed in *Gravity's Rainbow*, p. 317.
8. Pynchon's letter was written at the height of the Vietnam War. Early 1968 saw the battle for Hué, the virtual siege of Saigon and the struggle for control of the Mekong Delta.
9. Kleinstaaterei, i.e. system of little states. The Peace of Westphalia (1648) ended the Thirty Years War.
10. Although Pynchon has denied reading any Mumford, the two most relevant texts here would be *The Culture of Cities* (1938) and *The City in History* (1961). He actually consulted Jane Jacobs' *The Death and Life of Great American Cities* (1961).
11. Francisco Pizarro was born around 1471 in Truxillo, a town in Estremadura. He had no education as a youth and acted as a swineherd. In the 1530s he conquered the Inca kingdom.
12. Gottfried Wilhelm Leibniz (1646–1716) co-founder, as Pynchon states, of calculus, was also the proponent of the integration sign (cf. the layout of the Mittelwerke), inventor of a calculating machine, peacemaker in the Holy Roman Empire, and the author of a scheme to improve output from his patron's silver mines in the Harz Mountains. Johann Karl Friedrich Gauss (1777–1855) developed calculus and the theory of numbers, was also an astronomer and one of the founders of topology.
13. I have made a minor excision here at Pynchon's request.
14. At least one such book existed in 1968 – Horst Drechsler's *'Let Us Die Fighting'. The Struggle of the Herero and Nama against German Imperialism (1884–1915)* – although it was not published in English until 1980.
15. *Report on the Natives of South-West Africa and their Treatment by Germany* (cmd 9146) (London, HMSO, 1918).

Index